The Borders of the European Union in a Conflictual World

Antonina Bakardjieva Engelbrekt ·
Per Ekman · Anna Michalski · Lars Oxelheim
Editors

The Borders of the European Union in a Conflictual World

Interdisciplinary European Studies

palgrave
macmillan

Editors
Antonina Bakardjieva Engelbrekt
Faculty of Law
Stockholm University
Stockholm, Sweden

Per Ekman
Department of Government
Uppsala University
Uppsala, Sweden

Anna Michalski
Department of Government
Uppsala University
Uppsala, Sweden

Lars Oxelheim
Research Institute of Industrial Economics
Stockholm, Sweden

ISBN 978-3-031-54202-2 ISBN 978-3-031-54200-8 (eBook)
https://doi.org/10.1007/978-3-031-54200-8

Cover image: Lightspring

This Palgrave Macmillan imprint is published by the registered company Springer Nature Switzerland AG
The registered company address is: Gewerbestrasse 11, 6330 Cham, Switzerland

Paper in this product is recyclable.

Contents

1 **Perspectives on the Significance of Borders in Europe: Past Challenges, Future Developments** 1
Antonina Bakardjieva Engelbrekt, Per Ekman, Anna Michalski, and Lars Oxelheim

2 **EU Border Policy: Enhanced Border Security and Challenges to Free Movement** 23
Johanna Pettersson Fürst

3 **The Return of Borders in the World Economy: An EU-Perspective** 49
Fredrik Sjöholm

4 **The Boundaries of the Internal Market In- and Outside the EU** 73
Marja-Liisa Öberg

5 **EU Norm Promotion in a Conflictual World. An Existential Necessity with Obstacles?** 93
Ann-Kristin Jonasson

6 **The Ability of the EU to Extend Its Model of a Social Market Economy Beyond Its Borders** 119
Pär Hallström

7 **The EU's Dependence on Russian Energy—A Force that Divides or Unites the Union?** 147
Torbjörn Becker and Anders Åslund

8 **The EU's Fight against Money Laundering and Terrorist Financing in a Digital and Fragmented World** 177
Maria Bergström

9 **The European Security Order** 205
Kjell Engelbrekt

10 **A European Marshall Plan for Ukraine on the Way to the EU** 233
Anders Åslund and Torbjörn Becker

11 **The EU's Internal and External Borders in a World Torn by Conflict** 261
Antonina Bakardjieva Engelbrekt, Per Ekman, Anna Michalski, and Lars Oxelheim

Index 285

Notes on Contributors

Anders Åslund is a senior fellow at the Stockholm Free World Forum and an Adjunct Professor at Georgetown University. A leading specialist on the East European economies, he has authored 16 books. He has advised the Russian and Ukrainian governments and earned his D.Phil. from Oxford University.

Antonina Bakardjieva Engelbrekt is Professor of European Law at the Faculty of Law of Stockholm University. She has been chair of the Swedish Network for European Legal Studies (2011–2022) and Torsten and Ragnar Söderberg Professor of Legal Science (2015–2018). Her research interests include processes of Europeanization and globalization and their influence on national law and institutions.

Torbjörn Becker is the Director of the Stockholm Institute of Transition Economics at the Stockholm School of Economics since 2006 and a board member of several research institutions in Eastern Europe. He previously worked at the IMF. His primary research interests are in macroeconomics, international finance, and institutional development.

Maria Bergström is Associate Professor of EU Law at Uppsala University in Sweden. Her research expertise is focused on the area of EU Law and EU Criminal Law, and she has authored many publications within these fields of law. She holds a Doctor of Laws from the European University Institute in Italy. Bergström has contributed to various European projects funded by the European Commission.

Per Ekman is a researcher in Political Science at the Department of Government, Uppsala University, Sweden, and Coordinator for the Swedish Network for European Studies in Political Science (SNES). His research interests include foreign policy of countries in the EU's Eastern Partnership, state building, and historical institutionalism.

Kjell Engelbrekt is Professor of Political Science at the Swedish Defence University, Lifetime Member of the Royal Academy of War Sciences, and Non-Resident Senior Fellow with the Chicago Council on Global Affairs. He has published extensively on European and transatlantic security, foreign policy, and institution-building in Central and Eastern Europe.

Pär Hallström is Professor Emeritus of Legal Science at the Department of Law, Umeå University. His fields of research and publications are International and European Law and Comparative Constitutional Law.

Ann-Kristin Jonasson is Senior Lecturer at the Department of Political Science at the University of Gothenburg. Her research interests include the diffusion of norms, particularly, in relation to democracy.

Anna Michalski is Associate Professor in Political Science at the Department of Government, Uppsala University, a visiting Professor at the College of Europe, Bruges, and Senior Associate Research Fellow at the Swedish Institute of International Affairs. She is also Chair of the Swedish Network for European Studies in Political Science (SNES). Her research interests include European foreign policy, EU-China relations, and foreign policy roles in the Nordic countries.

Marja-Liisa Öberg is Associate Professor of EU Law at Lund University. Her research interests lie in the areas of EU constitutional and external relations law, third-country integration in the EU, the internal and external boundaries of EU integration, and interdisciplinary dimensions of EU integration.

Lars Oxelheim is Professor of International Business and Finance at the University of Agder, Professor Emeritus at Lund University, and affiliated with the Research Institute of Industrial Economics (IFN), Sweden. He is the founder of the Swedish Network for European Studies in Economics and Business (SNEE). His research interests include economic and financial integration, corporate governance, and risk management.

Johanna Pettersson Fürst, Ph.D. is a researcher at the Department of Government at Uppsala University. Her research interests include European integration, border and migration policy studies, and international relations.

Fredrik Sjöholm is Professor of Economics and CEO at the Research Institute of Industrial Economics. He specializes in the economic implications of globalization, encompassing diverse facets of international trade and investments.

List of Figures

Fig. 3.1	International trade as a share of GDP 1979-2021 (%). *Source* World bank development Indicators. https://data.worldbank.org/indicator	52
Fig. 3.2	Foreign direct investments as a share of GDP 1970–2022 (%). *Source* World Bank Development Indicators. https://data.worldbank.org/indicator/BX.KLT.DINV.WD.GD.ZS	52
Fig. 3.3	The share of global GDP in different regions 1970–2022 (%). Source World bank development indicators. https://data.worldbank.org/indicator/BX.KLT.DINV.WD.GD.ZS	55
Fig. 7.1	Energy balances of EU countries in 2020. *Source* Eurostat	151
Fig. 7.2	Sources of the dependence on Russian energy for EU countries	152
Fig. 7.3	Estimate of what EU countries paid Russia for energy in 2020	155
Fig. 7.4	EU countries' shares of total Russian energy exports in 2020. *Source* Eurostat, Central bank of Russia (cbr.ru), and authors' calculations	157
Fig. 9.1	Govermental support to Ukraine. *Source* 'Ukraine support tracker', website to a database on military, financial, and humanitarian aid to Ukraine, KIEL institute for the World Economy, 2023	226

List of Tables

Table 9.1 EU's enlargement following the signing of the European coal and steel community on april 18, 1951 (European Parliament 2023) EU's enlargement 226
Table 9.2 Sanctions imposed on Russia by EU and like-minded countries, Fall 2023 227

CHAPTER 1

Perspectives on the Significance of Borders in Europe: Past Challenges, Future Developments

Antonina Bakardjieva Engelbrekt, Per Ekman, Anna Michalski, and Lars Oxelheim

Borders as a Paradox in European History

Historically, the concept of borders has evolved differently in Europe compared to many other parts of the world, as geographical spaces in Europe have been shaped by organized human settlements for as long as historical accounts stretch, whereas on most other continents the

A. Bakardjieva Engelbrekt
Faculty of Law, Stockholm University, Stockholm, Sweden

P. Ekman
Department of Government, Uppsala University, Uppsala, Sweden

A. Michalski (✉)
Department of Government, Uppsala University, Uppsala, Sweden
e-mail: anna.michalski@statsvet.uu.se

L. Oxelheim
Research Institute of Industrial Economics, Stockholm, Sweden

A. Bakardjieva Engelbrekt et al. (eds.), *The Borders of the European Union in a Conflictual World*,
https://doi.org/10.1007/978-3-031-54200-8_1

geographical expanse of the land was defined by the reach of the settlers and envisaged as the frontier between settlement and wilderness (Maier, 2002, 17). As no such uninhabited lands existed in Europe, borders were often conceived of dividing lines between geographical areas according to the control of the dominant order, whether empires, kingdoms, principalities, or tribes, thus separating peoples from each other and ordering them into different political units. Where natural borders existed, such as mountains, rivers, and seas, they had an important function to delineate one political unit from another, often separating inhabitants effectively and making crossings important points of contact. Such borders constituted important defensive lines as they were easier to hold in the event of an assault of a neighbouring country. On the whole, throughout history, borders on the European continent changed quite frequently through wars and conquests, at times befitting the people inhabiting the lands while at other times dividing ethnic and linguistic communities.

In early European history, most of the then-known lands were directly incorporated into the Roman Empire, or strongly influenced by its might. In the Romans' conception, these borderlands became a demarcation line for the division between civilization and barbarism in Europe and around the Mediterranean and Black Seas, thus excluding Scandinavia and large parts of north-eastern Europe. The areas where the Roman Empire ended also constituted the limit of its jurisdiction. These border areas were referred to as *limes* and became formal demarcation lines between an advanced civilization and a political organization of space, and the lands that lay beyond (Maier, 2002, pp. 18–19). During the Middle Ages and into the Renaissance, borders in Europe, as elsewhere, took on a different meaning in loosely held together empires, first in the appearance of the Holy Roman Empire, then its successor, the Habsburg Empire, later Austrian Empire, dominating varying parts of the continent. These empires consisted of territories, often inherited or acquired through marriage, ruled over by dynastic monarchies, and characterized by multiple cultures, languages, religions, and ethnicities (Hassner, 2002). The territories of the empires were accorded high degrees of autonomy and various centralization attempts were resisted and subsequently failed. The empires found their raison d'être vis-a-vis their component provinces and principalities in the defence against foreign enemies, first against the Central Asian invaders, the Mongols, then against the Ottomans, which justified the sovereignty of the empire and the loyalty of its subjects. The boundaries between these multi-cultural, decentralized empires and the outside were often imprecise, not least because of their varying geographical composition as well as the nature of the attachment of these territories, especially those far away, to the political centre which varied over time. This turned the borders of the empire, in the sense of a dividing line, into a relative concept as the economic, social, and cultural exchanges over the border zones were flowing relatively freely, constituting areas of interchange, often referred to as borderlands where the exact physical border line had little meaning (Parker, 2010).

The notion of a border as a demarcation line, delineating one geographical space from another, separating a geographical territory from another, is associated with the Westphalian Peace Accords of 1648, purportedly laying the ground for the nation-state. These treaties instituted the principles of the inviolability of borders and non-interference in the domestic affairs of sovereign states and, as a consequence, weakened the political power of the Catholic Church. From these principles followed the concept of a nation-state as a defined territory over which the ruling power had judicial, political, and military control. This conceptualization of political power and territory was strengthened during the nineteenth century in parallel to the emergence of the industrial era, ushering in technological advances in production, transport, and communication (Maier, 2002). To uphold the power of the elite in the shift towards modernity, the state needed to have control over the territory and the inhabitants, both to protect its wealth against enemies and the prerogative to tax its citizens. Borders became strict lines to separate those on the inside from phenomena on the outside that threatened the national order. The juxtaposition of nation and state created the notion of a fairly homogenous, well-defined area where the state could exercise power, including the legitimate monopoly of violence, and in exchange provide order, guarantee civil and other rights, and deliver social security for its citizens (see, Max Weber quoted in Maier, 2002, p. 20). Sovereignty became the privilege of the ruling elite who could count on the loyalty of the citizenry which formed communities around a sense of national belonging.

During the twentieth century, the nation-state fell somewhat in disrepute because of its association with nationalism which in certain European states led to the emergence of radical ideologies, such as Nazism and Fascism, followed by two disastrous wars which redrew national borders in much of continental Europe. At the same time, in many other European states, the nation-state became firmly anchored in modern democratic welfare states which as a form of political organization is predicated on a stable citizenship as voters, taxpayers, and beneficiaries of political rights and social services. The concept of nation-state came therefore to mean different things to different people. For some, nation-states' territoriality, nationalism, and the quest for power were intrinsically linked to war and conquest (Krasner, 1999; Laitin, 2007), while for others, their ability to organize, the loyalty of their citizens and their ability to enshrine the principles and norms of democracy were prerequisites for welfare states and imagined communities (Anderson, 1991; Esping-Andersen, 1990). The Cold War effectively divided Europe into a western part, characterized by democracy and market economy, and an eastern part, dominated by Communist regimes and an inefficient command economy. As many scholars bear witness to, the dominance of Communist ideology in eastern Europe not only prescribed a particular form of organization of society and the economy but also froze ethnic, religious, and linguistic conflicts within the boundaries of the states (Liebich, 2002; Mungiu-Pippidi, 2002).

In the era of globalization, gaining speed from the end of the Cold War onwards, the notion of borders as necessary dividing lines between a well-defined area, political rule, and citizenry began to be seen as outdated, even anachronistic: something of the past that had not been at the service of humanity (see, for instance, Maier, 2002). Many predicted the end of the nation-state with its hard border and protected (gated) communities (Guéhenno, 1995; Ohmae, 1995). It is therefore something of a paradox that globalization in the early 2020s became associated with rising socioeconomic inequalities in advanced industrial societies, the spread of organized crime, and unprecedented levels of immigration, fuelling populism, in places even nativism, and a yearning for protection from these ills. However, the era of globalization lasted undisputed for only about 25 years as the rise of emerging powers, some of them with revisionist ambitions, set off a geopolitical shift, a weakening of the rules-based international system, and great power rivalry between the US and China (Cooley & Nexon, 2020).

Since World War II, the efforts to integrate Europe have been tightly associated with the processes of political, social, and economic modernization, first in western and southern Europe and since the fall of the Berlin Wall in 1989 also including countries in central and eastern Europe. Since its inception, the process of European integration has raised questions regarding the impact on the sovereignty of the member states and whether their statehood would be diminished through the pooling of competences and centralization of political power to the institutions of the European Union (EU) in Brussels. The control and management of the external border of the EU has been, and, still is, a sensitive issue in this regard. Nonetheless, the pressure, first on the European Community (EC) and later the EU, from the states on the outside has been constant as they have sought to end their exclusion from the ever-expanding political community by seeking association and membership. They fear that the exclusion from the European internal market and political alliance would have negative consequences for their socioeconomic wellbeing and safety. The process of an ever-closer union among European states has therefore engendered a twin-challenge of deepening and widening, thus shaping the nature of the internal and external borders of the EU (Amato & Batt, 1999). At the heart of this dilemma lies the question of how far the enlargement of the EU will go and where its outer boundaries will eventually be drawn. The answer to this question will have a significant impact on the states on the inside of those borders as well as for those on the outside.

European Integration and the Reshaping of Europe

At its inception in the early 1950s, it was far from certain that the efforts of the founding states to create the European Coal and Steel Community (ECSC) and then the European Economic Community (EEC) would be of a lasting impact on the organization of Western Europe. However, as steps were taken in the mid-1950s to set up a common market in western Europe, trading nations on the outside, led by the United Kingdom (UK), feared the exclusion from their closest markets. Already in 1961, the British government handed in an application to join the EEC, immediately followed by Denmark, Ireland, and Norway. The accession of the UK, Denmark, and Ireland to the EEC took over ten years to complete and two failed attempts, primarily due to resistance from the French President Charles de Gaulle, who feared that the inclusion of the British would water down the aims of political integration (Michalski, 2014; Michalski & Wallace, 1992). Part of his suspicion was triggered by the UK's initiative in 1960 to set up the European Free Trade Area (EFTA), regrouping most of the Nordic countries, Austria, and Portugal. Although the UK, Denmark, and Ireland joined the EC in 1973, EFTA continued to serve its member states well, not least by providing incentives for setting up bilateral free trade agreements between the EC and the remaining members of EFTA (Archer, 1979). In the early 1970s, most of western Europe was united through close economic and trading links which brought stability to the countries in western and northern Europe, including Finland and Sweden, as well as for Austria, which for reasons of military non-alignment were not members of the North Atlantic Treaty Organization (NATO). In 1962 and 1963, respectively, Greece and Turkey signed far-reaching association agreements with the EEC which envisaged an eventual membership application in the 1980s upon the completion of a customs union (Michalski, 2014). Their association with the EEC enlarged the common market to south-eastern Europe but without including the Balkan Peninsula with Yugoslavia still under the Communist regime of General Josip Tito.

Changing domestic political circumstances played a prominent role in the decisions of Greece, Portugal, and Spain to seek membership in the EC, eventually acceding in 1981 and 1986. Anchoring these states' transitions from military dictatorships to democracies and opening up their economies, especially significant for Spain, to trade on the European internal market were seen as prerequisites by the political elites. For the EC, enlargement to include countries in south-western and south-eastern Europe implied that its borders moved closer to Africa and the Middle East. It also meant that the affinities to Latin America were considerably strengthened. At this time, the migratory pressures on these borders were still quite modest, not least because of the geopolitical context which remained frozen.

The division of Europe during the Cold War acted as a natural border for the European states in the sense that joining the EC was excluded for Communist regimes in Central and Eastern Europe and the Communist regime in Yugoslavia. Yet, the mounting security threats from the Soviet Union in northern Europe also inhibited Finland and Sweden from seeking membership of the EC. Military neutrality also prevented Austria, Switzerland, and Malta from pursuing closer ties to the EC. However, the geopolitical situation in Europe was changing quickly. Towards the end of the 1980s, the Communist regimes in Central and Eastern Europe were crumbling, and soon newly elected democratic governments came to power. The end of the Cold War with the reunification of Germany in 1990 and the demise of the Soviet Union in 1991 lifted the Iron Curtain that had divided Europe since the end of World War II. It heralded a geopolitical shift that had fundamental implications for Europe and the EU for years to come.

With the threat of the Soviet Union dissipating, the neutral and non-aligned EFTA members—Austria, Finland, and Sweden—which had been in the process of negotiating an extensive association agreement with the EC since 1989, took the opportunity and applied for membership in 1989 and 1991, finally joining in 1995 (Michalski & Wallace, 1992; Preston, 1997). The so-called EFTA enlargement was, however, only the prelude to the big eastern enlargement that saw the inclusion of ten central and eastern European countries, Malta and Cyprus in 2004 and 2007. The eastern enlargement was in a preparatory stage for over 15 years, starting with the invitation in the early 1990s of the then European Commissioner, Frans Andriessen, to the former Communist states to conclude an associate membership with the EC, which they promptly refused out of fear of finding themselves in a perpetual waiting room for membership. By the mid-1990s, however, the forerunners had signed association agreements, the so-called Europe Agreements, with the EU, seen as precursors to full membership.

The accession of the central and eastern European countries was a significant step in the process of European integration, not only from an economic and social viewpoint but perhaps even more so from a political perspective (Zielonka, 2006). Three considerations stand out: firstly, the enlargement of the EU to include twelve new countries (on top of the three which joined in 1995) meant that the EU had become near synonymous with Europe. Geopolitically, this means that the EU had become an international player, which led to expectations both at home and abroad about its ability to conduct foreign and security policy to enhance Europe's security, and promote liberal norms and rule of law in the neighbourhood and further afield (Browning & Joenniemi, 2004).

Secondly, the EU's border would now stretch into eastern European heartlands as it now counted among its members former Soviet states and previous Comecon members and satellite states of the Soviet Union. The instability in the East after the demise of the Soviet Union meant that the EU had to think about the nature of the new border so that it did not become a new dividing line between peoples who had strong economic, cultural, and linguistic affinities, but at the same time would not undermine the economic, social, and political transitions of the countries that had just become members, nor the deepening of the EU as a political and economic community (Lavenex, 1998; Liikanen et al., 2016).

Thirdly, as a consequence of the completion of the single market, the internal border of the EU was lifted through the Schengen Convention of 1985. This augmented the challenges on the borders of the enlarged EU, and as a result, the succession of treaty reforms in the 1990s opened a new chapter of Justice and Home Affairs (JHA), which included the issue of borders and the management of asylum and refugees. Although JHA was strictly intergovernmental at first due to the sensitivity of the issue area, by the revisions of the Amsterdam Treaty 1997, it had evolved into a European policy competence in its own right (Monar, 2001).

The enlarged EU, along with new competences in foreign and security policy, migration, asylum policy, and border management gained through treaty reforms in the 1990s and 2000s, had a great impact on the regions bordering the EU. For this reason, the EU took the initiative of setting up the European Neighbourhood Policy (ENP) with the aim of drawing countries bordering the EU in the east and south closer to it (Schumacher et al., 2017). In regard to the states of the former Yugoslavia, apart from Slovenia and Croatia which joined the EU in 2004 and 2013 respectively, the enlargement process is long and uncertain. As a part of the ENP, the EU set up a special strategy for the western Balkans in the form of Stabilization and Association agreements concluded from 1999 onwards and updated several times since then. From the perspective of the internal and external borders of the EU, the management of its relationship with neighbouring states is of utmost importance. The EU's aim was to cushion the effects of a hard external border to the states in the neighbourhood, but also to strengthen the borders against unwanted pressures and activities. Nonetheless, because of reasons lying both within as well as beyond these countries' borders, the EU is now facing a dilemma of having to fortify the external border in order to keep the internal borders open, something which cannot be taken for granted judging from the experiences of the migration crisis in 2015–16 and the COVID-19 pandemic in 2020–21.

This exposé of the changing borders of the EU would not be complete without discussing the withdrawal of the UK from the EU, which took effect on 31 January 2020 (Diamond et al., 2018). The decision of the UK to leave the EU was seen at the time as a major setback for European integration, with some predicting that other member states would soon follow in Frexit, Swexit, or Grexit. To be sure, the withdrawal of the UK had significant implications for the EU in economic, social, and political terms and also from the perspective of European foreign and security policy as the weight of the EU in international politics was believed to shrink, not least because of the considerable military capabilities of the UK. However, the impact of Brexit was felt the most by Britain itself which lost the free access to the EU's internal market and its place around the table in the EU internal policy-making. The miscalculation of the conservative governments under Theresa May and Boris Johnson for seamless access to the market without abiding to the EU regulatory regimes or the rules of the EU's customs union led to acrimonious negotiations with the EU which resulted in a fairly modest free trade agreement. A main reason for leaving the EU was the urge to regain control over national borders and purportedly stem the flow of immigrants to the UK. Ironically, in the years following Brexit, immigration into the UK has increased as a result of an increase in labour migration from outside the EU and a growing number of illegal entries of migrants and asylum seekers. Despite its geographical, economic, and cultural closeness to the EU and its member states, the UK has a less advanced form of association with the EU than countries such as Canada, Japan, or South Korea, and certainly much less close than the countries in the European Economic Area, Norway, Liechtenstein, and Iceland. The EU was adamant to protect the integrity of the internal market, EU law, and political unity proved in concrete terms where the dividing lines between membership and non-membership lie and where the limits of association to the EU without becoming a member are.

Perspectives on the Evolving Borders of the EU in an Unsettled Neighbourhood

As discussed at length above, the admission of countries from Central and Eastern Europe and the south-eastern Mediterranean raised the question of the EU's future borders in a broader sense, not as barriers between peoples but rather as areas for contact—for economic, social, and cultural exchange (Amato & Batt, 1999). Over the subsequent 15 years, the Union succeeded in integrating these new member states. New external borders then emerged—vis-à-vis Russia in the northeast, the Black Sea in Eastern Europe, and the countries in the Balkans (Schimmelfennig & Sedelmeier, 2005). The EU has been clear, despite the new types of deeper cooperation it has established with its neighbours to the south and east, it is keen to distinguish membership from other (partial) forms of integration, as embodied in association agreements and various free trade arrangements. The external border of the Union remains a dividing line between a zone of material prosperity, democracy, the rule of law, and political rights and freedoms, on the one side, and an area of instability and a lack of socioeconomic development, on the other.

The EU has learned from previous crises on the border, to be sure. Just as surely, moreover, the unthinkable fact that war is again raging on European soil helped generate consensus within the Union. Nevertheless, the EU confronts major challenges that will put its capacity for consensus to considerable tests, over the short and the long term. In this seventh edition of Palgrave's Interdisciplinary European Studies, researchers in law, economics, and political science examine what it means for the EU's internal and external borders that it finds itself in a global environment marked by conflicting norms, rising strategic tensions, and competition between systems and regulatory frameworks. How has the European security order been reshaped by Russia's invasion of Ukraine? What does the geopolitical shift mean for the EU as a global trading power? Can the Union continue to disseminate norms internationally and within its neighbourhood? Beyond the physical border, how does the EU international market regime distinguish between insiders and outsiders on the market? And finally, how has the Union's border policy developed, what forms does it take, and how can it handle the tension between open borders internally and stricter surveillance of the external borders?

The evolution of the EU's border regime is the theme of the chapter by Johanna Pettersson Fürst who considers the dilemma of the hardening of the EU's external borders and the challenge to the freedom of circulation. She begins with considering the impact of growing tensions over border policy on the measures taken to control movement across EU borders. The main issue she addresses is how policies in this area challenge and contribute to European integration. Pettersson Fürst understands borders as political institutions created and maintained through processes in which material conditions, political decisions, and patterns of behaviour interact. In order to understand the consequences of border policy for European integration, she employs a theoretical framework with two dimensions: First, does a given policy apply to internal or external borders? Second, does it tend to dismantle or strengthen the borders in question? Pettersson Fürst analyses developments in three different dimensions of EU border policy. The first has to do with 'temporary internal border controls', the use of which increased significantly in connection with the refugee crisis of 2015, as well as later during the

COVID-19 pandemic. Here, she shows how internal border controls have challenged the very core of the Schengen Agreement, through the temporary halt to freedom of movement they have entailed. The second dimension concerns developments in the EU's external border policies, the aim of which is to control migration from outside the Union. External border controls have successively increased, both in terms of resources and mandates for the European Border and Coast Guard Agency (also known as Frontex), and geographically, as border controls are moved beyond the EU's external borders. The third dimension of border policy relates to EU investments in new technology for border control. To conclude, Pettersson Fürst discusses how these different trends can be understood from the standpoint of integration. The strengthening of both internal and external borders can be seen as defensive integration. As Pettersson Fürst sees it, there are risks associated with the tightening of borders as a simple solution to complex problems. She concludes with a call for a clear defence of free movement of people and fundamental rights.

The impact on the EU's role in the world economy and the return of a hard border policy is the theme of the chapter by Fredrik Sjöholm. In the chapter, he considers the return of borders in Europe and the world from the standpoint of trade. Trade within the EU, as well as between it and the rest of the world, is facing higher barriers. This trend can in part be explained, Sjöholm shows, by the distributive effects of globalization. More specifically, groups that have not benefitted from globalization—whose jobs were moved out of the country, for example—have voted for more protectionist and inward-looking policies. Noting the influence on the EU of developments in China and the US, Sjöholm further elaborates the view of globalization in those two countries. The rise of China, with its state-controlled economy, has helped to change views on economic policy in other countries as well—towards a more positive view of direct involvement by the state. The US, with its protectionist policies and big investments in industry, has also influenced the EU in various ways.

The result, according to Sjöholm, has been a general concern within the Union that the EU's companies are lagging behind competitors in other countries. A stronger focus on industrial policy is evident, both in the EU and in individual member states. A long series of planned measures, if introduced, will work as a regime change in European policy on the respective roles of the state and the market. This also involves a changed view of globalization, with openness to trade and foreign direct investment taking a backseat to a more inward-looking approach. Sjöholm argues that this emerging strategy—with its more active industrial policy, in which governments select companies and industries for special support and protect them against competition—is negative for growth and prosperity. Instead, Sjöholm contends, the EU should maintain open borders. This applies to both internal and external borders. In other words, the Union must ensure a well-functioning internal market, and it should work for an open and rules-based global trade regime.

In the fourth chapter, Marja-Liisa Öberg examines the outer limits of the internal market and their importance for EU foreign policy, particularly in relation to the Union's neighbours. The internal market, as Öberg sees it, is the core of European integration. It has also gained greater external importance for the Union. Through various types of international agreements, third countries are given the opportunity to participate in the internal market, in exchange for adopting the Union's regulatory framework in the areas concerned. The goals range from the establishment of initial partnerships with third countries to the full-scale integration of non-member states into the internal market. Öberg begins with a discussion of the importance of the internal market for relations within the Union. She then considers its impact on the EU's dealings with its immediate neighbours. Her treatment embraces both states that seek closer relations with the Union in hopes of eventually joining it and states that desire a close relationship with the EU but do not wish to become members, such as Switzerland and the UK.

Öberg believes the application of the internal market's regulatory framework, and the strong economic and political ties to the Union thereby forged, have become the key to a long-term commitment to the European project both within and outside the Union. Trade within the region is mainly conducted in accordance with EU regulations—a fact which confirms, in the view of the author, its status as the region's normative superpower. Russia's war in Ukraine has further underlined the importance of cooperation between the EU and its neighbours within the framework of the internal market. Besides being an important marketplace and a primary pillar of the Union's integration, the expanded internal market has gained greater symbolic importance as representing a choice between paths—between Europe's sphere of influence and Russia's.

Citing the importance of the internal market within the Union, as well as for EU policy towards neighbouring states, Öberg argues that the extended bounds of the internal market constitute a highly significant part of the EU's external policy, serving to consolidate its leading role in the region. The expansion of the internal market offers third countries an excellent opportunity to identify themselves as members of the wider European community, thereby cementing their long-term commitment to the project of European integration. Öberg contends that, while the formal, physical, and administrative borders of the Union persist, the borders of the internal market continue to fade, thereby broadening and deepening the project of European integration and promoting common security and prosperity. In conclusion, Öberg argues that the Union should continue to deploy the attraction of the internal market in its dealings with its neighbours. Flexible integration should serve as the benchmark here, without by virtue of that eliminating the formal boundary between member states and third countries which EU membership entails.

The chapter by Ann-Kristin Jonasson reassesses the attempts by the EU to disseminate norms in the southern Mediterranean neighbourhood in regard to its foundational values and norms and in regard to climate change mitigation. She begins by discussing how the EU, on the basis of its founding treaties, has undertaken to spread its fundamental values—democracy, human rights, and the norms based on these—in the international arena. At the same time, the Union has been subject to stinging criticism for not being the normative or 'good' actor it likes to portray itself as. Like all other international actors, critics claim, the EU pursues its own short-term interests above all—sometimes at the expense of its cherished values. Such a gap between word and deed is cause for concern, according to scholars in the field. It runs the risk of eroding the Union's legitimacy, thereby reducing its global influence. Indeed, Jonasson argues, the Union may be undermining the norms and values themselves, by failing to act in line with them or to defend them when they are challenged. In this time of conflict, when the democratic order is under threat worldwide, the Union must work to protect—both within its borders and beyond them—norms and values linked to democracy and human rights, even if the short-term effect of so doing conflicts with its own short-term interests.

In order to ascertain how the EU can best work to disseminate such norms, Jonasson reviews what commentators in this area regard as necessary if value-based norms are to be spread. She also considers the EU's own experiences in this context. In particular, she examines and compares its efforts to promote democracy and to promote climate goals in its southern neighbourhood. Success in promoting democracy has been notably absent, whereas work on the climate seems to have fared better. This, Jonasson argues, is because efforts on behalf of the climate, unlike those aiming to promote democracy, are based on what researchers highlight as crucial for the successful dissemination of value-based norms: i.e., they reflect a genuine desire on the part of both parties to embrace the norms in question and to promote their spread. The work of introducing such norms is thus locally owned, and their dissemination is based on reciprocity and dialogue between the EU and its partner countries. Jonasson stresses in conclusion that, instead of pursuing its own short-term interests, the Union should contribute to the development of democratic goals in its partner countries and encourage local ownership of their realization. By taking part in a true dialogue, the EU can work to spread the value-based norms which form the foundation for its existence.

The ability of the EU to spread its model of social market economy beyond its borders is the theme of the chapter by Pär Hallström. In the chapter, the author takes a broad approach to understanding the EU's role in the world. His point of departure is that the model of society on which the nations of Europe and the EU are based—with democracy, human rights, the rule of law, and a liberal economy that allows state intervention to achieve social goals—is not just being called into question by Russia's invasion of Ukraine; other developments too pose a challenge to the Union, among them Europe's diminishing role in the world economy, especially in relation to authoritarian China, and its declining share of the world's population, not least in relation to the countries of Africa.

Against this background, Hallström analyses the ability of the EU and its member states to meet these challenges by influencing the larger world, directly and indirectly, to adopt European values. He does this by compiling and systematically examining the factors he considers crucial in that process, with particular stress on their legal aspects. He begins with a look at different geopolitical theories and at the distinction between political, economic, and soft power. On this basis, he examines how a European-inspired social and legal system has been adopted globally, but often in such a way as to take on a local colour when it encounters a traditional culture. On the other hand, the EU's more technical and economic norms have undoubtedly inspired corresponding rules in other countries and its organization has served as a model for other regional associations. Internally, the EU took over decision-making power in the field of foreign trade from its member states, thus acquiring an important instrument with which to exercise economic/political power for its purposes. Externally, the EU proffered the support for the WTO on the basis of its inclination towards international free trade, a stance which has increasingly been challenged by China's aspiration to become the Middle Kingdom once again. Hallström concludes that the EU, despite the major challenges it faces, has an opportunity to influence the rest of the world in favour of the ideals that form its foundation. It possesses, namely, the economic and soft power needed, and it can use the law as a means to achieve this.

In the following chapter, Torbjörn Becker and Anders Åslund evaluate the EU's dilemma of being dependent on Russian energy imports at the start of the war in Ukraine. The authors first analyse how the mutual dependence of the EU and Russia has developed. Their focus is on Russia's energy exports to the Union. The question Becker and Åslund pose in their chapter is whether this dependence will lead to division or to greater cohesion within the EU, now that Russia's war of aggression against Ukraine has forced the Union to reconsider its dependence on Russian energy. Over the short term, sanctions and the war have put a halt to a large proportion of Russian gas exports to the EU, and energy prices have skyrocketed as a consequence. Becker and Åslund show how the interdependence between the EU and Russia looks with respect to different types of energy, and they discuss in the light of this the sanctions and counter-sanctions implemented and planned by both sides as a result of the Russian war in Ukraine. The short-term effects of these sanctions, Becker and Åslund contend, will be palpable both in Europe and in Russia; but Russia will lose more in the end, both with regard to its relationship with the EU and in terms of its own economic development. Energy exports are a fundamental driving force for the Russian economy, and the country will not be able to wean itself from dependence on the export of fossil energy without major political and institutional changes. Without new leadership in Russia that prioritizes law and order within the country over the exercise of power outside it, the economic prospects for the country are dim at best. For the EU, the big challenge will be to manage the internal cracks that come to light when the relationship with Russia is reconsidered.

The EU has a historic opportunity now, in the judgement of Becker and Åslund, to speed up its green transition, while at the same time improving its security by making itself independent of Russian energy.

This may require some transfers within the Union, in order to counteract divisions that may arise when countries with varying economic conditions and differing levels of dependence on Russian energy have to compromise on how the transition is to be achieved. Becker and Åslund conclude that if the EU and its member states are able to reach a consensus in such negotiations, the effect will be to strengthen both the EU's energy security and its external borders.

In the eighth chapter, Maria Bergström analyses the Union's law and policy against money laundering and the financing of terrorism in a digitalizing and fragmented world. Money laundering is an ever-changing threat that must be constantly combatted, for it continually facilitates new forms of criminal activity: drug trafficking in the 1980s; organized crime in the 1990s; terrorism after 11 September 2001; and tax fraud in the 2010s. Taking her point of departure in the development of the EU's regulatory framework, Bergström describes the various threats, interests, and actors involved. The main question she poses is what the legal challenges are, whether they are addressed by existing instruments and current legislative proposals, and whether there is room for further reforms.

Bergström identifies a set of challenges for the emerging regulatory framework: First, the increase in public–private cooperation, in which private actors are involved in designing the regulatory framework and are assigned 'police' tasks. Second, the exchange of information and the special problems posed by digitization. Third, the interface between administrative law and criminal law, as well as different types of sanctions. Fourth, the long-standing 'securitization' of money laundering and terrorism financing, which among other things has called forth an increased competence for the EU's institutions. With the increased fragmentation and digitization of central aspects of our modern world, recently updated regulatory frameworks face swiftly mounting challenges. The hope, according to Bergström, is that the diversity of tools that will be at the disposal of the Commission and of a proposed central Union agency will enable the EU to keep pace with the complex and rapidly shifting international environment in this area, with its fluctuating risks, without resulting in restrictions on fundamental rights. Bergström also looks at the latest legislative package, which is being discussed in the European Parliament and the Council. She considers it of special importance that developments be monitored in this area, so that society's efforts to respond to constantly changing threats do not result in restrictions on the fundamental rights of individuals.

The European security architecture is the theme of the chapter by Kjell Engelbrekt. In the chapter, the author raises the overarching question of whether Russia's war in Ukraine signals the definitive collapse of the European security order, or whether there are prospects for the latter's renewal in a more robust guise within the near future. Engelbrekt reviews the origins and nature of the European security order, whereupon he delineates its current exposure to an exceptional challenge. Said challenge consists in the fact that one of the guarantor powers for stability and security—not just regionally but globally as well—Russia, has attacked a neighbouring country with full force, thereby casting aside the most fundamental norms and principles of the United Nations Charter. It bears stressing in this connection that the members of a regional security order are so intertwined that both the actions of individual governments and significant events within each country potentially impinge on the security of the others. It is thus clear, according to Engelbrekt, that the Kremlin's brutal war of aggression against Ukraine directly threatens the whole of Europe, as well as making individual countries along Russia's border vulnerable and thus damaging them economically and socially.

Further, Engelbrekt discusses how Europe—via the EU, NATO, and other organizations—has sought to ensure that Moscow would fail in its ambition to reshape the European security order to its own advantage. The measures taken include sanctions; increasingly generous humanitarian, financial, and military support for Ukraine from Europe; and extensive diplomatic efforts to meet the challenge at a global level—in the UN, the G7, the G20, and other forums. One factor that Engelbrekt judges will be important for the rest of this decade will be how Germany uses the additional one hundred billion euros it has allocated to the Bundeswehr, its armed forces. This involves a potential defence capability of a level that can also prove significant outside of Europe and its immediate surroundings, at least if the forces in question are allowed to work together with those of other EU and NATO countries.

Engelbrekt argues in conclusion that the EU and its member states need to reassess the area of security policy. They must do what they can to preserve their political unity and to reduce their dependence on Russian energy, fertilizers, and other income-generating exports—all the while building up their capacity to defend themselves against the threat from the east by various societal and military means. Engelbrekt avers that most European states have already renewed or expanded their commitment to increase defence spending, as the US has long called on

NATO members to do. In addition, there are several signs the Union is about to shift the focus of its security policy away from an emphasis on economic investments in its neighbours to the south and east, and towards a more traditional geopolitical approach where the stress lies on military power, energy security, access to strategic raw materials, and investments in technological competence within areas important for the defence industry.

In the tenth chapter of the book, Anders Åslund and Torbjörn Becker ask if the EU has the ability to conceive a kind of European Marshall Plan for Ukraine on its road towards EU membership. They begin with outlining a plan for the reconstruction of Ukraine, with the aim of one day making the country a full member of the EU. Åslund and Becker remind us that the war in Ukraine will eventually end, at which point the EU must be ready to help the country build anew for a better future in the Union. Already in 2023, the costs for Ukraine's reconstruction were enormous, and they are increasing with each day the war continues.

Ukraine will therefore need far-reaching support, which should be managed within the framework of an EU agency devoted to the purpose. The task of such a body would be to coordinate donors and maintain a close dialogue with the government of Ukraine on goals and processes. Åslund and Becker also point out other vital principles for such a reconstruction: the aid must arrive quickly, but be subject to conditions ensuring it is used in the best manner for all of the country's citizens; the assistance should take the form of a grant and not a loan; and the focus of the rebuilding effort should be on creating a sustainable economy with a clear green transition in terms of energy and infrastructure. Ukraine's entry into the Union, moreover, must be a crucial factor in prioritizing institutional reforms that strengthen the reconstruction of all parts of Ukrainian society. Important points on the EU agenda ought to include securing the short-term financing of Ukraine's national budget while the war is ongoing; working for a start to negotiations on Ukrainian membership in the first half of 2023; and ensuring there is a clear plan for how the outside world is to organize and finance Ukraine's long-term reconstruction. A successful Ukraine within the EU, Åslund and Becker point out, will enhance the security and prosperity not just of Ukraine itself, but of the entire Union as well.

In the last chapter, Antonina Bakardjieva Engelbrekt, Per Ekman, Anna Michalski, and Lars Oxelheim set the paradox of the internal and external borders of the EU in perspective from the vantage point of past, present, and future developments. To begin with, the authors take stock of the challenges which are besetting the EU's internal and external borders from the perspective of contemporary events and evaluate them against previous economic, social, and political developments in the Union. They consider what can be learned from past experiences concerning internal borders which in the last decades have been lifted only to be reinstated again, as well as external borders which are unrelentingly hardening in order to keep unwanted pressure in terms of irregular immigration at bay while trying to prevent hard security threats, terrorism, and organized crime to enter. The chapter concludes by drawing some lessons from the geopolitical shift and the war in Ukraine regarding the EU's border policy, the European security architecture, the internal market, and a future enlargement towards eastern and south-eastern European countries.

References

Amato, G& Batt, J. (1999). *The long-term implications of EU enlargement: The nature of the new borders: final report of the reflection group*. Fiesole: European University Institute.

Anderson, B. (1991). *Imagined communities: Reflections on the origins and spread of Nationalism*. Verso.

Archer, C. (1976). Britain and Scandinavia: Their Relations within EFTA, 1960–1968, *Cooperation and Conflict*, XI, pp. 1–23.

Browning, C. S., & Joenniemi, P. (2004). The Challenges of EU and NATO Enlargement. *Cooperation and Conflict, 39*(3), 227–342.

Cooley, A., & Nexon, D. (2020). *Exit from Hegemony: The Unraveling of the American Global Order*. Oxford University Press.

Diamond, P., Nedergaard, P., & Rosamond, B. (2018). *The Routledge Handbook of the Politics of Brexit*. Routledge.

Esping-Andersen, G. (1990). *Three Worlds of Welfare Capitalism*. Princeton University Press.

Guéhenno, J.-M. (1995). *The End of the Nation-State*. University of Minnesota Press.

Hassner, P. (2002). 'Fixed Borders or Moving Borderlands? A New Type of Border for a New Type of Entity'. In E. Unbound (Ed.), *Zielonka, J* Enlarging and Reshaping the Boundaries of the European Union. (pp. 38–50). Routledge.

Krasner, S. (1999). *Sovereignty: Organized Hypocrisy*. Princeton University Press.

Laitin, D. (2007). *Nation, States, and Violence*. Oxford University Press.

Lavenex, S. (1998). Asylum, Migration and Central-Eastern Europe: Challenges to EU Enlargement. *European Foreign Affairs Review, 3*(2), 275–294.

Liebich, A. (2002). Ethnic Minorities and Long-term Implications of EU Enlargement. In E. Unbound (Ed.), *Zielonka, J* (pp. 117–136). Routledge.

Liikanen, I., Scott, J. W., & Sotkasiira, T. (2016). *The EU's Eastern Border: Migration, Borders and Regional Stability*. Taylor and Francis.

Maier, C. S. (2002). Does Europe Need a Frontier? From Territorial to Redistributive Community. In E. Unbound (Ed.), *Zielonka, J* (pp. 17–37). Routledge.

Michalski, A. (2014). The Enlarging European Union. In D. Dinan (Ed.), *Origins and Evolution of the European Union* (2nd ed., pp. 274–301). Oxford University Press.

Michalski, A., & Wallace, H. (1992). *The European Community: The Challenge of Enlargement* (2nd ed.). The Royal Institute of International Affairs, Chatham House.

Monar, J. (2001). The justice and home affairs dimension in EU enlargement. *International Spectator, 36*(3), 37–46.

Mungiu-Pippidi, A. (2002). Facing the 'Desert of Tartars': The Eastern Border of Europe. In E. Unbound (Ed.), *Zielonka, J* (pp. 51–77). Routledge.

Ohmae, K. (1995). *The End of the Nation State: The Rise of Regional Economies*. The Free Press.

Parker, N. (2010). Empire as a Geopolitical Figure. *Geopolitics, 15*(1), 109–132.

Preston, C. (1997). *Enlargement & Integration in the European Union*. Routledge.

Schimmelfennig, F., & Sedelmeier, U. (2005). *The Europeanization of Central and Eastern Europe*. Cornell University Press.

Schumacher, T., Marchetti, A., & Demmelhuber, T. (2017). *The Routledge Handbook on the European Neighbourhood Policy*. Routledge.

Zielonka, J. (2006). *Europe as Empire: The Nature of the Enlarged European Union*. Oxford University Press.

CHAPTER 2

EU Border Policy: Enhanced Border Security and Challenges to Free Movement

Johanna Pettersson Fürst

As the overarching theme of this book suggests, questions and problems relating to the external and internal borders of the European Union (EU) are becoming more prominent, as instability worsens and geopolitical tensions rise around the world. Many studies of borders and border politics have pointed out that the management of borders has become a prominent political issue globally and that border-control practices have gotten more expansive (Dodds, 2021; Jones, 2016; Longo, 2018; Simmons, 2017; Yuval-Davis et al., 2019). Borders are increasingly the subject of political debate, and walls and barriers are being erected across the world (Simmons, 2019; Vallet, 2020). The trend towards politicised borders and stricter border controls is also clearly visible in Europe. With Russia's invasion of Ukraine in 2022, moreover, the new geopolitical (dis)order came violently to a head, as did the challenges to territorial integrity. Even before then, however, several crises for the EU over the last decade have been understood as crises of the Union's borders.

J. Pettersson Fürst (✉)
Uppsala University, Uppsala, Sweden
e-mail: Johanna.Pettersson@statsvet.uu.se

A. Bakardjieva Engelbrekt et al. (eds.), *The Borders of the European Union in a Conflictual World*,
https://doi.org/10.1007/978-3-031-54200-8_2

Brexit, for example, redrew the borders of the EU. The 'refugee crisis' of 2015 brought an increased focus on the EU's external borders, and led to an internal border crisis as well. The latter was then renewed due to restrictions on mobility imposed during the COVID-19 pandemic, which challenged the principle of free movement within the Schengen Area. The war in the EU's immediate neighbourhood, combined with climate change and growing geopolitical tensions, indicates that many future challenges will be connected with EU border policy. The question of how borders are to be guarded is closely linked to the persistent question of what the relationship should be between the Union and its member states. The imposition of internal border controls, for example, raises the question of whether freedom of movement is threatened. Indeed, might the renationalisation of border controls even lead to the disintegration of the Union?

The issue addressed in this chapter is how the EU and its members deal with the various challenges facing them in the area of border policy. By highlighting three different trends in EU border policy, I seek to illustrate the questions involved. In the first section, I present a theoretical framework for understanding the role of borders in European integration. The second section, looking inward, deals with the use of 'temporary internal border controls'—i.e., the reintroduction of national border controls within the Schengen Area. The third section reviews the development of EU policy on the external borders, the aim of which is to control migration from the outside. In a striking shift in this area, border controls are being moved further and further away from the outer borders of the Union itself. Since the refugee crisis of 2015, moreover, there has been a dramatic expansion and reform of the EU's Border and Coast Guard Agency, commonly known as Frontex. In the fourth section, I take a closer look at the development and use of new technology, and the increasingly 'borderless' methods of border control. The chapter ends with a discussion of what these different trends say about the state of the Union's internal and external borders. Are integration and internal freedom of movement under threat? Or are we sooner seeing a consolidation of the external borders of the EU?

Borders as Political Institutions

Before moving on to the discussion of border politics and policies within the EU, I should clarify certain concepts and underlying assumptions. From a political-science perspective, borders are best understood as political institutions, which are created and maintained through processes in which political decisions, material conditions, and patterns of behaviour interact to establish and maintain the function of borders. Territorial boundaries are central to the existence of the modern state, and it is from them that much of what we understand as a state has its beginnings: without a clearly defined territory within which the state's political decisions can take effect, it is difficult to imagine the idea of the sovereign state. Once a state's territorial boundaries are established, they fulfil several important functions of both a practical and symbolic nature. It is at the borders that what belongs and what does not belong can be defined; thus, the marking of borders—with the help of buildings, fences, flags, and signs—has often been critical in the creation of a national 'we'. Borders thus perform functions of inclusion and exclusion. They are also important, however, as gates and bridges for regulating flows between different countries. The manner in which they are managed, therefore, has substantial consequences, not least on economic life and on people's rights and freedoms.

In the EU, many of the questions concerning the relationship between member states and the Union come to a head over questions relating to the management of borders. Questions of efficiency versus democratic control, of integration through intergovernmentalism or neofunctionalism, and whether power ultimately rests with the member states or with the supranational institutions—all are directly linked to decisions regarding the Union's internal borders and its shared external borders. The question I intend to address in this chapter is how the ongoing border politics of the EU can be understood based on the tension between European integration on the one hand and state sovereignty on the other.

A suitable framework for understanding the relationship in the EU between the politics of internal borders and that of external ones has been presented by Schimmelfennig (2021). This author starts from the concept of *bordering*, which is often used in studies of border politics to illustrate that borders are not something static; rather, they are constantly created and recreated through social and political processes.

In this regard, bordering refers to the activities and political processes involved in the creation of borders. In order to describe the creation of borders within the EU, I start from the two dimensions that Schimmelfennig (2021) identifies: first, the internal and external borders; and second, the different directions that bordering takes—from de-bordering (i.e., the dismantling of borders) to re-bordering (their strengthening). Based on these dimensions, according to Schimmelfennig (2021, p. 316), we can identify four positions in which territorial integration within the EU might find itself: (1) *diluted integration*, where both internal and external borders are dismantled; (2) *effective integration*, where external borders are reinforced at the same time that internal ones are dismantled; (3) *disintegration*, where national borders are strengthened at the same time that external borders are dismantled; and (4) *defensive integration*, where both internal and external borders are strengthened at the same time.

The relationship between bordering processes at the external and the internal borders can thus be said to generate four possible directions in which European integration can move. The polar extremes of this model, in terms of the level of integration, are maximum effective integration, where the endpoint is exemplified by the creation of a federal European state, and maximum disintegration, where the endpoint is a return to the national territorial framework (as through a departure of more states from the EU, along the lines of Brexit). In the case of the middling outcomes of diluted or defensive integration, by contrast, the level of integration is neither as total as in the case of effective integration, nor as weak as in the case of disintegration. In the case of diluted integration, integration is weakened by the lack of any consolidation of the external borders; in the case of defensive integration, it is weakened by the restrictions on internal movement. In the following three sections, I employ this theoretical framework to analyse the developmental tendencies that have been most evident with regard to European borders in recent years. The tension between the national level and the European one emerges most clearly in the first section below, which deals with the use of internal border controls. The next two sections describe the border-making processes for reinforcing the common external borders. I return, finally, to the theoretical framework in the concluding section, wherein I discuss how these different processes can be understood in terms of European integration.

Internal Border Controls as a National Response to the Migration Crisis and the COVID-19 Pandemic

Article 17 of the original Schengen Agreement, concluded by the Benelux countries, Germany and France in 1985, later incorporated as acquis of the EC, and subsequently as title VI, of the Treaty of Amsterdam in 1997, sets out the following long-term objective:

> In terms of the free movement of persons, the parties shall seek to abolish controls at the common borders and to transfer these to their external borders. To this end, they shall initially, if necessary, seek the harmonization of laws and other regulations concerning the prohibitions and restrictions underlying the controls and take complementary measures to protect the security and prevent illegal immigration of nationals from countries which are not members of the European Communities. (European Commission, 2000)

Thus, ever since the start of the Schengen Agreement, there has been an important connection between on the one hand the abolition of border controls between the member states, and on the other the security of external borders and the prevention of 'illegal immigration'. The basic principle is that the internal borders, which separate EU member states from each other, should be freed from border controls to the greatest extent possible. With the UK's exit from the Union, the only EU member states that are not part of Schengen are Ireland (which has special agreements) and Bulgaria, Croatia, Cyprus, and Romania (which will eventually join). Iceland, Norway, and Switzerland are in Schengen but not the EU. In this chapter, I focus mainly on the countries that are in both bodies. Freedom of movement for EU citizens is not just a cornerstone of European integration; it is also that EU policy which EU citizens themselves value most highly. According to the recent Eurobarometer (European Commission, 2022), as many as 84 per cent support freedom of movement within the Union. It bears adding, however, that the second and third most popular policies are a common defence and security policy (77%) and a common migration policy (70%). This suggests there is also strong support for increased cooperation on external border controls.

Moreover, freedom of movement within the Schengen Area requires each member state to help guard the Union's external borders—on land, at sea, and in the air. The absence of internal border controls thus requires that each member state have confidence in the willingness and capacity of all the other members to do their part to control the shared external borders. The Schengen Area is not based on supranational institutions for border control; instead, the responsibility for external border control lies primarily with each individual member state. At the same time, the responsibility for external borders is distributed unevenly among the member states, due to their differing geographical (and economic) positions. The Dublin Regulation stipulates that the country at which an asylum-seeker first arrives is responsible for the asylum process. This, in combination with a lack of legal routes into the EU, means that the main task of external border control falls mainly on the countries that have external land and sea borders in the south and southeast of Europe. The maintenance of internal mobility thus requires that certain member states take greater responsibility than others for guarding the external borders.

The EU's internal borders have been opened, then, even as its external borders are not guarded on a common basis. The latter, moreover, have changed constantly with the Union's enlargement. The tension thereby generated has always been an element of the EU's fundamental character. The territorial borders of the Union have never been consolidated, due to the repeated addition of new members (Bartolini, 2005)—or, as with Brexit, due to a member state's departure. The absence of strongly consolidated common borders also contributes to making the Union the *sui generis* entity that it is. Strongly consolidated external borders, namely, are primarily associated with a sovereign nation-state or federation. It would probably take a lot for member states to consider giving up control over their territory in the way that a fully shared external border would necessitate. During the 1990s and 2000s, national territorial control and open internal borders co-existed in a fairly conflict-free way; the internal borders were opened up without the external borders' being overly tested. This changed in the 2010s, however. First, the Arab Spring in 2011, and later the refugee crisis of 2015, put the system to the test and led to debates about Schengen's being in crisis (Börzel & Risse, 2018; Casella Colombeau, 2020; Votoupalová, 2018). Due to the arrival of large numbers of refugees in Greece and Italy, many of whom moved on to other EU countries, several Schengen states decided to reintroduce internal border controls on a temporary basis.

The reintroduction of temporary internal border controls does not directly violate Schengen rules, as it is part of these rules. In the event of a serious threat to national order and security, member states have the right to carry out such internal border controls. This exception was already included in the original agreement on the Schengen *acquis* from 1985, and it is provided for today by a series of provisions in the Schengen Borders Code (see Regulation 2016/399, Articles 25–35). Before 2015, temporary internal border controls were a tool that was used very rarely, usually for a few days to a week or so, in order to increase security around international events such as summits or sporting events (Groenendijk, 2004; Pettersson Fürst, 2023a). During the refugee crisis, however, controls were introduced in order to manage migration for the first time. Several countries decided to do so, and the controls they introduced were both more extensive and longer-lasting than had previously been customary. This prompted declarations that the border controls meant 'the death of Schengen', and worries that they would bring the end of freedom of movement in Europe (Brekke & Staver, 2018). Since border controls between member states challenge freedom of movement—the very core of European integration—commentators have described them as a serious problem and a 'crisis of Schengen' (Börzel & Risse, 2018). Furthermore, six of the countries that introduced temporary internal border controls during the height of the refugee crisis in 2015—Austria, Denmark, France, Germany, Norway, and Sweden—have continued their controls in some form ever since (European Commission, 2023a). Over the course of this time, the justifications proffered for the controls have changed somewhat—from the need 'to stop the large influx of asylum-seekers' to the need to prevent cross-border crime or to reduce the risk of terrorist acts (Pettersson Fürst, 2023a)—but the fact remains: these countries have continued their border controls far beyond the point where they can be considered temporary.

When the COVID-19 pandemic broke out in the spring of 2020, the question of internal borders came up again—with full force. As the virus spread, several countries chose to reintroduce internal border controls, often as one of several measures for reducing the spread of the virus. During the 2016–2020 period, it bears noting, internal border controls had been used very sparingly except for the continuations mentioned above. In the spring of 2020, however, that changed quickly. A total of 17 Schengen countries introduced internal border controls vis-à-vis their neighbours, as part of an effort to curb the spread of the new coronavirus (Pettersson Fürst, 2023a, 2023b). These border controls differed in several ways from previous ones. They were more far-reaching in scope, and they were used at the same time by a larger number of countries. Some border crossings were closed completely, and in many cases, travellers were stopped from crossing borders altogether. However, the closing of borders was by no means unique to the Schengen Area; rather, it was something that was done around the world in response to the pandemic, often in combination with restrictions on movement within countries. In view, however, of the central importance of freedom of movement for European integration, the border controls presented a clear challenge to solidarity within the Schengen Area, not least because they were aimed at EU citizens in general for the first time. Heinikoski (2020) has shown that, in the face of the health threat posed by the pandemic, different member states interpreted the Schengen regulations differently, and they cited different legal provisions in order to justify their controls. Moreover, the common guidelines that the European Commission set out for border controls were not implemented in a coordinated manner (Somer et al., 2020). Somer, Meissner, and Tekin (2020) refer to this absence of coordinated action as a 'sovereignty reflex': in the face of the perceived threat from the pandemic, most member states focused on controlling their own borders and protecting their own populations. On the one hand, this shows that the member states have retained the initiative, despite the far-reaching integration that has taken place within the EU. On the other hand, they behaved the same way despite the absence of coordination. However, the reflex to introduce border controls when faced with a threat also brings the question of European integration to a head, as it highlights the tension between cooperation and control in the EU. Furthermore, the introduction of controls during the pandemic had a major impact on EU citizens living in border regions, where daily trips across borders had been taken for granted. However, unlike the internal border controls introduced in response to the migration crisis (which several countries are still applying), those due to the pandemic have not lasted long: most were lifted in the autumn of 2020.

The rapid resort of so many countries to internal border controls in order to curb the spread of COVID-19 has also been described as breaking a taboo. According to Wolff et al. (2020), the refugee crisis and the continuation of internal border controls since 2015 have normalised the use of such controls as part of regular policy within the Schengen Area. Thus, the previously restrictive stance against limiting mobility across internal borders has become less of a taboo, making internal border controls more readily available as a political tool in crisis situations—as we saw during the first year of the COVID-19 pandemic when a majority of Schengen states introduced temporary internal border controls. However, member states that had done so on previous occasions were no more likely to use this tool than those that had not (Pettersson Fürst, 2023b). Thus, while the threshold for imposing internal border controls may have been lowered due to their use during the refugee crisis, the situation in this regard applies generally across the EU: it is not just a matter where certain member states have acquired the habit. For example, four countries that had never previously introduced temporary internal border controls—Czechia, Lithuania, Slovakia, and Switzerland—did so in 2020 in response to the pandemic.

The issue of open borders within Europe has often been described in terms of a trade-off between economic efficiency and security. According to this view, it is rational for member states to give up some autonomy and to agree to openness because it is economically efficient to do so. With such an explanatory model, it stands to reason as well that when a security problem arises—in this case a global pandemic—states reclaim control and prove to be willing to renounce the economic gains resulting from open borders in favour of increased security for their citizens. As Genschel and Jachtenfuchs (2021) have shown, this is what happened initially—when member states not only introduced internal border controls but also, in some instances, prevented the export and transport of medical equipment to other EU countries. However, these authors contend, the European Commission immediately began working to shift the focus to external borders, for example by introducing a common entry ban for the entire EU from other countries, while at the same time working to harmonise measures against COVID-19 within the EU and to remove internal border controls as quickly as possible (Genschel & Jachtenfuchs, 2021, p. 356). Interestingly, the authors also conclude that, although internal borders were hardened during the first year of the pandemic, a more long-term effect was to increase economic solidarity, as EU member states managed to agree on far-reaching economic measures to help each other deal with the economic consequences of the pandemic's closed borders. This echoes the views of other commentators as well, who have argued that the refugee crisis eventuated in more integration in certain policy areas (Rhinard, 2019).

The use of internal border controls on a much larger scale than was originally intended has posed a fundamental challenge to the Schengen Agreement, and there is an ongoing debate among researchers as to whether this should be seen as a sign of renationalisation and of European disintegration (see, for example, Eilstrup-Sangiovanni, 2021; Guild, 2021; Scipioni, 2017; Votoupalová, 2019). Many believe, however, that the introduction of internal border controls has not substantially reduced the willingness of member states to cooperate; on the contrary, it has in fact led to strengthened cooperation at the European level. The expansion of internal border controls has not been accompanied by criticism of European integration among the countries that have continued to apply the controls. Rather, these countries have made their view very clear that the challenges over border control can best be solved through European cooperation (Pettersson Fürst, 2023a). One consequence of the reintroduction of internal border controls, during both the refugee crisis and the pandemic, was a new focus on external border control. If the trend in the EU during the 1990s and 2000s was largely towards the removal of obstacles to mobility across both internal and external borders, it has to a great extent, since the 2010s, rather concerned the strengthening of European cooperation in the guarding of the external borders. The internal border controls introduced during the refugee crisis were largely justified by the member states as necessary due to shortcomings at the external borders. Accordingly, much of the EU's efforts since then have been devoted to strengthening surveillance of the shared external borders. In the next section of this chapter, I discuss how European cooperation in the area of border controls has developed.

Frontex and the Expansion of the EU's External Border Guard

The Schengen Agreement does not just require that the member states open their internal borders to each other; it also necessitates far-reaching trust between the member states that each will take responsibility for external border control. As part of this, cooperation on the external borders has been both broadened and deepened. A very important step was taken in this direction in 2004, with the creation of the European Agency for the Management of Operational Cooperation at the External Borders of the Member States of the European Union (commonly called Frontex, after the French '*frontières extérieures*'), which established the agency, Frontex was intended to act as 'a specialised expert body tasked with improving the coordination of operational cooperation between

Member States in the field of external border management' (Council Regulation 2007/2004, recital 3).

Already at the time of its creation, Frontex had a rather broad mission. This included facilitating the application of common measures in the management of the external borders and ensuring the coordination of these measures by the member states. This in turn involved assisting member states with the operational aspects of managing internal borders—such as returning third-country nationals, conducting risk analyses, and monitoring relevant current research—as well as contributing to the joint use of material resources, providing technical and operational assistance to member states when requested, and providing joint training at the European level for national trainers of border-guard personnel. The aim was also to develop common practices in the management of external borders.

After the refugee crisis of 2015, work was intensified to strengthen cooperation in the area of border surveillance. A new regulation was adopted in 2016, giving the agency a new name—the European Border and Coast Guard Agency (Frontex)—and a greatly expanded mandate (European Parliament and Council Regulation 2016b/1624). The Agency's new mission continues its previous one, with the difference that Frontex can now review the work of the member states to a much greater extent. It is also able to deploy its own operational personnel in emergency situations, and it has a clearer mission to fight crime and terrorism than before. In connection with this expanded mandate, moreover, its budgetary resources have been significantly strengthened. Two aspects of the new Frontex are (1) a stronger and more explicit focus on return as a central part of border-guarding, through the establishment of 'integrated border management' and (2) an explicit sharing of responsibility for this integrated management between the member states and the Agency (although the formal responsibility for border-guarding still rests with the member states): 'European integrated border management should be implemented as a shared responsibility of the Agency and the national authorities responsible for border management' (Regulation 2016b/1624, recital 6). Integrated border management has four parts: external border controls; measures in third countries; cooperation with third countries; and measures within the Schengen Area, including return policies. The aim is to integrate border management at the national and EU levels. The reform goes a long way towards bringing migration and border control to the EU level, through the expanded mandate given to Frontex.

Three years after the 'new' Agency was established, another major step was taken in the common management of the external borders, as Frontex underwent yet another institutional reform. The main mission of the Agency was largely the same in 2019 as had been set out in Regulation 2016/1624. The difference resided in the Agency's operational capacity, which was greatly expanded with European Parliament and Council Regulation 2019/1896 on the European Border and Coast Guard, a uniformed force was established: the 'standing corps'. A corresponding new long-term budget commitment was made, adding to the already growing budget of the agency, which has increased continually since 2005 and even more rapidly since 2014: from only six million euros in 2005 and 114 million euros in 2015, to 333 million euros in 2019, reaching 845 million euros in 2023 (Frontex 2005; 2014; 2019; 2023b). Its budget and personnel are furthermore slated to continue growing, with the goal of reaching 10,000 people in the standing corps by 2027, of whom 3000 will be Frontex staff (Frontex, 2023a). At the time of writing (the spring of 2023), approximately 2000 people are employed by Frontex, of whom approximately half belong to the standing corps. In the Agency's own words, this is a historical event:

> For the first time in history, the European Union has its own uniformed service—the European Border and Coast Guard standing corps. Trained by the best and equipped with the latest that technology has to offer, Frontex border and coast guards are ready for challenges at the borders... . (Frontex, 2023a)

The standing corps share many tasks with the national border-control authorities. For example, they have the right to check ID documents, patrol border crossings, and permit or refuse entry to the EU. This new operational capacity must be understood as part of an even stronger focus on return policies. This is emphasised in the 2019 regulation, which states that increasing the resources and strengthening the mandate of the Agency is being done 'with a view to ensuring effective external border control and *significantly stepping up the effective return* of irregular migrants' (European Parliament and Council Regulation 2019/1896, recital 8; author's emphasis).

From a political-science perspective, it is remarkable how little debate the establishment of the European standing corps has occasioned in public, political, or academic debate. If we take Sweden as an example, the Frontex standing corps was mentioned only once in the Swedish press during the first year after the adoption of the regulation that established the new force in 2019, when the Swedish police and coast guard participated in a Frontex operation in Greece. Nor did the creation of the corps result in any political debate to speak of in Sweden. (Of the 359 articles in the Swedish press in October–December 2019 that mentioned Frontex, not one was primarily about the expansion of the Agency.)[1] This is despite the fact that the practical and symbolic implications of this expansion for the relationship between national sovereignty and European supranationalism are far-reaching. Uniformed police and military are usually seen as an exclusive prerogative of the sovereign state. The establishment of such forces at the European level, therefore, raises many questions about how this has become possible, and what it will lead to in the long run. Do the standing corps set an example that may end up being extended to other types of uniformed missions on a European basis? In this case, the member states have prioritised streamlining control over the external borders over keeping said control as an exclusively national task. The member states, through the European Council, have thus agreed with the European Parliament that joint border surveillance is needed and that the question of the mandate is subordinate to getting the task done.

In addition, the reform of Frontex in 2016 and its subsequent expansion in 2019 must be understood in light of the internal border controls that several member states introduced during the 'refugee crisis' of 2015, and which they have continued since. One of the main arguments for the continuation of internal border controls proffered by the member states that use them has been that such controls are necessary as long as 'deficiencies at the external borders' remain (Pettersson Fürst, 2023a). The expansion of Frontex can thus be seen as a response to the demands of these member states, as well as a way of relieving the countries (such as Greece and Italy) that due to their geographical location have been tasked with the greatest responsibility for controlling the Union's external borders.

[1] Author's own calculations.

Regulation 2019/1896 states that the goal of Frontex is to manage the external borders effectively. As mentioned, this involves a clear focus on preventing irregular migration and countering cross-border crime. The opening paragraph, however, adds that *'[a]t the same time,* it is necessary to act in full respect for fundamental rights and in a manner that safeguards the free movement of persons within the Union' (Regulation 2019/1896, recital 1; author's emphasis). Furthermore, the introduction states that:

> The extended tasks and competence of the Agency should be balanced with strengthened fundamental rights safeguards and increased accountability and liability, in particular in terms of the exercise of executive powers by the statutory staff. (Regulation 2019/1896, recital 24)

The European Council and the European Parliament were thus aware when they adopted these regulations and increased the Agency's operational capacity, that such an expansion was not without risks for fundamental rights. Any government agency, regardless of policy area, that expands quickly in such a short time runs a significant risk of developing organisational problems. When migration is concerned, moreover, the issue of legality and the protection of fundamental rights become even more important, since the actions of the agency have direct consequences for people's lives.

The expansion of Frontex's mandate has not been without problems. Since 2019, the Agency has been accused of engaging in the illegal 'pushback' of refugees in the Mediterranean, where Frontex personnel have forced refugees out of European territory, thereby hindering their right to seek asylum and to obtain an individual trial (Luyten, 2022). Frontex has also been extensively investigated by OLAF (the European Anti-Fraud Office) for irregularities in the management of its resources. Among other things, this resulted in the resignation of Fabrice Leggeri, executive director of the Agency, with immediate effect in April 2022. On 18 October 2022, moreover, the European Parliament voted against granting discharge for the 2020 Frontex budget, due to the scale of the irregularities committed (European Parliament, 2022). Much of the existing research on the EU's structures and policies for guarding its external borders points to the problem of the intermingling of humanitarian and security-policy objectives in the Agency's work in the Mediterranean—where, according to the UNHCR, between 1500 and 5000 people died each year between 2014 and 2021 (UNHCR, 2022).

Stumpf (2006) has coined the term 'crimmigration' to describe the intermingling that occurs when more and more immigration-related actions are treated as crimes. The problem with this conflation is that all migrants are viewed as potential criminals, while actions by humanitarian organisations are criminalised (Mainwaring & DeBono, 2021). In this way, migration has become increasingly *securitised*: that is, it is treated more and more as a security problem rather than a humanitarian one, and migrants are increasingly described as a threat to Europe's internal security. This serves to legitimise a trend towards ever-stricter measures to prevent people from crossing the outer borders into Europe. This is not, however, a uniquely European development; on the contrary, the securitisation of migration and the continual hardening of border policies and barriers is a global trend (Pettersson, 2020). For example, border-related deliberations on the UN Security Council have not only increased dramatically but their focus has also shifted—from the establishment and legitimisation of borders to questions of border security, control, and management (Simmons, 2019). An estimated 80 border walls, moreover, have been built around the world—more than ever before in modern history (Vallet, 2020).

A further aspect of how the EU's external border controls have developed in recent years is the increased importance placed on border policies of *externalisation*. Externalisation means that external border control is moved away from the location of the actual border, often through agreements with neighbouring countries. An example of externalisation can be seen in how the United States supports Mexico with equipment and training for border guards in exchange for increasing surveillance by Mexico of its southern border, the object being to prevent people from proceeding north through Mexico to the United States (Galemba et al., 2019; Walker, 2018). The same principle applies to the EU's agreements with states that act as transit countries for migrants on their way to Europe, such as Algeria, Libya, Morocco, and Turkey (Mainwaring & DeBono, 2021; Pacciardi & Berndtsson, 2022). The agreement of this kind that has occasioned the most comment is the one that the EU concluded with Turkey in 2016, which charged the latter country with stopping people (mainly from Syria) from entering Europe via Turkey.

The point of externalisation from the EU's perspective is that it shifts border control away from EU territory, thereby reducing the number of people crossing the EU's external border. However, like any other type of border control, externalisation does not address the reasons why people try to cross the border—it just moves the problem out of the sight of Europe. As a means of preventing the entry of asylum-seekers, it has therefore been called an 'extremely fragile' strategy (Borevi, 2022). One problem raised by critics of externalisation is that it places responsibility for refugees with countries known for not respecting human rights. Another problem is that the demand for increased border controls in transit countries can create problems for mobility between the transit countries and their neighbours—including for residents of border regions who are not migrants, as they too are prevented from crossing the borders (Pastore & Roman, 2020). The EU's externalisation of migration control has also been criticised for neo-colonialism, since the EU uses its power to put pressure on countries in Africa—such as by making aid conditional on stricter migration controls.

The Border-Control Industry and the Digitisation of EU Borders

So far in this chapter, I have shown how political decisions in the 2010s and early 2020s sought to tighten control over Europe's borders. At the national level, this has occurred through the reintroduction by member states of temporary border controls vis-à-vis their European neighbours. At the European level, it has taken place through expanded cooperation in the surveillance of the EU's external borders, with the expansion of Frontex's mandate and resources. What these processes have in common is that they both result from and reinforce a trend whereby border policy and the management of borders have become increasingly linked to the issue of European security: there has been a securitisation of policy in connection with borders and migration (see, for example, Huysmans, 2000; Léonard & Kaunert, 2020; Moreno-Lax, 2018). This means that border guards are increasingly held out as the answer to very different types of problems, such as the reception of asylum-seekers and the fight against pandemics.

One development in border-security policy is the creation of various digital systems for coordinating and streamlining the surveillance of the Union's borders. These are intended for use by both national and joint authorities. Since the Schengen Agreement began, several such systems for surveillance and border control have been developed, and they are in use or about to be put into use. These shared systems collect and manage large amounts of information on border crossings, and they allow member states to exchange such information with each other. These systems can all be said to have been developed to compensate in part for the risks that each member state takes with open internal borders. As mentioned above, free internal movement requires member states to have great confidence in each other's contribution to external border control. The central systems for joint border surveillance and migration control are the Schengen Information System (SIS)—which has existed for a long time but has recently been expanded—and three newer systems: VIS, a system for exchanging Visa information; the Entry-Exit System; and Eurodac, a database for asylum applications.

The way in which such systems change border control in the EU is exemplified by the Entry-Exit System (EES). This is an automated digital system, not yet operational, that was planned to be put in use in May 2023 in order to replace existing procedures with stamps in passports. According to the European Commission, this new digital system will be more time-efficient; it will provide systematic information about border crossings; and, unlike current procedures, it will enable the systematic detection of travellers who have overstayed their permitted time within the Schengen Area (European Commission, n.d.). Historically, Frontex has primarily focused on 'illegal immigration': i.e., on people who cross the border irregularly, even though a large proportion of those staying irregularly in the EU do so after having entered regularly. It is very hard to know how many are 'visa-overstayers'—i.e., who have remained in the Schengen Area after their permitted (visa-free or visa-regulated) time has expired (Hansen & Pettersson, 2021). However, one development in recent years—not least since Frontex was assigned the additional task of 'significantly increasing returns'—has been that 'illegal stays' have also come into focus (a development enabled by the introduction of new systems such as the Entry-Exit System). Created to register all third-country nationals who cross an external EU border in a regular manner, this new digital technology affords new means of controlling movement in the EU after entry as well—which means that overstayers can increasingly be made subject to Frontex's securitisation of migrants (see Hansen & Pettersson, 2021).

Other digital systems have been expanded or developed recently. An example of this is the Schengen Information System (SIS), which allows national authorities to share or to search for information regarding for example wanted or missing persons, and which provides recommendations for action when wanted persons are found. In 2018, a series of new rules were adopted for the SIS, which among other things reflect the new ambition to increase returns. The changes, which became operational in March 2023, include making return decisions part of the information available in the common information system (European Commission, 2023b). As mentioned above, the budget for Frontex has been dramatically increased in recent years. The Agency's mission and resources have been expanded (it has its own ships now, for example), enabling it to assist member countries with equipment. Progressively greater financial resources are thus being put into border-control infrastructure. As mentioned earlier, this trend is by no means unique to the European context; similar patterns can be observed in many other countries, which also devote substantial resources to fortifying and guarding their borders. As new technology develops, novel and ever more advanced ways of controlling borders become available. Providing the EU (and other states) with equipment for border control is a large and growing industry. Drones, thermal-imaging cameras, and biometric technology (such as facial recognition) are just some of the equipment in which the EU is investing in order to strengthen its capacity to monitor borders (Dodds, 2021). The economy that has developed around border security has been called a 'border-industrial complex', where political demand and industrial development reinforce one another. Dodds cites the European expansion of border control as an example of this complex, where the border-control industry has blossomed as a result of increased governmental spending, and where both the expansion of Frontex and the development of several new digital systems for border control will require investments in (digital) infrastructure worth hundreds of millions of euros. The big winners from this, Dodds contends, are European data companies; while the EU and other states that expand their digital border-surveillance systems are locking themselves into intricate and costly digital infrastructures. This lock-in effect is worth noting for several reasons: (1) because of the risks with digital systems, which are often vulnerable for example to data breaches; (2) because there are risks with all surveillance that can encroach on the integrity of the population; and (3) because it is recognised within border research that stricter border controls do not act as the deterrent they are intended to be. In this regard, border controls are useful as a political tool—it is thought to show vigour and resolve to invest in 'increasing security'—but they have no impact on the underlying causes of migration. Instead, the imposition of more difficult border barriers usually prompts people to resort to more dangerous routes. It also favours organised human smuggling, which is exactly what the EU says it wants to stop with the help of more advanced methods of border control.

Stricter Border Controls Are No Quick Fix for Complex Problems

In this chapter, I have discussed three parallel and interconnected trends in European border policy: the imposition of internal border controls by several member states; the expansion of external border controls; and the expansion of technical systems aimed at facilitating border control. The migration crisis of 2015–16 and the COVID-19 pandemic in 2020 both led member states to impose internal border controls to a much greater extent than they had before. Due to this reaction, described by some as a 'sovereignty reflex' (Somer et al., 2020) and a 'knee-jerk reaction' (Wolff et al., 2020), it may be that the same measures will be taken in future crises as well. That is, member states may come to regard more and more political problems as border problems, and internal border controls as a useful tool for dealing with them. This is in line with the politicisation of borders in general. The use of internal border controls poses a major challenge to the Schengen Agreement, inasmuch as it suspends freedom of movement within the EU (albeit temporarily). Since several countries have continued to apply their controls after 2015—far beyond what Schengen regulations allow—the internal border controls also challenge the legitimacy of those regulations. The issue of EU borders is more than a matter of policy or management. Control over territorial borders is strongly linked to national sovereignty and to the idea of the sovereign state as a clearly bounded territorial unit. EU membership, therefore, has always made for a certain amount of tension in the relationship between national self-determination and supranational integration. The ability of member states to introduce internal border controls, then, illustrates the complex relationship between national sovereignty and integration in the EU.

As discussed in this chapter, it is clear that border politics has come to play a central role in the process of European integration. The reintroduction of internal border controls poses a major challenge to European integration, as it undermines internal freedom of movement. In crises where risks were connected with control over borders—as during the refugee crisis and the COVID-19 pandemic—it became clear that the member states often give priority to national territorial control. At the same time, these crises resulted in a wave of new political decisions regarding border controls, border-surveillance systems, and not least the expansion of Frontex. There are no indications that internal re-bordering has led to decreasing levels of cooperation; and even when member states have introduced internal border controls, they have often done so while stressing the importance of European cooperation. In terms of the theoretical framework presented at the beginning of this chapter, it can be said that we have partly seen a re-bordering of the internal borders—both in the use of internal border controls and in the development of more shared systems for monitoring third-country nationals who are present within the borders of the EU. We have also seen a re-bordering of the external borders, through the expansion of Frontex, the externalisation of border controls, and the development of digital border-control systems. A re-bordering of both the internal and the external borders, then, has taken place. The trends discussed in this text can therefore be said to place developments in EU border policy clearly in the *defensive-integration* corner.

In light of this, a first recommendation for action would be to clarify the rules in the Schengen Borders Code, so that they reflect the intentions of the member states regarding the possibility of introducing internal border controls. Such a process is already underway. In December 2021, the European Commission presented a proposal for changes in the Schengen rules (European Commission, 2021). The adoption of these new rules, however, has been stalled since then, and as of September 2023, they are yet to be adopted. The Commission recommends in this proposal that internal border controls be understood as temporary and that other methods of control—e.g., more police controls in border areas—be used instead. The idea of replacing border controls with more scattered police controls has been criticised, among others by the Swedish government, on the grounds that it is incompatible with other legislation, and also on the grounds that actual border controls are more effective. The new bill also seeks to clarify and strengthen demands on the member states, by requiring those that introduce internal border controls to communicate this in greater detail to the EU and the other member states. The proposed changes include new criteria for when internal border controls are to apply, as well as requirements for risk analysis on the part of member states that introduce such controls. The aim, among other things, is to prevent citizens who live in border regions and who often cross borders from suffering unnecessarily. The question that remains is whether the proposed changes will be adopted and whether they will be sufficient to get the member states which have continued to use internal border controls since 2015 to stop extending them for new periods.

Regarding the second developmental trend, it is clear that the member states have agreed to devote greater resources and effort to the identification and prevention of irregular border crossings, and to finding and turning away more people who have entered EU territory without permission. As both researchers and human rights organisations have shown, the risk is great that such policies will contribute to the criminalisation of actions that were previously seen as humanitarian, such as safeguarding the right to seek asylum or helping refugees who have crossed borders irregularly. Another major risk intimately connected with the expansion of large digital surveillance and information-sharing systems is that the ever-stricter border policies—the overall purpose of which is purportedly to protect the member states' own populations—will have negative effects on those very populations. Border controls, both internal and external, are not neutral: they often involve ethnic profiling, which also affects persons who are EU citizens but who do not belong to the majority ethnic population. Such controls are also often time-consuming, and thus disruptive of traffic in integrated EU regions. A second recommendation is therefore to closely monitor the infrastructure being built for surveilling the borders, so as to ensure that it does not restrict the personal integrity of EU citizens or their freedom of movement. As the external borders become harder, moreover, it is important to establish and maintain the functionality of safeguards for the right to asylum, especially in view of the advancing process of externalisation, which often stops people who are fleeing their homes long before they approach EU territory.

In practice, it is difficult to 'succeed' with harder borders. There is no obvious endpoint to the expansion of border-control infrastructure, and the more border control that is done, the more it comes to be seen as a solution to a range of problems of varied origins. Yet, since border controls do not address the core problems that cause migration—such as wars, inequality, and climate change—there is no upper limit to how many resources can be spent on border controls. A final recommendation is therefore to consider carefully what the opportunity costs of expanded border controls are, and what direction we think European integration should take. The risk is that harder borders will be seen as a one-size-fits-all solution to global problems that are much more complex. However, if defensive integration is the way forward, then the safeguarding of free internal movement becomes imperative, for much of the EU's legitimacy with its citizens lies in the benefits attendant upon freedom of movement.

References

Bartolini, S. (2005). *Restructuring Europe: Centre formation, System Building And Political Structuring between The Nation-State and the European Union*. Oxford University Press.

Borevi, K. (2022). Immigration and Asylum in the EU: A Resilient policy for integration? In Bakardjieva Engelbrekt, A., Ekman P., Michalski, A. and L. Oxelheim (eds.) *Routes to a Resilient European Union: Interdisciplinary European Studies* (pp. 195–218). Springer.

Börzel, T. A., & Risse, T. (2018). From the Euro to the Schengen Crises: European integration theories, politicization, and identity politics. *Journal of European Public Policy, 25*(1), 83–108.

Brekke, J. P., & Staver, A. (2018). The Renationalisation of migration policies in times of crisis: The case of Norway. *Journal of Ethnic and Migration Studies, 44*(13), 2163–2181.

Casella Colombeau, S. (2020). Crisis of Schengen? The effect of two 'migrant crises' (2011 and 2015) on the free movement of people at an internal Schengen Border. *Journal of Ethnic and Migration Studies, 46*(11), 2258–2274.

European Commission. (2021). Proposal for a regulation of the European parliament and of the council amending regulation (EU) 2016/399 on a union code on the rules governing the movement of persons across borders (COM/2021/891 final). Strasbourg: European Commission.

European Commission. (2023a). *Temporary Reintroduction of Border Control: Full list of MS notifications of the temporary reintroduction of border control at internal borders*. https://home-affairs.ec.europa.eu/policies/schengen-borders-and-visa/schengen-area/temporary-reintroduction-border-control_en. Accessed Sept 12, 2023.

Dodds, K. (2021). *Border Wars: The Conflicts That Will Define Our Future*. Ebury Press.

Eilstrup-Sangiovanni, M. (2021). Re-bordering Europe? Collective action barriers to 'Fortress Europe.' *Journal of European Public Policy, 28*(3), 447–467.

European Commission. (2022). Directorate-general for communication, (2022). *Public Opinion in the European Union: Summer 2022*. European Commission.

European Commission. (2023b). *What is SIS and how does it work? | Migration and Home Affairs* https://home-affairs.ec.europa.eu/policies/schengen-borders-and-visa/schengen-information-system/what-sis-and-how-does-it-work_en. Accessed Sept 12, 2023.

European Commission. (n.d.). *Entry/Exit System (EES)|Migration and Home Affairs*. https://home-affairs.ec.europa.eu/policies/schengen-borders-and-visa/smart-borders/entry-exit-system_en. Accessed Sept 12, 2023.

European Communities (EC) (2000). Agreement between the Governments of the States of the Benelux Economic Union, the Federal Republic of Germany and the French Republic on the gradual abolition of checks at their common borders, 14 June 1985. *OJ L 239*, 22.9.2000, 13–18.

European Council. (2004). Council regulation (EC) No 2007/2004 of 26 October 2004 establishing a European Agency for the Management of Operational Cooperation at the External Borders of the Member States of the European Union. *OJ L 349*, 25.11.2004, 1–11.

European Parliament and Council. (2016). Regulation (EU) 2016/399 of the European Parliament and of the Council of 9 March 2016 on a Union Code on the rules governing the movement of persons across borders (Schengen Borders Code) (codification), *OJ L 77, 23.3.2016*, 1–52.

European Parliament and Council. (2016). Regulation (EU) 2016/1624 of the European Parliament and of the Council of 14 September 2016 on the European Border and Coast Guard and amending Regulation (EU) 2016/399 of the European Parliament and of the Council and repealing Regulation (EC) No 863/2007 of the European Parliament and of the Council, Council Regulation (EC) No 2007/2004 and Council Decision 2005/267/EC. *OJ L 251*, 16.9.2016, 1–76.

European Parliament and Council. (2019) Regulation (EU) 2019/1896 of the European Parliament and of the Council of 13 November 2019 on the European Border and Coast Guard and repealing Regulations (EU) No 1052/2013 and (EU) 2016/1624. *OJ L 295, 14.11.2019*, 1–131.

European Parliament. (2022). *Frontex: MEPs refuse to discharge EU border agency over its management in 2020*. https://www.europarl.europa.eu/news/en/press-room/20221014IPR43210/frontex-meps-refuse-to-discharge-eu-border-agency-over-its-management-in-2020. Accessed Sept 12, 2023.

Frontex. (2005). *Budget 2005*. https://prd.frontex.europa.eu/document/budget-2005/, Accessed October 25, 2022.

Frontex. (2014). *Budget 2014.* https://prd.frontex.europa.eu/document/budget-2014/, Accessed October 25, 2022.
Frontex. (2019). *Voted budget 2019.* https://prd.frontex.europa.eu/document/voted-budget-2019/. Accessed October 25, 2022.
Frontex. (2023a). *Standing corps.* https://frontex.europa.eu/about-frontex/standing-corps/standing-corps/. Accessed September 12, 2023.
Frontex. (2023b). *Voted budget 2023.* https://prd.frontex.europa.eu/document/voted-budget-2023/. Accessed January 4, 2024.
Galemba, R., Dingeman, K., DeVries, K., & Servin, Y. (2019). Paradoxes of protection: Compassionate repression at the Mexico-Guatemala Border. *Journal on Migration and Human Security, 7*(3), 62–78.
Genschel, P., & Jachtenfuchs, M. (2021). Postfunctionalism reversed: Solidarity and Rebordering During the COVID-19 Pandemic. *Journal of European Public Policy, 28*(3), 350–369.
Groenendijk, K. (2004). Reinstatement of controls at the internal borders of Europe: Why and against whom? *European Law Journal, 10*(2), 150–170.
Guild, E. (2021). Schengen borders and multiple national states of emergency: From refugees to terrorism to COVID-19. *European Journal of Migration and Law, 23*(4), 385–404.
Hansen, F., & Pettersson, J. (2021). Contradictory migration management? Differentiated security approaches to visa overstay and irregular border crossings in the European Union. *European Security, 31*(1), 117–134.
Heinikoski, S. (2020). Covid-19 bends the rules on border controls—yet another crisis undermining the Schengen acquis? *FIIA Briefing Paper*, *281.*
Huysmans, J. (2000). The European union and the securitization of migration. *JCMS: Journal of Common Market Studies*, *38*(5), 751–777.
Jones, R. (2016). *Violent borders: Refugees and the right to move.* Verso.
Léonard, S., & Kaunert, C. (2020). The securitisation of migration in the European Union: Frontex and its evolving security practices. *Journal of Ethnic and Migration Studies*, *48*(8).
Longo, M. (2018). *The politics of borders : Sovereignty, security, and the citizen after 9/11.* Cambridge University Press.
Luyten, K. (2022). Addressing Pushbacks at the EU's External Borders. *European Parliamentary Research Service*, *October*. https://www.europarl.europa.eu/RegData/etudes/BRIE/2022/738191/EPRS_BRI(2022)738191_EN.pdf. Accessed Sept 12, 2023.
Mainwaring, Ċ, & DeBono, D. (2021). Criminalizing solidarity: Search and rescue in a Neo-Colonial Sea. *Environment and Planning c: Politics and Space, 39*(5), 1030–1048.
Moreno-Lax, V. (2018). The EU humanitarian border and the securitization of human rights: The 'rescue-through-interdiction/rescue-without-protection' paradigm. *Journal of Common Market Studies, 56*(1), 119–140.

Pacciardi, A., & Berndtsson, J. (2022). EU border externalisation and security outsourcing: Exploring the migration industry in Libya. *Journal of Ethnic and Migration Studies, 48*(17), 4010–4028.

Pastore, F., & Roman, E. (2020). Migration policies and threat-based extraversion. Analysing the impact of European externalisation policies on African polities. *Revue Européenne Des Migrations Internationales, 36*(1), 133–152.

Pettersson Fürst, J. (2023b). Differentiated implementation of controls: The internal border regimes of Schengen. *Politics and Governance, 11*(3), 68–78.

Pettersson Fürst, J. (2023a). Defensive integration through cooperative re-bordering? How member states use internal border controls in Schengen. *Journal of European Public Policy*, 1–23.

Pettersson, J. (2020). Higher fences and wider nets ? Global trends in bordering policies. *UI Paper, 2020*(2).

Rhinard, M. (2019). The Crisisification of policy-making in the European union. *Journal of Common Market Studies, May 2017*, 1–18.

Schimmelfennig, F. (2021). Rebordering Europe: External boundaries and integration in the European union. *Journal of European Public Policy, 28*(3), 311–330.

Scipioni, M. (2017). Failing forward in EU migration policy? EU integration after the 2015 Asylum and migration crisis. *Journal of European Public Policy, 25*(9), 1–19.

Simmons, B. A. (2019). Border rules. *International Studies Review, 21*(2), 256–283.

Simmons, B. A. (2017). *The Built Environment: State Presence at Border Crossings in the Modern World*. https://papers.ssrn.com/abstract=3251398

Somer, M. De, Tekin, F., & Meissner, V. (2020). *Schengen under Pressure: Differentiation or Disintegration?* (No. 7; EU IDEA Policy Papers, Issue 7).

Stumpf, J. P. (2006). The crimmigration crisis: Immigrants, crime, and sovereign power. *American University Law Review, 56*(367), 1689–1699.

UNHCR. (2022). *No End in Sight*. https://storymaps.arcgis.com/stories/07502a24ce0646bb9703ce96630b15fa. Accessed September 12, 2023.

Vallet, É. (2020). State of border walls in a globalized world. In A. Bissonnette & É. Vallet (Eds.), *Borders and border walls: Insecurity, symbolism, vulnerabilities* (pp. 7–24). Routledge.

Votoupalová, M. (2018). Schengen in crisis? Why subjective critique matters. *Central European Journal of International and Security Studies, 12*(3), 10–34.

Votoupalová, M. (2019). The wrong critiques: Why internal border controls don't mean the end of Schengen. *New Perspectives, 27*(1), 73–99.

Walker, M. (2018). The other U.S. border? Techno-cultural-rationalities and fortification in Southern Mexico. *Environment and Planning A, 50*(5), 948–968.

Wolff, S., Ripoll Servent, A., & Piquet, A. (2020). Framing Immobility: Schengen governance in times of pandemics. *Journal of European Integration, 42*(8), 1127–1144.

Yuval-Davis, N., Wemyss, G., & Cassidy, K. (2019). *Bordering*. Cambridge, UK: Polity.

CHAPTER 3

The Return of Borders in the World Economy: An EU-Perspective

Fredrik Sjöholm

Introduction

Almost 20 years ago, Thomas Friedman (2005) described in his best-selling book how the world appeared to be "flat" with no major barriers to the movement of goods and people between countries. National borders were said to be a relic of a bygone era and of no practical significance. This was in many ways a fair and accurate description of the world as it was at the time of writing, but it was also the end of an era of ever-increasing globalization. Two events in 2016 provided definitive proof that this was the case. In June, the United Kingdom voted to leave the European Union (EU), a lengthy process, as it turned out, that was not

I gratefully acknowledge financial support from Marianne and Marcus Wallenberg Foundation (2020.0049) and from Jan Wallander and Tom Hedelius stiftelse (P23-0186).

F. Sjöholm (✉)
The Research Institute of Industrial Economics (IFN), Stockholm, Sweden
e-mail: Fredrik.Sjoholm@ifn.se

A. Bakardjieva Engelbrekt et al. (eds.), *The Borders of the European Union in a Conflictual World*,
https://doi.org/10.1007/978-3-031-54200-8_3

completed until more than three years later. On the other side of the Atlantic, in November of the same year, Donald Trump was elected President of the United States after campaigning on the slogan "Make America great again", which would be achieved through more inward-looking economic policies.

These developments reflect a return to the importance of geographical borders, both between the EU and the rest of the world, as well as within the EU. More specifically, trade between the EU and the rest of the world faces higher tariffs and more of other types of trade barriers, and trade within the EU has also encountered obstacles, such as trade in medicine and health-related products during the coronavirus pandemic. The seeds of this development were sown decades ago. Already in the 1990s, we started to see a change with the emergence of anti-globalization movements backed by both intellectuals (e.g., Klein, 2000) and violent groups that literally fought for their ideas in Genoa, Seattle and Gothenburg. The gradual impact of these ideas meant that for the first time in decades, globalization seemed to stall. In particular, after the 2008–09 financial crisis, an increasing number of countries started to introduce various types of trade barriers, in stark contrast to the trade liberalization of the previous decades (Evenett & Fritz, 2019).

The EU has a tradition of promoting a rules-based and open trade policy. This stance is being challenged by the protectionist measures introduced in both the US and China. An aggravating factor is that the World Trade Organization (WTO) has been damaged by international conflicts. At the same time, we are also seeing increased protectionism within the EU, which in turn can damage the very foundations of the Union.

This chapter ventures to unravel a perplexing question: In light of these transformative events and the rise of protectionist measures, how should the EU navigate its trade and economic policies? Particularly, does the EU's burgeoning emphasis on a selective industrial policy, favouring certain sectors over others, risk stunting its growth and prosperity? Or should the Union reconsider its stance and steer towards embracing an open, rules-based global trade regime?

The main argument of this chapter is that the EU's emerging strategy of a more active industrial policy, whereby authorities select companies and industries for special support and protection from competition, is negative for growth and prosperity. Instead, the EU should open its borders. This applies to both internal borders, to ensure a well-functioning internal market, and external borders, to work for a global open and rules-based trade regime.

This chapter relates to the book's overall theme of borders by discussing the reasons for the decline of globalization, the increasing importance of borders and the implications for the EU. I start by showing how globalization has stalled and continue with a discussion of what drives globalization, which is then used as a basis for explaining current developments. Developments in the EU are largely influenced by what is happening in China and the US, which is why I discuss the view on globalization in these two countries in the next two sections. The chapter then continues with a description of the shift in the view of globalization that can be discerned in the EU, after which a concluding section offers a number of different policy recommendations.

The Era of Ever-Increasing Globalization Is Over

The decline of globalization is illustrated, for example, by the development of world trade in Fig. 3.1. World trade rose from just under 30% of world income (GDP) in 1970 to just under 40% in 1990. With the collapse of the Soviet Union and the progress of market economies around the world, world trade then increased to 60% in 2007. The 2008–09 financial crisis caused a sharp but rather short-lived decline in trade. However, after the upturn in 2010, the share has stagnated, being 57% in 2021, roughly the same level as in 2005. Part of the global decline in trade is due to the COVID-19 pandemic, but it is worth noting that the share of trade declined even before the pandemic. There are exceptions to the general pattern of a relative decline in international trade, including in the EU where trade has increased slightly after the financial crisis (Sjöholm, 2023).

A very large share of international trade is carried out by multinational companies, which have been a key player in globalization. Figure 3.2 shows foreign investments by multinational companies as a share of GDP. These grew quite modestly from 1970 to 1990. As with international trade, direct investment as a share of GDP then increased, reaching over 5% in 2007. The financial crisis brought a decline to around 3% of GDP and investments have since stagnated or even decreased in importance.

When discussing the rise and fall of globalization, it is crucial to first understand what drives it. As Baldwin (2006) elucidates, the development

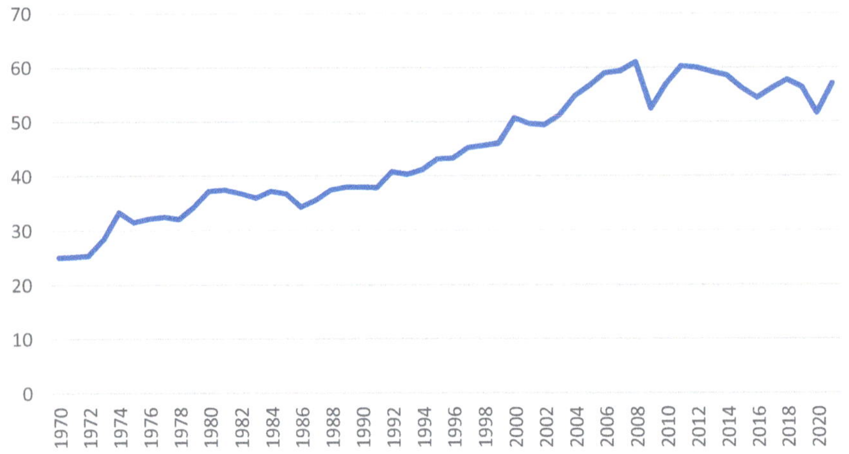

Fig. 3.1 International trade as a share of GDP 1979-2021 (%). *Source* World bank development Indicators. https://data.worldbank.org/indicator

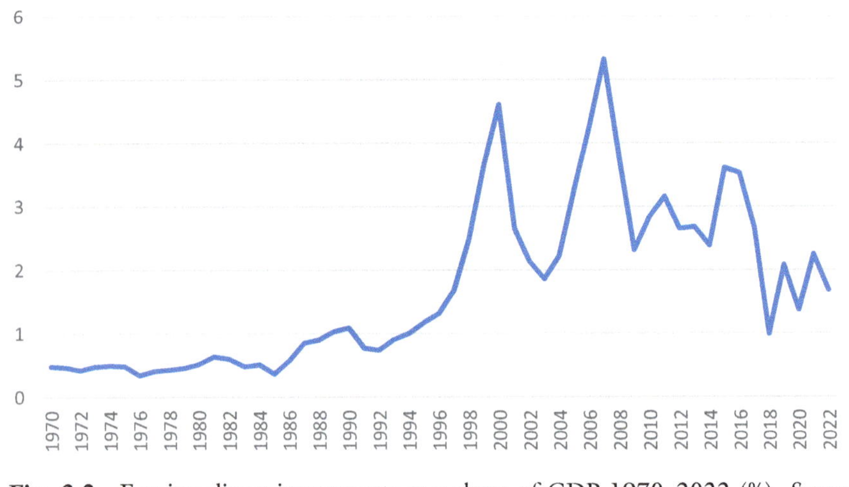

Fig. 3.2 Foreign direct investments as a share of GDP 1970–2022 (%). *Source* World Bank Development Indicators. https://data.worldbank.org/indicator/BX.KLT.DINV.WD.GD.ZS

of globalization can be broadly segmented into two overarching determinants. The first revolves around the political will for augmented global integration; the strength of a nation's inclination for trade and integration directly dictates its engagement level. This political intent subsequently shapes a nation's tariffs and trade barriers. The second determinant pertains to the capability to transfer goods and services across borders, often steered by technological advancements. The drive for global integration has surged since the mid-twentieth century, with the creation of the EU exemplifying this trend. The EU has successfully implemented a plethora of measures and reforms to promote the seamless movement of capital, labour, goods and services across member states. According to Moravcsik (1998), the EU's accomplishments include not only economic integration but also the enhancement of political stability and the establishment of shared regulations and standards, making it a benchmark for integration worldwide. These achievements have clearly served as an inspiration for other regions, prompting the development of integration projects like ASEAN in Southeast Asia, NAFTA (now USMCA) in North America and Mercosur in South America.

Parallel to increased regional integration, such as the EU, there has been a significant effort to increase global integration. This has been supported by the establishment and work of international organizations such as the WTO (formerly GATT), which has been successful in reducing tariffs and trade barriers between its member countries. The political will to increase trade and reduce protectionism has both political and economic explanations. In particular, the creation of the EU had the stated aim of preventing future wars through greater economic integration in Europe. In terms of economic explanations, it became increasingly clear in the decades after World War II that increased growth and living standards were difficult to achieve with protectionist economic policies. This shift in thinking about international integration has been gradual. In the 1950s and 1960s, many academics and politicians advocated a development strategy based on domestic industrial expansion under the protection of high import tariffs (Krueger, 1978). The experience with this so-called import substitution policy was in many places very negative, leading countries to open up to trade and capital flows. This is a development we have seen since the 1990s in some of the world's most populous countries such as China, India, Brazil and Indonesia and which has had a major impact on global production and trade patterns.

Technological progress and improved infrastructure are other important determinants of the increased globalization. Moving goods and services between countries requires affordable transportation. About 80% of world trade is carried by sea and the development of container traffic has greatly reduced transportation costs and increased trade (Bernhofen et al., 2016). Similarly, the deregulation of air travel in many countries since the 1980s has led to increased trade in goods that need relatively fast transport.

The development of information and communication technologies (ICT) has also had a major impact on trade. In particular, it has opened up trade in services, which was previously very difficult as proximity between production and consumption was necessary. Before the digital revolution, it was said that anything that can be packed in a box can be traded, nowadays it is anything can be sent as an attachment to an email.

Falling transport costs and the development of ICT services have also affected the way companies organize their activities. Multinational companies in particular have fairly complex structures. Production chains have developed where different components are produced in different countries, leading to increased efficiency and reduced costs. The production of components usually takes place both in the company's own foreign plants and in independent companies. Overall, this has led to an increase in the volume of trade but also to a change in the structure of trade, with more trade in inputs and relatively less trade in finished products. Finally, a significant share of world trade takes place between multinational companies' establishments located in different countries.

Why Has the Political Will Changed?

The discussion above highlights the importance of technology and political will in the development of globalization. So why has globalization stagnated? It is not because of technological developments, which on the contrary continue to open up new sectors for international trade (e.g., Baldwin, 2016). Instead, the political will for globalization has diminished and in some places been replaced by much more inward-looking policies. This leads to the next question—why are we seeing a change in the political attitude towards globalization?

A first attempt at approaching the issue is provided in Fig. 3.3, which shows the shares of three regions in the world economy: Europe, the US and East Asia. Europe and the US each accounted for just over a third of the world economy in 1970 and East Asia only 14%. The share of the latter region increased continuously until the mid-1990s when it stabilized at a level of around 20–25%. After the financial crisis of 2008–09, East Asia's share increased again and was about one-third of the world economy in 2020. At the same time, the shares of Europe and the US have decreased to around 25% each. Asia's increased relative size is largely due to China's high growth. Between 1979, when the country started reforming, and 2021, growth has averaged 9% per year, which in turn has led to China's share of the world economy increasing from around 2 to 17% over the same period.

This change has had both political and economic effects. On the political side, it is clear that in recent years China has pushed its global interests harder. China has advanced its positions in the South China Sea, increased pressure on Taiwan and crushed the relative freedom of Hong Kong. The repression of Uyghurs and other minority peoples can be added to this development, which has led to increased geopolitical conflicts. This is one reason behind a more cautious approach to globalization in many countries.

The economic development also reflects significant changes in production pattern. After joining the WTO in 2001, China's exports increased

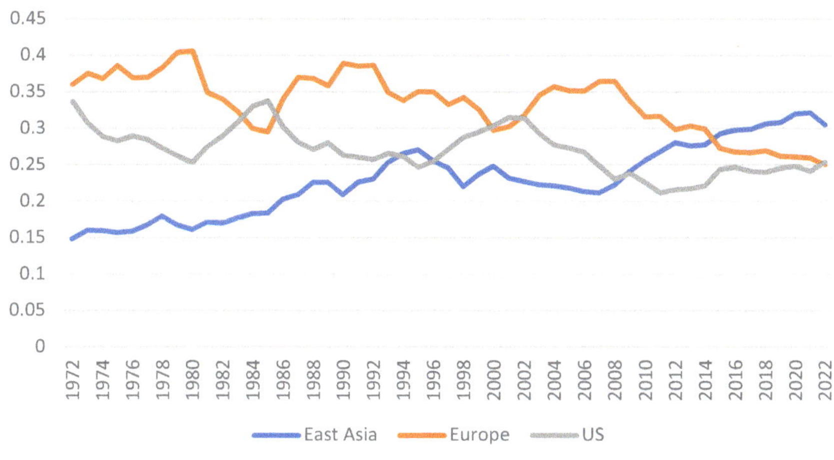

Fig. 3.3 The share of global GDP in different regions 1970–2022 (%). *Source* World bank development indicators. https://data.worldbank.org/indicator/BX.KLT.DINV.WD.GD.ZS

sharply. In ten years, China's share of world exports increased from less than 5% to more than 15%. This led to major socio-economic gains but also to structural changes. Above all, much of the industrial production has moved out of Europe and the US to China. In the literature, the concept of job polarization has been established to denote a development where low- and high-wage jobs increase their share of total employment and middle-wage jobs decrease in importance. Such developments have been documented in many countries (e.g., Heyman, 2016). While the trend has, somewhat surprisingly, had a modest impact on income inequality in most EU countries, it has meant that parts of the workforce in the US and UK, for example, have seen their real wages fall.[1]

This job polarization has had political consequences. At a general level, we see that populist parties have grown in importance in a large number of countries on many continents (Rodrik, 2017). Within EU member states, around one-fifth of citizens vote for what can be characterized as populist parties. In 2022, the election of Giorgia Meloni as Prime Minister of Italy was a sign that populism continues to thrive in Europe.

The existing research literature does not show that increased globalization always increase support for populist parties (Bergh & Kärnä, 2021), but there are studies on individual countries that find a causal relationship between globalization and various specific political effects that are sometimes referred to as populism (e.g., Dippel et al., 2015). In particular, Autor et al. (2020) show that it led to increased political polarization in the US. Their results show that the surge in Chinese imports to the US has affected voters' political preferences. More specifically, Democratic voters in districts negatively affected by Chinese imports have become more left-leaning in their views. Even stronger is the effect on Republican voters in districts affected by the import shock, who have moved to the right to the Tea Party movement and to the Donald Trump camp.

Another study by Colantone and Stanig (2018) finds that globalization contributed to Brexit. International trade was not debated in the election campaign. The major issue was rather national self-determination from Brussels, as evidenced by the Yes-side's motto "Bring back control." But the negative view of the EU was very much influenced by economic factors, which in turn were affected by globalization. Imports from China negatively affected parts of the population and led these people to vote

[1] Data on income distribution in the EU can be found at Eurostat https://ec.europa.eu/eurostat.

relatively strongly in favour of leaving the EU. In the election, 52% of the population voted in favour of leaving, but there were large differences between different parts of the UK. More specifically, the share of yes-votes was high in regions that produced goods that competed with Chinese imports. This was the case, for example, in the traditional industrial towns in central and northern England. At the other end of this spectrum is London, whose labour market was hardly affected at all by Chinese imports and where the no-vote was in the vast majority. Of course, the EU has nothing to do with Chinese imports, which may make the voters' choice seem illogical. A reasonable explanation is that both imports and the EU were associated with globalization, which evokes negative associations in those parts of the population affected by its negative aspects.

The war in Ukraine has also affected the EU's approach to trade and borders. In particular, the war has resulted in the closure of the border with Russia. Many EU member states are refusing entry to Russian citizens. Perhaps even more importantly, the trade boycott against Russia and Belarus was introduced fairly soon after the outbreak of the war and has since been tightened in various stages. Before the war, Russia was the EU's fifth-largest trading partner. At the same time, the EU was the largest trading partner for Russia, Belarus and Ukraine. This means that the trade boycott against Russia and Belarus has a significant impact on the economies of these countries, as described by Becker and Åslund in their chapter. It also means that the trade liberalizations with Ukraine that started before the war and deepened in 2022 are important and of more than symbolic value.

Finally, the change in economic policies in the EU depends to some extent on the development in China and the US. Both these countries have become increasingly inward-looking, which has had a direct effect on the EU. We therefore continue by discussing below how views on globalization have evolved in China and the US.

The US Turns Its Back on the World

Donald Trump has always seen trade as a way to move income and jobs between countries, and he entered the 2016 election campaign with a clear protectionist line (Jones, 2021). More specifically, his core instinct seems to be that any trade deficit is due to other countries manipulating prices and exchange rates, thereby stealing income and jobs from the US.

If there were any doubts whether Donald Trump would actually implement protectionist policies, they were dispelled almost immediately after he took office. On his first day, he withdrew from negotiations on a free trade area in the Pacific region. This alone was not so controversial. President Barack Obama had failed to gain support for the plans during his presidency and Hillary Clinton said during the presidential campaign in 2016 that she was willing to scrap the project. However, this was only the beginning of a policy that drastically changed US trade policy. In 2017, a renegotiation of the Free Trade Agreement with Canada and Mexico (NAFTA) was initiated. President Trump was unhappy that the US was running trade deficits with both Mexico and Canada and made the usual claim that it was costing the country jobs and revenue.

New protectionist programs followed (Bown & Kolb, 2020). In 2018, for example, tariffs were imposed on almost all steel and aluminium imports, all under the slogan "If you don't have steel you don't have a country." This affected a wide range of countries on many continents. Other types of protectionist measures were also introduced, and the most significant trade dispute was with China. Donald Trump successively imposed high tariffs on almost all imports from China. The average tariff on Chinese imports rose from around 3 to 24%. China responded by raising tariffs on US imports from around 7 to 26%. The trade conflict was about to escalate out of control when, in 2019, the parties reached an agreement that cooled the worst of the conflict and stabilized the situation, albeit at a high protectionist level. More specifically, the average US tariff on Chinese imports was then around 20% and the average Chinese tariff on US imports around 19%. But the deal was deeply problematic by design. In particular, it included quantitative import targets for Chinese imports from the US. In other words, China committed to import certain specific products of a certain value from the US. One difficulty with such a procedure is that it is not states but companies that trade with each other and it is not obvious that there are American companies that want to sell these products to China and Chinese companies that want to import. An even more problematic aspect of quantitative targets is that they obviously risk affecting other countries' exports to China.

The change in US trade policy has resulted in economic costs for the US and the rest of the world. Import tariffs imposed by large countries such as the US are theoretically paid for either by domestic consumers who have to pay more for imported goods and services, or by foreign producers who may be forced to reduce prices when demand falls. Studies show that in the case of the US, prices have been passed on to American consumers (Amiti et al., 2019; Redding et al., 2019). When import prices go up, workers cannot consume as much as before. Real wages and welfare for US citizens have therefore declined. The idea behind the policy was possibly that higher prices could be a cost worth taking if the number of American industrial jobs increased. But prices have risen without much job creation, and Amiti et al. (2019) estimate that each new job has costed $195,000 in reduced welfare, or about four times the average annual income of steelworkers, an occupational category often mentioned in the US trade policy debate.[2]

The biggest cost of US protectionist policies is the erosion of the rules-based trading system that has successfully governed international trade over the past decades. US policy changes have been in direct conflict with the WTO rules system: the US has threatened Mexico with import tariffs unless its migration policy is changed, pressured South Korea to impose voluntary export restrictions on steel, used security arguments to impose tariffs and violated the WTO principle of non-discrimination between members when China was pressured to impose quantitative targets on US imports.

Canada, the EU, China and Mexico have in turn responded by imposing their own tariffs on imports from the US, tariffs that also violate WTO rules. The consequence is that the WTO is playing a diminishing role in world trade. There are, of course, other reasons for the WTO's decline, such as its apparent difficulty in reaching new multilateral trade agreements. The latest round of negotiations, the Doha Round, has been ongoing since 2001. But the trade war has made it even more difficult for the WTO to operate. So has another US practice that cripples the WTO's operations—blocking the appointment of new judges, which is necessary to resolve trade disputes between member countries. The US has traditionally been reluctant to let decisions affecting it to be made by an international court. One way to hinder the court's work is to veto new judges to replace those who leave. This procedure was already used on a few occasions during President Obama's time in office but was used more consistently and wholeheartedly by President Trump. Nowadays, the WTO dispute settlement mechanism does not work.

[2] One reason for the importance of the steel industry in US trade policy is that this industry is important in swing states, states that are particularly important to win in US elections (Bown, 2019).

President Joe Biden can be said to have put forward a new ideological basis for his foreign policy, talking about making a common cause with other democracies (Wong & Swanson, 2022). This policy has been reinforced by the Ukraine war. But Biden also talks about making life easier for the middle class by encouraging American companies to bring back production from China in particular, a clearly protectionist policy. Tariffs imposed by President Trump remain in place, and no real broader attempts to return to the situation before the trade wars have been initiated. Rather, new trade barriers are being introduced, such as a ban on exports of high-tech goods to China and on the import of goods produced in whole or in part in Xinjiang, a province where Chinese authorities commit abuses against the indigenous population (Zenz, 2019). Furthermore, the US continues to block the work of the WTO. Thus, the US protectionism introduced under President Trump remains in place and there are no clear indications in 2023 that the situation is about to change.

The Chinese Wall

It is hardly surprising that China is the main target of the US in its changing trade policy. The EU, the US and many other individual countries are united in their dissatisfaction with China's trade policy. When China joined the WTO in 2001, there was a relatively broad expectation that the country would take further steps to liberalize and become more of a market economy. This has not been the case and the country is characterized by a state capitalist system that is difficult for the WTO to deal with and which is causing great irritation to the outside world.

The first problem is the large subsidies paid to Chinese companies, which means that companies from other countries do not compete on equal terms. These subsidies are most evident in the case of state-owned enterprises, which are of great importance in China. For example, of the world's 500 largest companies in 2020, 130 were Chinese, a sharp increase from only 15, fifteen years earlier (Huang & Véron, 2022). Even though private Chinese companies have increased their share of the list, state-owned enterprises still dominate the list with about 75% of the number of companies and 80% of the revenue.

State-owned enterprises are often pressured by the authorities to achieve objectives other than purely economic ones, such as avoid laying off workers or participate in different types of projects. In return, the company gets access to a variety of support from the authorities. Private companies also receive support if they follow government instructions. Since the Chinese state controls access to land and capital, for example, this is rational behaviour on the part of companies.

One consequence of the system is that, due to subsidies, a very large surplus capacity has been built up in Chinese industry, which depresses world market prices and affects foreign companies (Lai, 2021). The mechanism behind the excess capacity is in turn a result of the Chinese political system pushing for more and more investment to sustain economic growth (Chen et al., 2021). Chinese leaders at all levels need to deliver high growth to advance within the state bureaucracy. Ideally, growth in their own region, city or district should be higher than growth elsewhere. Pushing companies to sell more is difficult, but pushing for increased investment in machinery, premises and technology is more feasible. The result, as mentioned above, is an industrial capacity that far exceeds what can actually be sold on the domestic market or exported.

Another problem concerns the lack of transparency, which makes it difficult for the WTO to intervene. An illustrative example is China's production of aluminium products. Coal production is subsidized, which leads to lower prices for aluminium. In turn, aluminium producers are prohibited from exporting their production, which leads to lower prices for Chinese users of aluminium, that is, producers of various aluminium products. Finally, exporters of aluminium products pay lower taxes than other Chinese companies. Taken together, these measures constitute a significant but hard-to-identify subsidy for Chinese exporters of aluminium products and a negative competitive situation for foreign producers. Similar arrangements exist in other industries.

The third major problem concerns technology issues. Accusations that China improperly appropriates foreign technology are regularly made by other countries. It is common for less developed countries to use foreign technology in their industrialization efforts. What makes the Chinese case different from the experience of many other countries is that the state is said to be (more) involved and that technology transfer to Chinese firms is said to be institutionalized. There are often requirements that foreign companies cooperate with local Chinese companies, use local subcontractors, conduct research and development in China and use the latest technology in their Chinese operations. Overall, the requirement for technology and local Chinese partners is said to lead to the diffusion of firm-specific technology to Chinese competitors.

There is reason to believe that China will become more inward-looking in the future. The "Made in China 2025" strategy launched in 2015, and the "Dual Circulation" strategy included in the 14th five-year plan for 2021–2025, stress that China will become less dependent on the outside world by producing more inputs and especially more technologically sophisticated products. In reality, China's dependence on foreign markets has already decreased. For example, the share of exports in GDP has halved in the last 15 years to a modest 17%. Chinese economic policy aims to enable the country to make the difficult transition from a middle to a high-income country. China should become less of a country with a competitive ability to assemble imported inputs into finished products for export. Instead, the domestic share of value added will increase. This requires significant technological upgrading. The hope is that Chinese high-tech companies will emerge and grow as a result of an appropriate combination of subsidies and protection (Sjöholm and Lundin, 2010).

The EU Turns Inward

Developments in the US and China have affected the EU and its approach to globalization. In the case of China, the European view is that there is no level playing field and that China, through subsidies and trade barriers, unfairly favours domestic companies at the expense of European companies. Furthermore, increased US protectionism has led to European tariffs on imports from the US and, perhaps more importantly, to a reduced belief in free trade. Contributing to the rise of protectionism is also the view in some quarters that large state-led industrial initiatives in China and the US, which include protection from foreign competition, are successful and should be replicated in the EU.

Traditionally, the EU has advocated free trade, although there are exceptions, such as agricultural policy. The EU has also been a driving force in global trade liberalization and the development of the WTO. Finally, over the last 20 years, the EU has concluded bilateral trade agreements with Chile, Egypt, Georgia, Israel, Japan, Mexico, South Korea, Ukraine, Singapore, Canada, South Africa, Vietnam and New Zealand.

But the situation has changed. Some important trade liberalization negotiations collapsed in the second half of the 2010s, most notably the 2016 free trade agreement negotiations with the US and Canada. Negotiations with China have also encountered difficulties. A 2020 investment agreement has faced increased political resistance and has in 2023 not yet been approved by EU member states.

The EU also broke its tradition of promoting a rules-based trading system when it responded to rising protectionism in the US by imposing tariffs on US imports. Under the leadership of European Commission President Ursula von der Leyen, the EU has moved in a more interventionist and protectionist direction. The European Commission talks about tariffs on imports from countries that subsidize their production, while advocating an industrial policy that will foster successful companies in sectors considered to have high growth potential. The EU has also increasingly talked about taking into account a variety of issues, such as child labour and the environment, in its trade policy.

The war in Ukraine has contributed to a growing concern in the EU about being dependent on vital imports from authoritarian countries. The dependence on Russian oil and gas led to a severe energy crisis after the war broke out and imports from Russia declined (see Becker and Åslund, Chapter 7, this volume). Similar concerns are increasingly voiced over imports from China, and there is a discussion on the possibilities of moving production home to the EU or to more friendly countries (Goldberg and Reed, 2003). This is one example of how trade and security issues are increasingly intertwined.

An increased degree of introspection in the EU is even more due to the fact that China and the US appear to be successful in some areas of their industrial policies. As mentioned earlier, China has used subsidies and other measures to support domestic companies, and in the US, government industrial policy has also become more important. A general concern in the EU is that its companies are perceived as lagging behind competitors in other countries, in particular in so-called high-tech industries. An increased focus on industrial policy is seen in the early 2020s both in the EU and in individual member states. The fact that these sentiments are heard in France is in line with a long tradition in the country, but it is surprising to hear similar arguments in Germany. In 2019, Germany launched a strategic plan for German and European industries (Altmeier, 2019). The plan focuses mainly on the manufacturing industry rather than, for example, the service industry, and the policies advocated are strongly interventionist (Zettelmeyer, 2019).

More specifically, the plan mentions quantitative targets for the size of the industry. For Germany, the target is 25% of GDP and for the EU 20%, an increase from the current 23% and 14% respectively. These are high figures for countries at such high-income levels. In comparison, the share in the US is about 12%.

The plan aims to achieve the objective of a larger industrial sector through a number of measures (Zettlemeyer, 2019, p. 1).

- Purchases of inputs will be increasingly sourced from companies within the EU. Value chains will therefore be regional rather than global.
- Companies that are considered particularly important will receive various forms of support. For example, it is proposed that competition law be changed to make it easier for these companies, even if it means less competition in the European market.
- Foreign takeovers of domestic companies can be stopped by the state buying up shares in private companies.
- Key industries should be identified and supported.

The above measures represent a significant regime change in the European view of what the market should stand for and what is the role of the state. It also implies a changed view of globalization where openness to trade and foreign direct investment is replaced by a more inward-looking policy. Exactly how much of the measures that actually will be implemented is uncertain, but it is clear that the idea of a more interventionist industrial policy has gained a foothold and is spreading across the Union. It is also interesting that the measures are not based on market failures, a standard argument for state interventionism. Rather, there is a more fundamental belief in the ability of the state to bring about changes in a positive direction, changes that private industry is not believed to be able to bring about on its own. That this would be the case seems highly uncertain. Identifying future important projects is difficult for both the state and companies, but the latter are much better at dismantling unsuccessful initiatives (Zettlemeyer, 2019, p. 11). When the state makes targeted investments that do not pay off, various interest groups tend to make it difficult to dismantle the project in question.

The European Commission's 2020 industrial policy strategy echoes many of the German proposals. Again, the emphasis is on selective packages of measures to target certain companies and industries. In terms of strategic industries that the EU wants to focus on, important raw materials, batteries, hydrogen, processors and semiconductors, industrial data, cloud and e-services and circular plastics are mentioned (Flam, 2021, p. 4). It is questionable how many of these industries have the potential to be competitive in the EU. A likely future global overcapacity in for instance semiconductors will be a difficulty for European production and in the case of batteries the market seems to be able to meet demand without government subsidies (*ibid*).

In 2022, the US' introduction of the Investment Reduction Act (IRA) stirred unease within the European Union. Aimed at significant cuts in greenhouse gas emissions, the IRA positions the US closer to its 50% reduction goal by 2030. The IRA subsidizes purchases of electric vehicles, clean-tech production and production of carbon–neutral fuels, exclusively for US producers (Kleinman et al., 2023). This exclusion, however, contravenes World Trade Organization regulations.

The EU is anxious that the IRA might catalyse a shift of clean-tech production to the US, lured by subsidies and low energy prices. This anxiety is pronounced in the automobile industry, given the IRA's potential to slash US electric car production costs by 20%, thereby threatening EU's car exports and possibly leading European manufacturers to move operations to the US (Kleinman et al., 2023). Thus, while the EU appreciates the US's renewed environmental commitments, it fears potential damage to its green sectors (Holtzhausen, 2023). In response, the EU has launched initiatives like the "Green Deal Industrial Plan" and the "Net Zero Industry Act," providing support comparable to the US's support of its green industries.

In addition to internal support initiatives, the EU is also exploring external measures to safeguard its green industries and ensure a level playing field. One notable mechanism is the proposal of the EU's Carbon Border Adjustment Mechanism (CBAM), commonly referred to as "climate tariffs." Designed as a part of the European Green Deal, the CBAM aims to impose taxes on carbon-intensive products imported from countries with less stringent environmental regulations, thereby discouraging European companies from relocating to such countries and importing back into the EU. The rationale is to prevent "carbon leakage", where companies might move to countries with laxer emissions standards. By doing so, the EU intends to protect its green sectors from unfair competition while simultaneously encouraging other nations to elevate their environmental standards (European Parliament, 2021).

It is evident from the above discussion that the EU has glanced at developments in China and the US and advocates a more active industrial policy and a more restrictive trade policy. The argument that political decisions should govern industrial production and choice of technology has been increasingly used. An alternative strategy for the EU could be based on improving the business environment through general measures but without hindering trade and foreign direct investment.

Improving the functioning of different markets would be positive for European competitiveness and growth. This could include aspects such as competition law, intellectual property rights and digital services legislation (Flam, 2021, p. 2.). In particular, competition should be strengthened as it is the basis for growth and development. Companies that rely on government support and protection from foreign competition tend to spend too little time developing their business. Large industrial investments also tend to favour large and already established companies and disadvantage small and midsize enterprises. This is a further argument that politics works against a dynamic business community.

One way to create the necessary pressure for change is to ensure that the internal market works as intended with full freedom for goods, capital, people and services to move across national borders. Signs of various restrictions on freedoms are beginning to emerge in the second half of the 2010s. For example, the migration crisis in 2015 led to the reintroduction of border controls within the EU, while the pandemic crisis led countries to introduce new travel restrictions and stop the export of goods that were considered particularly important, such as medicines and medical equipment. In the case of the trade freeze, countries seemed to learn from the cost of this type of policy and in the later stages of the pandemic trade flowed more normally, but the fact that a fundamental aspect of the free market could be compromised at all is a cause for concern. Work is now underway in the EU to prevent similar measures in future crises.

Another discussion in the EU focuses on trade in services. More specifically, work is underway to harmonize regulations around services markets, which would facilitate trade. Other areas would also benefit from more harmonization in order to deepen and improve integration and the functioning of the common market.

Making the single market work better is important. But it is also important to work towards a better functioning and more rules-based global economy. As noted above, the WTO is facing major problems and a number of different measures are likely needed if the world is to return to a rules-based trading system. It is in the EU's interest that this happens, which means that a thoughtful and coherent strategy from the Union is needed. The EU has historically been important to the global trading system and can hopefully play a leading role in addressing the major challenges that exist.

The problems cannot be solved with the existing rules; a major change is needed (Mavroidis & Sapir, 2021). Changing the WTO will not be an easy task, not only because of developments in recent years but also because the organization has grown to include more than 160 countries with different interests and preferences.

Multilateralism, joint commitments by all member countries, is an important part of the WTO guidelines. However, it is likely that a larger number of agreements with groups of member countries will be necessary. There is nothing to prevent such agreements as long as they do not adversely affect other members. Such work is already taking place in a number of areas. More specifically, in 2017, working groups were established between different countries focusing on reforms in various trade-related areas: e-commerce; trade in services; investment frameworks; and internationalization of small businesses (Hoekman & Sabel, 2021). Different countries are involved in the different working groups. For example, the EU and China are in all four groups while the US is only in one (e-commerce). The advantage of this approach is that it allows countries to cooperate in different areas rather than liberalizing all trade, as is the case in many other free trade agreements.

China's entry into the WTO has been problematic. The WTO's rules are not designed to deal with state capitalist systems like China's. Furthermore, the belief that China would change and become like any other market economy country has been proven wrong. On the contrary, China under Xi Jinping is moving towards less market economy and more of state control and governance. This was made clear at the 20th Party Congress of the Chinese Communist Party in Beijing in October 2022. The desire to increase self-sufficiency and reduce dependence on the outside world was clear, as was the emphasis on continuing to develop capacity for domestic innovation and technology.

Again, the WTO fails to address more unconventional protections for domestic industry. It seems necessary to address this shortcoming, in particular, to create an effective mechanism to prevent subsidies to domestic firms (Wu, 2018) and to counteract various types of "theft" of foreign technology (Branstetter, 2018). In their research, Mavroidis and Sapir (2021) show that both phenomena are particularly associated with China. Pressure has therefore increased since China's entry to create an effective WTO to tackle a new type of trade barrier (Payosova et al., 2018). The US trade war with China has shown that unilateral action is costly and rather ineffective, which is a lesson for the EU.

At the same time, one should be aware that it is not easy to change the regulatory framework in this direction. State-owned enterprises, where government subsidies are significant, are not covered by the WTO framework, which means that the role of these companies must be explicitly put on the table and included in the reform process (Ahn, 2021). Naturally, this is a development that China may well oppose. Furthermore, subsidies of various kinds are present not only in China but also in Japan, the US and the EU. These may be industrial subsidies, which are rapidly increasing in importance, not least in the EU, but also agricultural subsidies that are important in many countries. Removing these subsidies would improve global welfare, but this is politically very difficult to achieve (Evenett & Fritz, 2019). Increased imports resulting from the removal of subsidies will hit some groups hard and these groups will do what they can to politically secure their livelihoods.

When it comes to forced technology transfer, the problems are perhaps even greater. Many observers doubt that the WTO can deal with the issue (Mavroidis & Sapir, 2021).

Furthermore, a functioning dispute settlement mechanism needs to be put back in place. Over the years, around 600 trade disputes have been handled by the WTO, but as described above, the process has collapsed (see also Hoekman & Mavroidis, 2021). It is important that the US stops blocking this activity. It should be noted, however, that for this to happen, reforms of the WTO are required, roughly along the lines described above. The fact that the US is blocking the Dispute Settlement Body is, at least in part, due to the WTO's inability to handle different types of conflicts, and countries other than the US have also expressed dissatisfaction with the situation (Bown, 2019; Fiorini et al., 2019). Finally, even if new judges were appointed, the dispute settlement mechanism cannot be expected to play the same role as before. Many countries use trade barriers that violate WTO rules. This in turn means that these countries are likely to be wary of taking other countries to the WTO court. Otherwise, the accused countries are likely to respond with the same action (Evenett & Fritz, 2019). Again, this shows the complexity of the problem and a solution will require many different types of measures.

Remove Border Barriers for a Successful EU

Political attitudes towards globalization have changed in many parts of the world. From a positive to a more sceptical one. As a result, tariffs and trade barriers have increased. For the rest of the decade, the development of globalization will be determined by the evolution of political will and technological developments. New technologies, such as digitalization and AI, open up for trade in new products and industries, and these developments are largely beyond the control of politicians. Technological developments may therefore compensate for a lack of political will.

However, relying on technological progress is too defensive a strategy. The trend towards stronger internal and external borders that Johanna Pettersson Fürst highlights in her chapter in this volume is also evident in international trade. A continued trend towards less globalization makes the world poorer (Irwin, 2019), since less international specialization and less competition are negative for growth and welfare. The EU therefore needs to intensify its efforts to open both internal and external borders.

With regard to internal borders, a much greater focus is needed on improving the functioning of the internal market. Ensuring the free movement of people, capital and goods is the most important thing the EU can do to ensure future growth and prosperity. The tendencies towards new trade barriers that were evident during the pandemic should be pushed back. Similarly, proposals for an active industrial policy inspired by developments in China and the US are not the way forward. Selective selection and support of certain companies and industries by public authorities is a strategy that has been tried in many parts of the world. The negative experiences of such policies are well documented.

Ensuring the functioning of the internal market is important but not enough. The EU benefits from open global markets. Furthermore, as China and the US turn increasingly inward, the EU needs to step up and take greater responsibility for global trade liberalization. The challenge is great and requires a focused effort to both establish new trade agreements, particularly with the US and to revitalize the WTO.

References

Ahn, D. (2021). Why reform is needed: WTO "public body" Jurisprudence. *Global Policy, 12*(3), 61–70.

Altmeier, P. (2019). *National industrial strategy 2030: Strategic guidelines for a German and European industrial policy*. Federal Ministry for Economic Affairs and Energy.

Amiti, M., Redding, S. J., & Weinstein, D. E. (2019). The Impact of the 2018 tariffs on prices and welfare. *Journal of Economic Perspectives, 33*(4), 187–210.

Autor, D., Dorn, D., Hanson, G., & Majlesi, K. (2020). Importing political polarization? The electoral consequences of rising trade exposure. *American Economic Review, 110*(10), 3139–3183.

Baldwin, R. (2006). *Globalisation: The great unbundling(s)*. Helsinki: Economic Council of Finland.

Baldwin, R. (2016). *The great convergence: Information technology and the new globalization*. Harvard University Press.

Bergh, A., & Kärnä, A. (2021). Globalization and populism in Europe. *Public Choice, 189*(1–2), 51–70.

Bernhofen, D. M., El-Sahli, Z., & Kneller, R. (2016). Estimating the effects of the container revolution on world trade. *Journal of International Economics, 98*, 36–50.

Bown, C. P. (2019). The 2018 Trade war and the end of dispute settlement as we know it. *Vox*, 19 June 2019.

Bown, C. P., & Kolb, M. (2020). Trump's trade war timeline: An up-to-date guide. *Peterson Institute for International Economics*.

Branstetter, L.G. (2018). China's forced technology transfer problem—and What to Do About It. *Peterson Institute for International Economics*, Working paper 18–13.

Chen, J., Chen, X, Hou, Q. & Hu, M. (2021). Haste doesn't bring success: Top-down amplification of economic growth targets and enterprise overcapacity. *Journal of Corporate Finance, 70*.

Colantone, I., & Stanig, P. (2018). Global competition and Brexit. *American Political Science Review, 112*(2), 201–218.

Dippel, C, Gold, R. & Heblich, S. (2015). Globalization and its (dis-)content: Trade shocks and voting behaviour. NBER, Working Paper 21812.

European Parliament. (2021). *EU carbon border adjustment mechanism. Implications for climate and competitiveness*. https://www.europarl.europa.eu/RegData/etudes/BRIE/2022/698889/EPRS_BRI(2022)698889_EN.pdf

Evenett, S.J. & Fritz, J. (2019). Jaw Jaw not War War: Prioritizing WTO Reform Options. *The 24th Global Trade Alert Report*. London, Centre for Economic Policy Research.

Fiorini, M., Hoekman, B., Mavroidis, P.C., Saluste, M. & Wolfe, R. (2019). WTO dispute settlement and the appellate body crisis: Detailed survey results. *Bertelsmann Stiftung Working Paper*.

Flam, H. (2021). EU Satsar för Mycket i Industripolitiken (The EU invests too much in industrial policy). *SIEPS Report, 2021*, 1.

Friedman, T. L. (2005). *The world is flat: A brief history of the twenty-first century*. Farrar.
Goldberg, P. K., & Read, T. (2023). Is the global economy deglobalizing? And if So, Why? And What is Next? *NBER Working Paper 31115*. Cambridge, MA.: National Bureau of Economic Research.
Heyman, F. (2016). Job polarization, job tasks and the role of firms. *Economics Letters, 145*, 246–251.
Hoekman, B., & Mavroidis, P. C. (2021). WTO reform: Back to the past to build for the future. *Global Policy, 12*(3), 5–12.
Hoekman, B., & Sabel, C. (2021). Plurilateral cooperation as an alternative to trade agreements: Innovating one domain at a time. *Global Policy, 12*(3), 49–60.
Holtzhausen, A. (2023). *A Faustian Bargain: Europe's Answers to the US IRA*. Allianz Research, February 7.
Huang, T. & Véron, N. (2022). The private sector advances in China: The evolving ownership structures of the largest companies in the Xi Jinping Era. *Peterson Institute Working Paper* 22–3.
Irwin, D.A. (2019). Does trade reform promote economic growth? A review of recent evidence, NBER Working Paper 25927. Cambridge, MA.: *National Bureau of Economic Research.*
Jones, K. (2021). *Populism and trade: The challenge to the global trading system*. Oxford University Press.
Klein, N. (2000). *No logo*. Flamingo.
Kleinmann, D., Poitiers, N., Sapir, A., Tagliapitera, S., Véron, N., Veugelers, R. & Zettelmeyer, J. (2023). *How Europe should answer the US Inflation Reduction Act*, Policy Contribution 04/2023, Bruegel.
Krueger, A. O. (1978). *Foreign trade regimes and economic development: Liberalization attempts and consequences*. Ballinger Publishing Company.
Lai, H. (2021). The rationale and effects of China's belt and road initiative: reducing vulnerabilities in domestic political economy. *Journal of Contemporary China, 30*, 330–347.
Mavroidis, P. C., & Sapir, A. (2021). All the tea in China: Solving the ´China Problem´. *Global Policy, 12*(3), 41–48.
Moravcsik, A. (1998). *The choice for Europe: Social purpose and state power from Messina to Maastricht*. Routledge.
Payosova, T., Hufbauer, G.C. & Schott, J.J. (2018). The dispute settlement crisis in the world trade organization: Causes and cures. *Peterson Institute for International Economics, Policy Brief* 18–5.
Redding, S.J., Amiti, M. & Weinstein, D.E. (2019). Who's paying for the U.S. tariffs? A longer-term perspective. *CEPR Working paper 6701.*
Rodrik, D. (2017). Populism and the Economics of Globalization. *CEPR Discussion Paper Nr. 12119.*

Sjöholm, F. (2023). Navigating the new normal: The European union's changing stance on globalization in the Era of trade conflicts. *Asian Economic Papers*, 23(1), 29–45.

Sjöholm, F., & Lundin, N. (2010). The role of small firms in the technology development of China. *The World Economy*, *33*(9), 1117–1139.

Wong, E. & Swanson, A. (2022). Ukraine war and pandemic force nations to retreat from globalization. *The New York Times*, 22 March 2022.

Wu, T. (2018). *The curse of bigness: Antitrust in the new gilded age*. Colombia Global Reports.

Zenz, A. (2019). "Wash brains, cleanse hearts": Evidence from Chinese government documents about the nature and extent of Xinjiang's extrajudicial internment campaign. *Journal of Political Risk*, 7(11). (2019).

Zettelmeyer, J. (2019). The return of economic nationalism in Germany. *Peterson Institute for International Economics, Policy Brief* 19–4.

CHAPTER 4

The Boundaries of the Internal Market In- and Outside the EU

Marja-Liisa Öberg

Introduction

Russia's full-scale invasion of Ukraine[1] has led to the enlargement of NATO as well as, potentially, the European Union (EU), with Moldova and Ukraine being granted candidate status in 2022. Moldova and Ukraine's candidate status is based on an ambitious agenda of integration with the EU via association agreements (AAs) concluded in 2014 and 2016, respectively. The AA/Deep and Comprehensive Free Trade Areas (DCFTAs) are characterized by close cooperation with the EU by means of the non-Member States' adoption of the EU's *acquis* in relevant areas in exchange for access to the EU's internal market. Third-country

[1] * This chapter is based on an article published as Öberg. M.-L. (2020). Internal Market Acquis as a Tool in EU External Relations: From Integration to Disintegration. *Legal Issues of Economic Integration*, *47*(2), 151–178, and the book Öberg. M.-L. (2020). *The Boundaries of the EU Internal Market: Participation without Membership*. Cambridge University Press.

M.-L. Öberg (✉)
Lund University, Lund, Sweden
e-mail: marja-liisa.oberg@jur.lu.se

A. Bakardjieva Engelbrekt et al. (eds.), *The Borders of the European Union in a Conflictual World*,
https://doi.org/10.1007/978-3-031-54200-8_4

integration in the EU via norms transfer offers a possibility for the Union to expand its sphere of influence, whereas for third countries it provides an opportunity for deep cooperation with the Union in preparation for membership or as an alternative thereto.

The expansion of the internal market to the neighbouring countries by means of norms export is a significant element of the EU's foreign policy towards the neighbourhood. Norms export also constitutes a crucial external dimension of individual policy sectors, such as energy and transport. Since AAs, through which the export of norms usually takes place, also aim to facilitate integration into the EU's political community, the agreements assume a security policy aspect that is particularly illustrated by the political developments surrounding the conclusion of the EU-Ukraine AA/DCFTA (Van der Loo, 2016). The EU's post-Brexit relationship with the United Kingdom and its relationship with Ukraine and Moldova after the currently raging war suggest that discussions about the participation of non-EU Member States in the internal market and its significance for EU integration on a broader plane are as crucial as ever.

This chapter examines how the expanded boundaries of the EU's internal market affect the Union's role as a regional power. The chapter argues that the expansion of the internal market offers third countries a solid opportunity to identify themselves as belonging to the wider European community and ensures their long-term commitment to the European integration project. The chapter begins with an account of the importance of the internal market within the EU. It is followed by a discussion on the significance of the internal market in the EU's external relations with a particular emphasis on the EU's neighbourhood and the role of association agreements as preparatory stages to (potential) membership. The chapter concludes with a discussion on the extent to which integration through internal market *acquis* can constitute a sustainable alternative to membership.

Definition and Meaning of the Internal Market Within the EU

The underlying economic ideal of the EU is the creation of an 'integrated economy in which the factors of production, as well as the fruits of production, can move freely and without distortion, thus achieving a more efficient allocation of resources and a more perfect division of labour' (Opinion of Advocate General Jacobs in Joined Cases C-92/

92 and C-326/92 Phil Collins EU:C:1993:276, point 10). Within the framework of these broad principles, ample scope is left to both the Member States and the Court of Justice of the EU (CJEU) to determine the exact shape of the single market, thereby determining the breadth and depth of market integration within the EU.

The concept of the internal market comprises rights and principles. First, the definition provided in Article 26(2) of the Treaty on the Functioning of the EU (TFEU) focuses on the four fundamental freedoms—the free movement of goods, persons, services and capital. Second, the Preamble to the TFEU makes references to fair competition between undertakings. Third, regulation of the relationship between the market participants is further underpinned by the principles of non-discrimination and equality.

The concept of the internal market is flexible as well as constantly evolving. Pescatore (1981) has classified the components of the internal market *acquis* in accordance with their legislative, political and judicial origins. The *acquis* consists of primary and secondary law, policy instruments and jurisprudence of the CJEU that shed light on the functioning and establishment of the internal market.

The legislative *acquis* includes a body of legally binding and non-binding acts; the founding Treaties of the EU and their amendments; secondary law comprising regulations, directives, decisions, recommendations and opinions; the internal acts of the EU's institutions, inter-institutional agreements as well as international agreements concluded by the EU.

The political *acquis* comprises legally non-binding acts, such as the political objectives of the Treaties, as well as various resolutions, declarations, positions, guidelines and principle, including decisions and agreements adopted by the European Council and the Council. Despite not being legally enforceable, non-binding acts can have certain legal consequences.

The third category, judicial *acquis* consists of the jurisprudence of the EU's judiciary. The latter is a source of fundamental principles framing the Union's legal order, such as the principles of direct effect and primacy of EU law but also effectiveness and unity.

The regulatory framework governing the EU's internal market thus includes all primary and secondary law, political instruments and jurisprudence of the EU courts regarding the establishment and functioning of the internal market. The latter includes the four freedoms as well as overarching provisions on, for example, competition, environment, social policy, consumer protection and fundamental rights to the extent that they have a connection to the internal market (Öberg, 2020).

Within the European integration project, the internal market plays a central role. The foundations for the internal market were laid in 1957 with the conclusion of the Treaty establishing the European Economic Community (EEC) between the then six Member States. The common European market was not created as an independent goal, but rather as a means of achieving the wider purpose of the Union, which was to increase economic prosperity through 'an ever closer association between the peoples of Europe' (Preamble, EEC Treaty). Neither the EEC Treaty nor the subsequent amending treaties provided a clear definition of the common market. Kapteyn and VerLoren van Themaat have defined the common market as 'a market in which every participant within the Community in question is free to invest, produce, work, buy and sell, to supply or obtain services under conditions of competition which have not been artificially distorted wherever economic conditions are most favourable' (Kapteyn & VerLoren van Themaat, 2008, p. 127). The definition includes the four fundamental freedoms—the free movement of goods, services (including the freedom of establishment), persons and capital and provisions on competition.

During the 1970s and 1980s, the common market experienced a period of stagnation. As an attempt to give impetus for increased integration, the Single European Act, which entered into force in 1987, set a deadline of 31 December 1992 for the completion of the 'internal market'. The European Commission's 1985 White Paper had outlined the actions necessary to achieve that goal accompanied by a precise timetable (European Commission, 1985). The White Paper was exceptionally detailed and contained a total of 279 legislative initiatives to remove trade barriers between the Member States. However, despite high ambitions and partial success, the internal market could not be completed by the set deadline. While efforts continued, the European Commission stressed that the legal framework of the internal market essentially requires the addition of other policy instruments, first and foremost a single currency, marking the transition from a common market to a monetary union. Subsequently, the European Commission (1997) published the 'Action Plan for the Single Market ' (CSE (97) 1 final) focusing on four strategic objectives: (1) increasing the effectiveness of existing regulations by improving their implementation, enforcement and problem solving; (2) addressing significant market distortions in the fields of taxation and competition; (3) removing barriers to market integration in individual sectors and (4) strengthening the role of citizens by abolishing internal borders within the Union and strengthening the social dimension of the single market.

Since the 1990s, the European Commission no longer pursues its original goal of 'completing' the internal market. In the 2000s, the European Commission instead began to emphasize the dynamic nature of the internal market and its need to adapt to changes over time. This new perspective takes the internal market beyond the idea of removing barriers to cross-border trade. Instead, as presented in European Commission (2007) Communication 'A Single Market for the Europe of the Future' of 20 November 2007 (COM (2007) 724 final), it supports the need for the internal market to respond to the challenges of globalization and increased competition, new economic, environmental and societal challenges and the enlarged Union. The principles underlying the internal market remain relevant. Their application, however, must be adapted to new realities and the right balance must be struck between a borderless market and considerations of labour law, health, safety and the environment. The fact that the common policies that have relevance for the internal market will never be 'completed' also means that the definition of the internal market will remain dynamic.

Integration Through the Internal Market as a Path to Membership

In addition to the internal context, the dynamic character of the internal market is also reflected externally in third countries' different possibilities to participate therein. The EU's competitive position in the world depends not only on economic power (Gehring et al., 2017) but also on the Union's ever-increasing normative power (Bradford, 2020; Cremona, 2004). This dynamics is prominently reflected in the role of the internal market in the Union's relations with third countries in its neighbourhood. On the one hand, the Union actively participates in multilateral fora that create global rules and practices. On the other hand, the EU exports its norms and values to non-Member States in exchange for the latter's access to the internal market. The latter phenomenon where the integration of third countries with the EU takes place through the Union's own *acquis* is most noticeable in the Union's immediate neighbourhood and is exemplified by different types of agreements that vary in both form and intensity.

The objectives of the export of EU *acquis* to third countries, too, vary in accordance with the economic development of the Union and its neighbouring regions as well as the need to coordinate solutions to common challenges and responses to common threats. The approximation of legislation between the EU and the neighbouring countries creates increased political and economic stability in the EU's immediate neighbourhood while assisting the non-Member States in achieving their internal political goals. The latter aspect concerns especially states that are in a phase of modernization or transition, such as countries in Eastern Europe. Providing neighbouring countries an alternative to membership through access to the internal market combined with financial and technical support is, furthermore, a means for the Union to manage its accession capacity.

Certain categories of agreements concluded between the EU and neighbouring countries are specifically aimed at exporting EU norms, policies and institutions. In these agreements, both the scope of the *acquis* and the depth of intended integration vary greatly. Elements that distinguish between the agreements include (1) the broad political goals of the programmes which the agreement forms part of (such as the European Neighbourhood Policy); (2) the specific aims of the agreement as well as (3) the third-country's geographical proximity to the EU, its economic situation and attitude and potential to become an EU Member State.

Unlike the enlargement process, agreements concerning legal approximation between the EU and neighbouring countries do not aim at total regulatory convergence that would cover the entire EU *acquis*. Norm export is usually, as exemplified by the Agreement on the European Economic Area (1994) (EEA), limited to the *acquis* of the internal market and is, thus, directly devoted to providing third countries access to the EU internal market. In some cases, the process of legislative approximation is based on international or bilateral norms. In other cases, legal homogeneity is to be achieved on the basis of the internal market *acquis*. Overall, the role of the internal market in the EU's external relations is characterized by a move towards deepening and broadening within a variety of political frameworks, types of agreements and perspectives of future EU membership.

Exporting the internal market *acquis* to third countries and, especially, the goal of thereby expanding the internal market is the most prominent example of third countries' legal approximation with the EU. The EU's close regulatory cooperation with neighbouring countries dates back to the early days of the European Communities. The European Economic Community (EEC) signed the first Association Agreements with Greece and Turkey in 1961 and 1963, respectively. Over the next 60 years, the EU has concluded numerous association, cooperation and partnership agreements with its near and more distant neighbours. Almost all countries in the EU's neighbourhood have formalized relations with the EU through one or more bilateral or multilateral agreements. The agreements vary considerably in terms of the wider political context in which they are situated, their stated aims, and the scope of EU *acquis* contained therein. Nevertheless, the central element in the rapprochement between the EU and the third countries concerned is the regulatory framework of the EU's internal market.

Third countries can cooperate with the EU, and be integrated with the internal market, to different degrees. The lowest level is constituted by cooperation agreements which envisage third countries' gradual integration into the EU's wider area cooperation, such as through the European Neighbourhood Policy, Partnership and Cooperation Agreements concluded in the 1990s with the countries of Eastern Europe, or the Euro-Mediterranean Association Agreements. The second level comprises the liberalization of trade through internal market *acquis*, either by means of a free trade agreement or the establishment of a customs union. Examples of such agreements include the EEC-Turkey Association Agreement, the Europe Agreements concluded with the countries of Central and Eastern Europe that became EU members in the consecutive enlargement rounds of 2004 and 2007, the Stabilisation and Association Agreements concluded with the countries of the Western Balkans, as well as the new AA/DCFTAs concluded within the framework of the Eastern Partnership.

Association agreements constitute the main instrument for the liberalization of trade between the EU and the neighbouring countries. Association agreements can have many different aims. They can be used to prepare neighbouring countries for EU membership, provide an alternative to membership, or a framework for development cooperation or interregional assistance (Hanf & Dengler, 2004). One common feature of the various association agreements is reciprocity, although the extent of concrete rights and obligations in individual agreements varies. According to the CJEU, an association agreement gives rise to 'special, privileged links with a non-member country which must, at least to a certain extent, take part in the Community system' (Case 12/86 Demirel EU:C:1987:400, para. 9). In practice, the reciprocity of rights and obligations usually includes third countries adopting EU acquis or acceding to international conventions in exchange for financial and technical assistance and, to a varying degree, access to the internal market.

For example, the 1963 EEC-Turkey Association Agreement aims to promote trade and economic relations between the EU and Turkey and to create a customs union covering all trade in goods. The specific regulatory framework to be adopted by Turkey is set out in decisions of the Association Council which, together with the Agreement, form the 'law of association'. Legal adaptation to the EU's regulatory framework must, however, only take place 'as far as possible' (EEC-Turkey Association Council, 1995, Article 54(1) of Decision 1/95, 22 December). The EU-Turkey law of association covers significant parts of the internal market's regulatory framework notably excluding the free movement of persons. Pursuant to Article 12 of the EEC-Turkey Association Agreement, for example, the Parties must gradually ensure the free movement of workers which, to this date, has not been achieved (Case C-81/13 *United Kingdom v Council* EU: C:2014:2449, para 57).

The EU's current integration strategy for the neighbourhood includes both a political and an economic dimension. Together with DCFTAs, association agreements form the basis of the cooperation. The combined AA/DCFTAs envisage the approximation of third countries' legal systems to the EU *acquis*, the entry of the third countries into the internal market and are expected to lead to increased competition within the neighbourhood. So far, new AA/DCFTAs have been concluded with Georgia, Moldova and Ukraine. Negotiations with Azerbaijan on a DCFTA, but excluding an association agreement are ongoing. Negotiations with Armenia on a DCFTA were completed in 2013, but as Armenia's membership in the Eurasian Economic Union proved incompatible with the provisions of the DCFTA, the latter agreement was never concluded. Instead, in 2017, an agreement—the Comprehensive and Enhanced Partnership Agreement (CEPA)—was signed that is narrower in scope and more modest in terms of access to the internal market. The purpose of the CEPA is to establish legislative cooperation between the EU and Armenia without an association. The scope of the EU's regulatory framework within CEPA is largely limited to the field of energy and envisages market integration and gradual approximation of legislation with 'the key elements of EU acquis' (Preamble to the Comprehensive and Enhanced Partnership Agreement between the European Union and the Republic of Armenia (2018)).

AA/DCFTAs are ambitious in terms of the gradual integration of third countries into the internal market. The agreements intend to provide far-reaching market access and extensive legislative approximation, however, without clearly leading to future membership in the Union. AA/DCFTAs cover several sectors of the internal market, such as energy, transport, services and agriculture. They also incorporate all four fundamental freedoms, albeit with significant exceptions regarding the free movement of persons. Unlike other free trade agreements, integration on the basis of the EU *acquis* in the AA/DCFTAs is a legal obligation and subject to strict conditions. The intended scope and depth of integration within AA/DCFTAS is significant: in the areas of services, establishment and public procurement, for example, the EU-Ukraine AA/DCFTA comes close to the level of integration envisaged in the EEA Agreement. The ambitious substantive scope of the AA/DCFTAs is supported by an institutional and procedural framework that includes features of other agreements that aim at comprehensive integration, such as the EEA Agreement, but does not, however, reach the same level of complexity as the latter.

The diversity of different types of integration agreements reflects the different functions that the internal market and its regulatory framework play not only within the EU but also outside the Union. In the EU's relations with third countries, internal market *acquis* can be said to encompass five main functions. First, internal market *acquis* is used to gradually integrate non-Member States into Europe's wider area of cooperation; second, the *acquis* contributes to the liberalization of trade when a free trade area or customs union is established; third, the *acquis* is used to prepare potential candidate countries for EU membership; fourth, the *acquis* serves as a means for more extensive integration of third countries into the internal market and fifth, as a limited version of the latter, the *acquis* contributes to the integration of non-Member States into a sector of the internal market, such as transport or energy. A sixth function relates to the management of a relationship between the EU and a former Member State, as exemplified by Brexit. The various functions of the *acquis* may overlap both within a single agreement and be included in several agreements concluded between the Union and a non-Member State. A case in point is the accession process, where total convergence with the EU's regulatory framework is usually preceded by less intensive forms of political and legal cooperation between the Union and the country concerned, including in the area of the internal market.

Integration Through the Internal Market as an Alternative to Membership

From the perspective of the EU, the export of internal market *acquis* via multilateral agreements is primarily a matter of foreign policy vis-à-vis third countries. However, it also constitutes a means of expanding the internal market by allowing third countries to participate therein, albeit to a limited extent. By adopting EU *acquis*, third countries are integrated into the EU's internal market rather than a separate, expanded market being set up with a legal system based on different norms than those that apply within the EU. The pursuit of legal homogeneity within the expanded internal market, such as in the example of the EEA, constructs a bridge between the EU's regulatory framework and the regulatory framework of the legal order created by the *acquis*-exporting agreement in question.

On the whole, the EU's external action towards the neighbourhood countries is thus not limited to bilateral trade relations, democratization and the improvement of security at the Union's external borders, but is increasingly aimed at integrating the neighbouring countries both into a wider area of cooperation and, more concretely, in the EU's internal market. The boundaries of the latter thus become more blurred. The expansion of the single market serves both the external and internal interests of the Union. In the gradual integration of third countries without immediate membership of the Union, the role of the internal market as the engine behind the EU's economic and political success has been infused into the Union's external relations. This is reflected in the evolving role played by internal market *acquis* in agreements concluded by the EU with the neighbourhood countries over time and across different countries and country groups. In these agreements, the obligation to adopt and implement internal market *acquis* has become standard, and the role of the agreements to integrate third countries either gradually or completely into the internal market has become increasingly relevant.

One of the most prominent functions of the internal market *acquis* in the EU's external relations is to integrate third countries into the internal market regardless of the membership aspirations of the latter. Such integration can either embrace the internal market in its entirety or be limited to one or more specific policy areas. Despite differences in the breadth of cooperation, both categories share roughly the same depth of integration in terms of relevant free movement provisions.

The only example of an agreement that exports the EU *acquis* in order to extend the internal market outside the Union in a comprehensive manner without explicit membership ambitions is the agreement establishing the EEA. The Agreement was signed in 1992 as a multilateral association agreement between the European Community and its Member States, on the one hand, and the countries of the European Free Trade Association (EFTA) excluding Switzerland, on the other hand. The agreement entered into force in 1994. Most of the former EEA EFTA countries have by now joined the EU, rendering Iceland, Liechtenstein and Norway the only non-EU members of the EEA. Despite the low number of participating countries, however, there are no indications that the EEA would cease to exist in the foreseeable future as it provides for the countries that have chosen to remain outside the Union an opportunity to continue to be closely connected to it in both political and economic terms.

The EEA Agreement aims to create a 'homogeneous European Economic Area' based on equal conditions of competition and respect for the same rules (Article 1.1 of the EEA Agreement). This express aim of legal homogeneity distinguishes the EEA Agreement from all other neighbourhood agreements discussed in this chapter. The EEA Agreement covers almost the entire internal market *acquis* (the Agreement does not include the Customs Union, the Common Commercial Policy and the Common Agricultural and Fisheries Policy), making the EEA EFTA countries nearly full-fledged participants in the internal market.

The annexes to the EEA agreement which contain the 'EEA-relevant provisions' are continuously reviewed by the EEA Joint Committee with the aim of guaranteeing legal security and homogeneity within the EEA. In order to ensure that the common rules are applied in a uniform manner, the EEA features an elaborate institutional framework. Unlike the association agreements discussed above, which mainly establish an association council, the EEA Agreement establishes both a Joint Committee, an EEA Joint Parliamentary Committee, and the EFTA Court. The latter is a body that adjudicates disputes between the EFTA parties to the EEA Agreement arising from the interpretation of the EEA

Agreement. The system established by the EEA Agreement thus goes far beyond exporting the internal market *acquis* to third countries and has become a legal system of its own (Case E-9/97 Sveinbjörnsdóttir v. Iceland [1998] EFTA Ct Rep 95, para. 59).

EFTA member Switzerland is not a party to the EEA Agreement. Although Switzerland participated in the negotiations of the Agreement along with the other EFTA members, a negative referendum in 1992 led to the country not signing the EEA Agreement. Instead, the relationship between the EU and Switzerland is governed by over a hundred bilateral agreements. These agreements notably include the two packages of sectoral bilateral agreements: 'Bilateral I' and 'Bilateral II' which were signed in 1999 and 2004 and contain seven and nine agreements, respectively. Examples of the policy areas covered by the agreements include the free movement of persons, air transport, rail and road transport, trade in agricultural products, public procurement, mutual recognition of conformity assessment, environment, etc.

The aim of the cooperation between the EU and Switzerland, which is based on the bilateral agreements, is to strengthen deep sectoral cooperation rather than to offer full participation in the internal market on equal terms with EU Member States in line with the EEA agreement. Similarly to the latter, the annexes to the bilateral agreements contain lists of applicable EU *acquis* and strive towards homogeneity with the EU regulatory framework. The fact that the provisions of the bilateral agreements must be interpreted and applied in the light of the jurisprudence of the CJEU confirms that the relationship between the EU and Switzerland is to some extent comparable to the *sui generis* character of the EU and the EEA legal orders (Breitenmoser, 2003).

A new form of sectoral cooperation between the EU and neighbouring countries has emerged since, by Steven Blockmans and Bart Van Vooren called 'legally binding sectoral multilateralism' (Blockmans & Van Vooren, 2012). This form of cooperation constitutes a viable alternative to bilateral agreements such as those concluded between the EU and Switzerland. Multilateral sectoral agreements, such as the Energy Community Treaty (signed in 2005), the Agreement on the European Common Aviation Area (2006) and the Transport Community Treaty (2017) are 'homogeneous' regulatory spaces that include both the EU and a number of third countries (Öberg, 2020).

Within sectoral integration, the internal market *acquis* plays a significantly different role. In the examples discussed above, the *acquis* is mainly used as a tool within the EU's foreign policy and a platform for political and economic cooperation between the EU and individual third countries or country groups. However, deep sectoral cooperation is based on the foundation of the European Neighbourhood Policy, Stabilization and Association Agreements and Euro-Mediterranean cooperation, which have gradually prepared the neighbouring countries to adopt the EU's regulatory framework. Deep sectoral integration fulfils the EU's internal as well as external policy goals. On the one hand, it serves to further integrate the energy markets of the Eastern Partnership into the EU's energy market, and deepen cooperation in the aviation sector within the Euro-Mediterranean policy framework. On the other hand, sectoral integration adds a structured external dimension to the EU's respective internal policies.

In addition to aiding the process of third countries gradually approaching the EU, internal market *acquis* serves to maintain a link between the EU and a country that is not approaching but instead moving further away from the EU and its internal market. Brexit is a case in point with the internal market *acquis*, specifically in the case of Northern Ireland (Weatherill, 2020), acting as a lifeline to hold on to in the continued relationship between the Union and the United Kingdom (UK).

The Brexit process aimed at a complete exit from the EU. Under the most radical of scenarios, all ties between the UK and the EU's supranational legal order would be dissolved. During the transition period, the internal market *acquis* played the role of maintaining economic and personal exchanges between the Union and the UK and enabling the UK's continued participation in the internal market. However, in the Trade and Cooperation Agreement (TCA) that now regulates the UK's relations with the EU, strong ties between the UK and the EU's internal market have not been (re-)established. The exception is Northern Ireland where free movement for goods under the Ireland and Northern Ireland Protocol still applies. Brexit, thus, constitutes a peculiar example of a third country first being bound by the EU's entire internal market *acquis* within the framework of membership to then needing to redefine cooperation in order to reduce the EU's influence.

Despite losing its immediate binding character in the UK, the internal market *acquis* has not become irrelevant, at least in relation to Northern Ireland. Moreover, some parts of the *acquis* continue to apply in the UK as 'sensible' rules approved by the national government despite its origins in the EU constitutional system (Barnard, 2016). The TCA ensures that close ties are maintained with the EU and the internal market, but not too close. At the beginning of the negotiations on the withdrawal agreement, the UK wished to continue adopting EU *acquis* in certain policy areas and was in the Political Declaration of 14 November 2018 open to further development of the relationship with the Union. However, after intense negotiations on the future relationship following the UK's formal withdrawal on 1 February 2020, the parties could only agree on cooperation at a low level which is not based on internal market *acquis*.

The experiences from EU integration show that close cooperation with the Union is normally a process of gradual deepening and significant spillover effects to other areas of cooperation. It is, therefore, very difficult to place a permanent limitation on the depth or breadth of a country's future cooperation with the EU. During the negotiations on the UK's future relationship with the Union, the EU constantly rejected a piecemeal approach to the future partnership with the UK. In a progressive integration process, third countries are granted gradual access to the internal market in exchange for implementing the EU's *acquis*. The European Council's Brexit negotiating guidelines of 29 April 2017 stated the firm position of the Union's negotiator insisting on a partnership 'as close as possible' while maintaining the 'balance of rights and obligations' and ensuring 'a level playing field' between the parties (European Council, 2017). The partnership would be based on the idea of indivisibility of the four fundamental freedoms that form the core of the single market, and essentially reject a sectoral approach that would 'undermine the integrity and proper functioning of the Single Market' (European Council, 2017). On the other hand, the UK's approach to the internal market was selective. The UK welcomed continued access to the internal market for manufactured goods and agricultural products, as well as in-depth cooperation in a number of priority areas such as energy and transport. On the other hand, the UK ruled out continued application of the bulk of the internal market *acquis*.

Generally, the EU considers sectoral integration of third countries in fields such as energy and transport as beneficial for the internal market in situations where the non-Member State in question has chosen a sectoral form of integration from the beginning. This includes, for example, the partnership between the EU and Switzerland which excludes the free movement of services and the freedom of establishment. In such cases, partial integration of third countries into the internal market is considered to be advantageous for the Union, the adverse impact on the integrity and functioning of the internal market notwithstanding. However, in the case of a Member State's withdrawal, future sectoral cooperation is considered more detrimental to the unity of the internal market. Although the Union's position in the Brexit negotiations was inconsistent with previous practice, it can be justified by the size of the UK and its former prominence as a Member State, as well as the inequality of the parties' respective negotiating positions. The EU's position was essentially driven by the perceived existential threat of Brexit to the entire European integration project rather than a firm understanding of the future function of the internal market in the Union's relationship with the UK.

Every country in the Union's neighbourhood for whom the EU constitutes the biggest trading partner depends on a well-functioning trade relationship with the Union, especially if they share a common border. In the UK's post-Brexit relationship with the EU, the internal market plays a very different role than in the agreements already concluded with the eastern neighbouring countries. This applies particularly to the aim of maintaining economic integration, as the previous agreements rather sought to 'achieve' such integration.

The EU's Internal Market as a Multifunctional Integration Tool

Over time, the EU's integration with the neighbourhood has developed towards deeper and more legally binding forms of regulatory cooperation. The internal market *acquis* has evolved from merely providing a legal framework for the Union's internal market to also integrating third countries into the Union's sphere of influence and even membership. The internal market should, therefore, not be regarded as an 'internal' and exclusive concern of a limited number of committed countries that offer inspiration and limited access to others, but rather as a dynamic and geographically inclusive form of cooperation between the Union and its periphery.

The most common tool for the Union's cooperation with third countries continues to be bilateral agreements, which enable tailor-made solutions to meet the individual interests and integration goals of both the Union and the third countries. The internal market *acquis* included in the agreements usually functions as a first step towards deeper regulatory cooperation with the EU. Alternatively, as in the case of AA/DCFTAs, EU *acquis* can constitute a further step in deepening integration in the area of the internal market building on less intense and mostly political cooperation. In the case of Ukraine and Moldova, integration with the EU has now resulted in EU candidate status without, however, rendering the AA/DCFTAs obsolete (Van der Loo & Van Elsuwege, 2022 regarding Ukraine; Emerson et al., 2022 regarding Moldova). The comparatively less flexible multilateral sectoral agreements are fewer in number but have become the EU's preferred option for integrating into the internal market economically highly developed countries capable of complying with EU standards, or for cooperating with less developed countries in policy areas characterized by strong cross-border dimension, such as transport and energy. Overall, bilateralism provides breadth to third-country integration in the internal market whereas multilateral frameworks provide depth.

For the EEA EFTA states, the EEA Agreement currently provides a satisfactory alternative to EU membership while multilateral sectoral cooperation is gaining ground by offering a 'fast track' option to EU integration in selected areas of cooperation. Multilateral agreements create common market spaces outside the borders of the Union, including among the third countries themselves. This facilitates further trade within that space, commitment to the EU as an integration project and the creation of a European market that resembles a domestic market as closely as possible and that extends beyond the borders of the Union.

On a general level, integration agreements strengthen the Union's relations with third countries while also strengthening the internal market. The internal market has proven to be suitable for expansion beyond the EU's borders. However, its partial dissolution through Brexit was perceived by the Union as a threat to its unity. This indicates firmness of principle in the Union's approach to integration with third countries. Gradual access to the single market is an option for countries whose legal and political systems require extensive upgrades to meet EU standards. A former Member State must choose between all or (almost) nothing, either full participation in the internal market or a more modest free trade agreement. From the EU's perspective, the expansion of the internal market is thus not an altruistic project but one pressing strong demands of loyalty on the EU partners. Despite this, even less intensive cooperation based on internal market *acquis* is expected to bring greater benefits for both the Union and the third country in question than the absence of any ties.

In sum, internal market *acquis* has been omnipresent in the Union's relations with neighbouring states since the Union's early days. Internal market *acquis* has been used for many different purposes of integration, ranging from the establishment of initial partnerships with third countries to full-scale integration of the latter into the internal market and maintaining a relationship with a former Member State. Over time, the internal market has become an indispensable part of the Union's policy towards the neighbouring countries. The extensive application of the *acquis* by non-Member States is the key to being able to secure a long-term commitment to the European project both within the Union and beyond. The fact that trade predominantly takes place according to the Union's *acquis* confirms the Union's status as the region's leading normative power. Criticism has been raised against the Union's normative 'hegemony' that arises when third countries adopt the Union's legal acts without being able to influence their content but only being able to decide on the validity of the rules in their legal order (Eriksen & Fossum, 2015). However, in this case, the hegemony is not intentional on the part of the Union but stems from the complex interdependence of the EU and third countries and the European integration process. Giving non-Member States a formal opportunity to participate in the decision-making processes within the EU would also blur the formal boundaries of membership of the Union and question its continued existence (Öberg, 2023).

Russia's war in Ukraine has further strengthened the importance of cooperation between the EU and neighbouring countries in the context of the internal market. In addition to constituting the main pillar of EU integration and an important economic space, the enlarged internal market has gained increased symbolic importance as a path choice between Europe's and Russia's spheres of interest. Integration through the internal market within the framework of the ambitious AA/DCFTAs has provided Ukraine, as well as Moldova and Georgia, an opportunity to confirm their belonging to the community of European states and a basis on which to build further membership ambitions. While the formal, physical and administrative borders of the EU remain, the boundaries of the internal market continue to be blurred and the European integration project broadened and deepened for the benefit of security and prosperity in the region.

The Way Forward: Strengthen the Internal Market's Force of Attraction and Maintain Its Flexibility

In order for the Union to best use the advantages of its internal market in the external context, it is suggested that the Union maintain the flexibility of the internal market as well as its openness to participation by non-Member States.

- Expansion of the internal market

The internal market has proven attractive for the Union's Member States as well as for countries in the EU's neighbourhood. For security and economic reasons, it is desirable for the EU to continue to actively seek to integrate third countries into the internal market via third countries' adoption of the relevant *acquis*. Participation in the internal market on the same terms as EU Member States has a strong attraction for non-Member States, which should continue to be taken into account in the development of the Union's policies towards the neighbourhood countries. Cooperation via the internal market strengthens the third countries' economic situation, institutions and societies, is conducted in accordance with the EU's values and interests and, not least, offers a future perspective in the form of gradual integration into the EU for countries that wish to choose or continue on the path towards European integration.

- Flexible integration

Integration requires adaptations on behalf of the third countries as well as the EU and the internal market. The internal market is not a homogenous concept. It has enabled the participation of both Member States and non-Member States on different terms but around a core set of principles that sustain its functioning. This flexibility should be maintained without modifying the formal boundary between Member States and third countries constituted by membership.

References

Agreement on the European economic area. 1994. [1994] *OJ* L1/3.

Barnard, C. (2016). The practicalities of leaving the EU. *European Law Review, 41*(4), 484–486.

Blockmans, S., & Van Vooren, B. (2012). Revitalizing the European 'neighbourhood economic community': The case for legally binding sectoral multilateralism. *European Foreign Affairs Review, 17*(4), 577–604.

Bradford, A. (2020). *The brussels effect: how the european union rules the world.* Oxford University Press.

Breitenmoser, S. (2003). Sectoral agreements between the EC and Switzerland: Contents and context. *Common Market Law Review, 40*(5), 1137–1186.

Case 12/86 *Demirel* EU:C:1987:400.

Case C-81/13 *United Kingdom v Council* EU: C:2014:2449.

Case E-9/97 *Sveinbjörnsdóttir v. Iceland* [1998] EFTA Ct Rep 95.

European Commission. (1997). 'Action Plan for the Single Market' (Communication) CSE (97) 1 final.

Cremona, M. (2004). The Union as a global actor: roles, models and identity. *Common Market Law Review, 41*(2), 553–573.

EEC-Turkey Association Council. (1995). Decision No 1/95 of the EC-Turkey Association Council of 22 December 1995 on implementing the final phase of the Customs Union [2014] OJ L13/74.

Emerson, M., Cenusa, D., Blockmans, S., & Akhvlediani, T. (2022). *Opinion on Moldova's application for membership of the European Union (CEPS Policy Insights No 2022–18).* CEPS.

Eriksen, E. O., & Fossum, J. E. (2015). Introduction: Assymmetry and the problem of dominance. In E. O. Eriksen & J. E. Fossum (Eds.), *The European Union's Non-Members: Independence under hegemony?* (pp. 1–14). Routledge.

European Commission. (2007). 'A single market for 21st century Europe' (Communication) COM (2007) 724 final.

European Commission. (1985). '*White Paper—Completing the Internal Market' COM* (85) 310 final.

European Council. (2017). 'Guidelines following the United Kingdom's notification under Article 50 TEU', EUCO XT 20004/17, 29 April.

Comprehensive and enhanced partnership agreement between the European union and the republic of Armenia. (2018). [2018] *OJ* L23/4.

Gehring, T., Urbanski, K., & Oberthür, S. (2017). The European union as an inadvertent great power: EU actorness and the Ukraine Crisis. *Journal of Common Market Studies, 55*(4), 727–743.

Hanf, D. & Dengler, P. (2004). *Accords d'association* (2004/1 college of Europe research papers in law 2004/1). Bruges.

Kapteyn, P. J. G. & VerLoren van Themaat, P. (2008). *The Law of the European Union and the European Communities.* Kluwer Law International.

Öberg, M.-L. (2023). Friend zone forever? The essence of and justifications for the EU's decision-making autonomy. *Journal of Common Market Studies, 61*(6), 1622–1638.
Öberg, M.-L. (2020). *The Boundaries of the EU Internal Market: Participation without Membership*. Cambridge University Press.
Opinion of Advocate General Jacobs in Joined Cases C-92/92 and C-326/92 Phil Collins EU:C:1993:276.
Pescatore, P. (1981). Aspects judiciaires de l''acquis communautaire'. *Revue Trimestrielle De Droit Européen, 17*(4), 617–651.
Van der Loo, G. Van Elsuwege, P. (2022). *Association agreement after Ukraine's EU membership application: Still fit for purpose* (EPC Egmont discussion paper, Europe in the World Programme, 14 March 2022).
Van der Loo, G. (2016). *The EU-Ukraine Association Agreement and Deep and Comprehensive Free Trade Area: A New Legal Instrument for EU Integration Without Membership*. Brill Nijhoff.
Weatherill, S. (2020). The protocol on Ireland/Northern Ireland: protecting the EU's internal market at the expense of the UK's. *European Law Review, 45*(2), 222–236.

CHAPTER 5

EU Norm Promotion in a Conflictual World. An Existential Necessity with Obstacles?

Ann-Kristin Jonasson

The treaties of the European Union (EU) commit the Union to promote the norms and values upon which it is founded in relations with countries outside of its borders. At the same time, the EU has often been criticised for not being the self-professed global 'force for good' that it sets out to be, not least regarding democracy and human rights. Instead, the EU is denounced for promoting its own short-term interests, sometimes in ways that contradict its stated values, much in line with most other global actors, in the current state of geopolitical conflict.

Such a gap between discourse and practice is fraught with problems. Some scholars argue that too great a discrepancy between what is said and what is done risks eroding the EU's legitimacy and policy efficiency (Chaban & Elgström, 2021; Lucarelli, 2018), which in turn may lead to a decrease in global influence for the EU. Other scholars downplay these risks, arguing that other international actors are not deceived by the EU's

A.-K. Jonasson (✉)
Department of Political Science, University of Gothenburg, Gothenburg, Sweden
e-mail: ann-kristin.jonasson@gu.se

A. Bakardjieva Engelbrekt et al. (eds.), *The Borders of the European Union in a Conflictual World*,
https://doi.org/10.1007/978-3-031-54200-8_5

normative discourse, expecting little else than interest-based behaviour from the EU (Chaban & Elgström, 2021; Jurgelaitytė, 2023). Both sides point out that there is a discrepancy between the EU's statements and its actions. Still, the EU upholds its treaty-based values in its foreign policy, even if the normative discourse was downplayed in the EU's new security strategy, the 2016 Global Strategy (EEAS, 2016; Barbé & Morillas, 2019).

This chapter argues that a failure of the EU to stand up for its value-based norms globally risks challenging not only its legitimacy but ultimately also its survival. By failing to stand up for its norms and values when they are challenged, the EU risks undermining the very same values and norms that it claims to promote globally, especially regarding democracy and human rights. In this era of geopolitical conflict, in which the democratic order is facing a frontal assault by authoritarian regimes, it is crucial that the EU stands by the rules-based world order, especially in terms of democracy and human rights. When the world order is at stake, the EU needs to stand up for its values, also to protect its long-term interests, even if doing so may counteract interests short-term. The question is how this best can be done.

Here, we look at how the EU works in practice to promote treaty-based values and with what effect against the backdrop of the theoretical discourse on the EU as a normative power. The analysis centres on the EU's promotion of democracy, contrasted with the promotion of climate action with a focus on the EU's southern neighbourhood, a region in which the EU has been active albeit with seemingly different levels of success. This chapter discusses possible reasons for these outcomes and suggests possible ways for the EU to promote values and norms globally, focusing on democracy.

EU Norm Promotion in Treaties and Policies

'Norm' is an ambiguous concept. Theoretically, norms are often closely associated with formal or informal rule-based behaviour. In some contexts, norms are linked to legal standards (see, for instance, Marja-Liisa Öberg in this volume). It is important to distinguish between adopted and implemented norms or laws, since experience—not least from the EU's own enlargement—shows that the adoption is not always followed by implementation (Schimmelfennig & Sedelmeier, 2005). In other contexts, norms are linked to more fundamental principles of thought (see, for instance, Pär Hallström's chapter in this volume).

This chapter focuses on what the EU refers to as the foundational values of the Union. At times, policy documents refer to 'principles' rather than values, although the Treaty on European Union (TEU, 2012), replaces 'principles' with 'values' at certain places. Sometimes, the EU uses the term 'norms' instead, particularly in relation to international agreements on democracy and human rights.

Even if different terms are used, the literature in the field has, as will be seen, consistently referred to the EU's efforts to promote its values globally as norm promotion, arguing that the EU could be seen as a normative power. This conflation of 'norms' with 'values' and 'principles' may complicate the analysis. In this chapter, in line with the literature, values and (value-based) norms refer to what EU policy documents define as values and principles.

What are these values, then? Article 2 of the TEU states that 'the Union is founded on the values of respect for human dignity, freedom, democracy, equality, the rule of law and respect for human rights, including the rights of persons belonging to minorities' (TEU, 2012). Article 3(5) states that the Union shall uphold and promote its values and interests in its relations with the wider world, and contribute to peace, security, the sustainable development of the Earth and the protection of human rights.

These values inform the EU's external action. Article 21(1) of the TEU states that the Union's action on the international scene shall be guided by the principles that have inspired its own creation, development and enlargement, and which it seeks to advance in the wider world, such as democracy, the rule of law and the universality and indivisibility of human rights and fundamental freedoms. Article 21(2) declares that the Union shall define and pursue common policies and actions and shall work for a high degree of cooperation in all fields of international relations in order to, among other things, safeguard its values, fundamental interests, security, independence and integrity; consolidate and support democracy, the rule of law, human rights and the principles of international law and to foster the sustainable economic, social and environmental development of developing countries.

The TEU thus establishes a catalogue of values that underpins the Union internally, which are also to be promoted externally. The EU's neighbourhood is particularly targeted in this respect. Article 8 of the

TEU states that a special relationship shall be developed with neighbouring countries, aiming to establish an area of prosperity and good neighbourliness, founded on the values of the Union and characterised by close and peaceful relations based on cooperation.

The EU launched the European Neighbourhood Policy (ENP) following the eastern enlargement in 2004, which established new external borders for the Union (European Commission, 2004). As we shall see, the ENP is based on the mutual commitment to common values, in particular the rule of law, good governance, respect for human rights (including minority rights), the promotion of good neighbourly relations and the principles of market economy and sustainable development (European Commission, 2004, p. 3). However, the 2015 ENP Review recognised significant shortcomings in the partner countries' implementation of the values underpinning the ENP and declared that more effective ways to promote reforms were needed (European Commission/High Representative of the Union for Foreign Affairs and Security Policy, 2015, pp. 1–5). Overall, the Review placed less emphasis on common values than before, although it reiterated the EU's commitment to promoting good governance, democracy, the rule of law and human rights in the neighbourhood, as well as cooperation on climate change.

The 2016 Global Strategy declared that the EU's interests and values go hand in hand and that the Union has an interest in promoting its values abroad. Peace and security, prosperity, democracy and a rules-based global order are the vital interests underpinning the EU's external action (EEAS, 2016, p. 13). It is further stated that the EU will be guided by clear principles, which stem as much from a realistic assessment of the current strategic environment as from an idealistic aspiration to advance a better world emphasising that 'principled pragmatism' will guide the EU's external action in the years ahead (EEAS, 2016, pp. 8, 16).

The EU as a Normative Power?

The EU as a normative power has long been debated in the literature. The debate began in the 1970s with a discussion on what kind of actor the EU should be in the global arena and whether it ought to be seen as a civilian power, with civilian forms of influence (Duchêne, 1972), or if it should be regarded as (the embryo of) a military power, defending its interests strategically (Galtung, 1974). In 2002, Ian Manners (2002) coined the concept Normative Power Europe (NPE). With this concept,

Manners argued that the EU is qualitatively different from other actors in the global arena by virtue of its normative, value-based foundations, and could be described as a normative power. However, Manners was strongly opposed by scholars, such as Adrian Hyde-Price, Richard Youngs and Helene Sjursen, who argued that the EU, like other actors, promotes its interests internationally, even if it does so using a normative discourse (Hyde-Price, 2006; Sjursen, 2006; Youngs, 2004).

In this debate, many scholars have shown that the EU has been poor at living up to its normative ideals in its external action (Youngs, 2004; Sjursen, 2006; Jonasson, 2013), a shortcoming which at times has also been recognised by the EU itself (Füle, 2011). As already mentioned, major problems have been identified with this gap between discourse and practice, although not everyone agrees that it is a problem (Chaban & Elgström, 2021; Lucarelli, 2018). The gap between discourse and action is deeply problematic, as it jeopardises both the legitimacy of the EU and the values themselves.

But what, then, should the EU do to promote its values and the norms based on these? The literature discusses different ways for actors to promote value-based norms internationally. Manners argues that the EU diffuses its norms by putting itself forward as an example, by being founded on treaty-based norms, and by its external action which is informed by and conditional on these norms (Manners, 2002, pp. 241–242). More specifically, Manners lists six ways in which the EU acts as a norm-diffuser. These range from *contagion*, i.e. unintentional diffusion e.g. by the setting of a virtuous example; *informational diffusion* resulting from strategic and declaratory communications and *procedural diffusion* involving the institutionalisation of relationships with third parties, to trade-related norm *transference* (e.g. in the form of export standards and conditionality), *overt diffusion* as a result of the EU's physical presence, and, finally, providing a *cultural filter*, impacting political learning in third states, leading to learning, adaptation or rejection of norms (Manners, 2002, pp. 244–245). In this way, norms are diffused by the fact that the EU is founded on the norms in question, which predisposes the EU to act in accordance with them (Manners, 2002, p. 252). Thus, according to Manners, the EU is a normative power with the ability to define what is considered 'normal' in international relations (Manners, 2002, p. 253).

The debate that followed Manners's highly influential article has centred on the extent to which the EU in fact is a normative power, and whether it actually does promote its value-based norms globally. Many scholars have convincingly pointed out that this is often not the case and that there is indeed a significant gap between the EU's discourse and practice in this regard making the EU's position as a normative power highly questionable (Youngs, 2004; Sjursen, 2006; Jonasson, 2013).

Value-based Norm Diffusion

The literature on value-based norm diffusion has often applied a social constructivist perspective to the EU's norm promotion. This perspective emphasises two basic mechanisms of norm diffusion: a positive, socialisation-based mechanism (e.g. persuasion, diplomacy and moral support) and a negative, incentive-based mechanism (e.g. positive or negative conditionality) (Jonasson, 2013, p. 11). These mechanisms are in turn based on the two basic logics identified by James March and Johan Olsen (March & Olsen, 2004). According to the rational choice-based logic of consequentiality, an actor's behaviour is driven by rational calculation, motivated by interest-based incentives and personal gain. According to the institutionalist logic of appropriateness, actors act in accordance with a role, an identity, or a membership of a political community. They act in ways they consider appropriate in the current situation based on the ethics, practices and expectations of the institution, making their behaviour in line with expectations and therefore legitimate. According to this literature, a value-based norm is considered as diffused when the logic of appropriateness replaces the logic of consequentiality as the basis for behaviour, and when actions are carried out in accordance with the norms of the group because 'this is what we do', rather than on the basis of rational calculation, because 'this is in accordance with my own (material) interest' (Jonasson, 2013, p. 12).

This norm diffusion process consists of different steps, which in turn are based on the two basic logics. Thomas Risse and Kathryn Sikkink (1999) argue that strategic, instrumental adaptation takes place when actors adapt their behaviour to international norms without necessarily accepting the validity of the norms, in line with the logic of consequentiality. Socialisation, on the other hand, occurs through moral discourse, emphasising communication, argumentation and persuasion, leading to the acceptance of norms in line with the logic of appropriateness. According to this argument, norm diffusion comes about as the first process evolves into the second, resulting in institutionalisation and internalisation, allowing norms to be fully accepted by the actors (Risse &

Sikkink, 1999, pp. 12–17). Genuine and authentic acceptance of the norm is seen as crucial for a norm to be considered as diffused. To achieve such acceptance, positive, socialisation-based methods are usually preferred to negative, incentive-based methods in this norm diffusion discourse. Positive methods facilitate genuine, as opposed to temporary, acceptance and only positive methods ensure authentic embracement of the norm (Jonasson, 2013; Risse & Sikkink, 1999). Adoption of the norm along the logic of appropriateness is thus favoured over adoption along the logic of consequentiality, even if the latter is considered as (potentially) leading to the former (Jonasson, 2013, p. 14). Importantly, it is pointed out in the literature that norm adoption along the logic of consequentiality risks creating only token change, not resulting in genuine norm acceptance.

It can be noted that most of the six processes that Manners outlined for EU norm diffusion are based on socialisation, even though there are elements of rational calculation, not least regarding conditionality linked to trade. It can also be noted that the norm diffusion literature has long indicated that socialisation-based norm diffusion is usually more successful. However, one crucial exception to this conclusion is often brought forth, namely the success of the EU's enlargement process, especially the eastern enlargement of 2004. EU enlargement is based on a logic of consequentiality, where negotiating countries become members only if they fulfil a (very large) number of conditions. As a consequence of this unprecedented success, the norm diffusion debate, not least in relation to the EU's promotion of democracy and human rights, came to emphasise the importance of external incentives in bringing about normative change in candidate states, in line with the logic of consequentiality (Schimmelfennig & Sedelmeier, 2005).

It is however important to note that Frank Schimmelfennig and Ulrich Sedelmeier recognise that the incentive-based approach is premised on a more fundamental orientation towards the norms in question (Jonasson, 2013, p. 15). They argue that the conditional external incentives, based on the logic of consequentiality, were crucial in bringing about rule adoption in candidate states, and that conditionality is thus the EU's most successful enlargement tool (Schimmelfennig & Sedelmeier, 2005, pp. 210–211). Nonetheless, they acknowledge that the whole process of Europeanisation was embedded in a larger process of socialisation and social learning as the eastern enlargement was based on the candidate states' fundamental identification with the EU and the high legitimacy of the European integration project (Schimmelfennig & Sedelmeier, 2005, p. 220; Jonasson, 2013, p. 16). They also note that norms adopted as a result of socialisation are far less contested locally and that actual implementation of and compliance with these norms therefore is far more likely. On the other hand, norms adopted as a result of external incentives, along a logic of consequentiality, are likely to generate more domestic resistance and risk facing lack of implementation (Schimmelfennig & Sedelmeier, 2005, pp. 219–220; Jonasson, 2013, p. 16).

Other scholars also suggest that there are crucial differences in how policymakers respond to external demands depending on their initial stance. According to this argument, policymakers cannot be enticed to change their minds if the external requirements are completely contrary to their initial stance and norm diffusion will fail when policy stances are too foreign to domestic policymakers. However, they can be enticed (even if it is difficult) or persuaded (more easily) if the external requirements are not completely contrary to their initial stance (Kelley, 2004, p. 432; Jonasson, 2013, p. 15; Dandashley & Noutcheva, 2022).

According to this argument, a certain orientation towards the norms in question is thus necessary for their acceptance. On this basis, the necessity to study the recipients of norms is increasingly recognised in the literature through the so-called 'local turn' emphasising the agency of norm-takers (Grimm, 2019; Checkel, 1998; Jonasson, 2013; Dandashley & Noutcheva, 2022). In line with this local turn, for the norm to take root, it requires not only a local orientation but also local ownership, both in terms of goal setting and implementation of the norm in question, as well as a genuine dialogue between the norm-maker and the norm-taker (Jonasson, 2013, pp. 23–37). However, prior research recognises that it is difficult to realise local orientation, ownership and dialogue (Checkel, 1998; Jonasson, 2013; Dandashley & Noutcheva, 2022). A case in point is the EU's external norm promotion which is criticised for failing to ensure local ownership when introducing norms, based on a locally rooted—at least nominal—orientation towards the norms, and to establish a genuine dialogue on norms. Instead, the EU is often accused of wanting to do things its own way, based on its own material self-interests. The EU is also at times accused of acting in ways that counteract its own norms in ways regarded as counterproductive (Jonasson, 2013, p 189; Dandashly & Noutcheva, 2019). A prerequisite for successful norm promotion is therefore that the norm-maker actually wants to promote the norm in question, something that is not always as self-evident as it may seem.

Based on the premise that norms are diffused either through strategic adaptation that (potentially) leads to normative change along the logic of consequentiality, or socialisation into the norm along the logic of appropriateness, the question arises whether different logics apply to specific norms? It may be argued that the conditions for norm diffusion vary depending on the nature of the norm, although the basic logic remains the same. While norms related to the social contract of a community, for instance, democracy, require a socialisation-based embracement of the norms, interest-related norms, for instance, related to trade, are more easily diffused following the logic of consequentiality. However, when interest-related norms challenge the social contract, problems will arise, and the outcome depends on the handling of these problems. Ultimately, what matters most is the extent to which both norm-makers and norm-takers are genuinely oriented towards the norm, providing a foundation for local ownership and mutual dialogue.

Following this argument, the conditions for norm diffusion can differ between norms related to democracy, on the one hand, and norms related to climate goals, on the other. Norm diffusion related to democracy, which directly affects the social contract, requires a process of socialisation on the part of the norm-taker, based on a local orientation towards the norm and local ownership of the democratisation process. It also requires a genuine dialogue with the norm-maker—and a true willingness by the norm-maker to promote democracy. Norms related to climate goals may be easier to diffuse through material incentives, at least initially. Fairly soon, however, the interventions affecting the social contract are likely to be so extensive that a deeper socialisation-based embracement of the norms is required for norm diffusion. In both cases, successful norm diffusion requires the norm-maker to want to diffuse the norm, and that the norm-taker is willing to embrace it.

The EU as a Norm Promoter

How, then, does the EU work to promote value-based norms, and how well does it succeed in doing so? In the following, we turn the focus to the promotion of norms linked to democracy and climate goals, in relation to the EU's southern neighbourhood. The EU has promoted these norms with seemingly different rates of success. It is argued that these two fields of norm promotion differ in fundamental respects. It may be questioned whether the EU in fact wants to promote norms related to democracy in the southern neighbourhood and whether the partners really want to take them on, whereas regarding climate mitigation goals these prerequisites seem met to a greater extent.

The EU as a Promoter of Democracy?

Promoting democracy, especially in the neighbourhood, became important for the EU after the end of the Cold War, even if the EU has worked at a general level to promote democracy beyond its borders since the 1970s. Since the early 1990s, the EU has thus developed more specific policies to promote democracy in third countries in the framework of its development policy. However, through the adoption of the 1992 Maastricht Treaty, democracy promotion became an explicit objective of the EU's foreign policy. Today, the EU institutions are surpassed only by the US when it comes to the funding spent on the promotion of democratic values and institutions, as well as human rights and the rule of law globally (Khakee, 2022).

The EU has developed different policy instruments to promote democracy. These include:

- Conditionality clauses related to human rights, democracy and sustainable development in agreements with third states
- The European Instrument for Democracy and Human Rights (EIDHR)/The Global Europe Human Rights and Democracy programme
- The European Neighbourhood Policy (ENP) and
- The Enlargement policy

The conditionality clauses define human rights and democracy as essential elements in the EU's political agreements with third states. Such clauses are also included in trade agreements, regardless of whether these agreements are linked to political agreements or not. Violations of these essential elements are grounds for various sanctions, including the suspension of the agreement. Since 1995, negotiations on agreements with states outside Europe have always included one or more such clauses, even if they have not always become part of the final agreement. Moreover, for more than a decade all trade agreements have included a clause on the three pillars of sustainable development—economic, environmental and social sustainability, which also includes social justice and human rights. Democracy is not directly included here, but there is mentioning of good governance.

The European Instrument for Democracy and Human Rights (EIDHR) was launched in 2006 mainly to support non-governmental organisations working for democracy and human rights in third countries, enabling the EU to fund the organisations directly without having to go through the formal channels of the host state. In 2021, EIDHR was succeeded by the Global Europe Human Rights and Democracy programme, incorporated in the Neighbourhood, Development and International Cooperation Instrument (NDICI)—'Global Europe' (European Neighbourhood Policy and Enlargement Negotiations (DG NEAR), 2021).

The European Neighbourhood Policy (ENP) was developed after the eastern enlargement in 2004, as the EU sought to establish good relations with its new neighbours, both to the east and, later, to the south. Since 2005, the ENP has offered the EU's neighbours a privileged relationship, based on mutual commitment to common values such as democracy and human rights, the rule of law, good governance, market economy principles and sustainable development. It is emphasised that the level of ambition of the relationship depends on the extent to which these values are effectively shared. It is further established that neighbouring countries that are part of international organisations for cooperation such as the Organisation for Security and Cooperation in Europe (OSCE) and the Council of Europe, or that have signed the Barcelona Declaration, are also committed to democracy and human rights (European Commission, 2004, pp. 3, 12–13).

Since the 1960s, the EU (and its predecessors) has undertaken different enlargements. Since 1993, the Copenhagen criteria were adopted stating that in order to be eligible for EU membership the candidate country must have achieved stability of institutions guaranteeing democracy, the rule of law, human rights and respect for and protection of minorities, in addition to a functioning market economy and the ability to cope with the competitive pressure and market forces of the EU. Moreover, the country is required to align with the EU's acquis, which also includes requirements related to democracy and human rights (EUR-Lex, 2023).

The policies to promote democracy are based on partly different logics. While the conditionality clauses are based on negative conditionality, as sanctions can be imposed if democracy and human rights are violated, the neighbourhood and enlargement policies are based primarily on positive conditionality, based on incentives, as benefits are rewarded if the partner state meets the objectives. In its democracy promotion, the EU thus attaches great importance to conditionality (positive and negative) and largely works in close cooperation with the partner states. However, a different logic underlies the EIDHR/the Global Europe Human Rights and Democracy programme, targeting support directly at non-governmental organisations.

In addition to these four policy areas, democracy promotion is also included in a range of other EU instruments, both short-term (such as the Instrument contributing to Stability and Peace) and long-term (such as development cooperation). Since 2013, the EU also collaborates with EU Member States to support democracy promotion, particularly in the neighbourhood, through the European Endowment for Democracy. Another instrument is the EU's Global Human Rights Sanctions Regime from December 2020, designed to support human rights by imposing sanctions on targeted individuals, entities and bodies, both governmental and non-governmental, in the form of travel bans, freezing of funds and prohibitions on making funds available to those listed (Official Journal, 2020).

Along the argument pursued here, material incentives and an incentive-based logic of consequentiality thus play an important role in the EU's democracy promotion. However, democracy promotion is sometimes—in the ENP and, especially, in the enlargement policy—embedded in an approach based on more comprehensive socialisation, presupposing at least a nominal orientation towards the project of democratisation. The question is how well these different approaches work.

In practice, the EU's promotion of democracy is not considered particularly successful beyond Europe's borders due to the problems associated with its implementation (Jonasson, 2013; Dandashly & Noutcheva, 2019). The literature points out that conditionality clauses are often manipulated politically, both in the negotiation phase and in the implementation phase. The EU is accused of requiring varying levels of compliance by different partners. Deterioration in democracy and human rights does not always lead to significant action, even in the case of authoritarian states. Even if the conditionality clauses lead to discussions between the partners about democracy and human rights, the effects of these discussions are often largely absent, as exemplified by one expert in the southern neighbourhood: 'I think maybe the Europeans would like to promote their own values, because they think ultimately that is the only thing that will change these crazy terrorists. But at the receiving end here, this is all for toasting ... at dinner parties' (Jonasson, 2013, p. 62).

The EIDHR/the Global Europe Human Rights and Democracy programme support non-governmental organisations that promote democracy and human rights. While it is stressed by the EU that this support can also be given to organisations critical of the sitting regimes, this is difficult to implement in practice as the control over organisations is often very strict in authoritarian states. Regime-critical organisations are often banned from operating in the country and are not allowed to receive foreign funds. If they do so, they risk being deemed as subversive and punished, directly or indirectly. Therefore, organisations supported by the EU are in fact often close to the regime and therefore unlikely to work against it by promoting true democratisation.

Regarding the ENP, the EU's 2015 ENP Review shows significant shortcomings in its democracy promotion (European Commission/High Representative of the Union for Foreign Affairs and Security Policy, 2015). On the one hand, the incentive-based conditionality approach is considered to have been successful in supporting reforms to strengthen the norms when there has been political will to do so locally. On the other hand, the Review points out that such political will does not always exist. It is questionable whether an authoritarian state has an interest in democratisation. The EU therefore stresses the need to work in more effective ways to promote reforms, upholding and promoting universal values (European Commission/High Representative of the Union for Foreign Affairs and Security Policy, 2015, pp. 1–5). Interestingly, it can be noted that the emphasis on common values has been replaced by a reference to universal values in the review of the ENP. It is emphasised that the EU will pursue its interests and that these include the promotion of universal values, such as democracy, human rights, the rule of law and economic openness. It is declared that stabilisation is the EU's main political priority in the new Neighbourhood Policy (European Commission/High Representative of the Union for Foreign Affairs and Security Policy, 2015, p. 2).

The enlargement policy, based on both conditionality and cooperation, is the EU's most successful approach to democracy promotion.

Here, the incentive-based logic of consequentiality is embedded in a larger socialisation-based logic of appropriateness, where Europeanisation includes a general orientation towards democracy, local ownership based on this orientation, and a dialogue with the EU, supposedly resulting in 'true' democratisation. It can be argued that the democratic decline that we see in some EU Member States today, for example, Hungary and Poland, shows that material incentives do not necessarily secure a genuine local orientation towards democratic values and a willingness of the state to attain them. As Daniel Silander (2022) points out, the anchoring of democracy in the political culture is lacking in several European countries. Democratic success can only be ensured to the extent that democracy is culturally rooted. If this is not the case, backsliding is likely.

Despite the emphasis on democracy in the ENP, and in the 2021 New Agenda for the Mediterranean (Council of the European Union, 2020), the states in the EU's southern neighbourhood show a glaring lack of genuine orientation towards democracy and local ownership of a democratic process. Research shows that while the sitting governments in the southern neighbourhood often express willingness to adopt democratic principles, this means little in practice (Dandashly & Noutcheva, 2019; Jonasson, 2013). Authoritarian regimes are rarely interested in true democratisation, contrary to their assertions. Furthermore, even if the EU sets out to ensure local ownership of the democratic process, the work envisaged is often based on conditions set out by the EU, often lacking a local contextualisation, which makes it difficult to talk about local ownership. Also, the principles of conditional support counteracts the ideal of mutual dialogue and the input from both parties on equal terms.

While EU democracy promotion in the southern neighbourhood presents major shortcomings in terms of orientation, local ownership and dialogue, the EU repeatedly demonstrates that it prioritises stability and security over democracy in the region. In 2022, the European Democracy Support Annual Review stated that '(i)n a year dominated by the rhetoric of defending democracy, EU democracy support policies were adjusted in important ways to align with the new geopolitical context. However, the union also seemed to treat commitments in this area as second-order priorities compared to security' (Youngs & Ventura et al. 2022, cp. also Jonasson, 2013; Dandashly & Noutcheva, 2019). The southern neighbourhood is marked by a substantial degree of instability and insecurity, and the EU has witnessed the consequences of this in the form of large migration flows. While the EU's discourse emphasises that democracy leads to stability and security, experience shows that whereas this often is true in the long term, things often get worse in the short and medium term before they get better again (Alizada, et al. 2022). This is clearly seen in the wake of the political uprisings dubiously dubbed the Arab Spring. At such critical junctures, the EU has often extended de facto support to authoritarian regimes in the southern neighbourhood, for them to maintain stability and security, rather than prioritised democratisation. The migration deals with authoritarian regimes in Turkey, Libya and, more recently, Tunisia, which offer support to socioeconomic development, without any mention of democracy, are examples of this practice (Directorate-General for Neighbourhood & Enlargement Negotiations, 2023).

The success of EU democracy promotion in the southern neighbourhood has thus been faltering. In line with the argument here, this is because the essential prerequisites for a successful norm promotion are missing. There is neither a genuine orientation towards, local ownership of, nor a mutual dialogue on, democratisation. This—together with the fact that it is questionable whether the EU wants to promote democracy in the region—makes the prospects for successful democracy promotion in the southern neighbourhood look bleak.

The EU as a Promoter of Climate Action?

The EU has long been considered a pioneer in adopting climate policies internally and in promoting such policies externally (Delreux & Ohler, 2019). At the international level, the EU partakes in the climate negotiations hosted by the United Nations (United Nations Framework Convention on Climate Change, UNFCCC), both as an entity in itself and through its Member States, negotiating under a common umbrella according to a common negotiating position. The EU's efforts in the international climate change negotiations led to a failure in Copenhagen in 2009. However, the EU learnt from its mistakes, and the 2015 Paris Agreement was a major success for the EU for reasons we will return to (Delreux & Ohler, 2019; Oberthür & Groen, 2017).

The United States (US) long led the fight against climate change through its strong climate ambitions under the democratic presidents, Bill Clinton and Barack Obama. Under the rule of republican administrations, however, it withdrew from the Kyoto Protocol in 2001 and the Paris

Agreement in 2017. Under Joe Biden, the US re-entered the Paris Agreement in 2021. By the time of the 2015 Paris meeting, China had also stepped forward as an important climate actor, along with other emerging powers with large emissions. With its new strategy, the EU however managed to manoeuvre skilfully in Paris. While the goal is the same for everyone involved in the fight against climate change, the approaches and priorities differ (Oberthür & Groen, 2017). By virtue of its ambition to lead by example and basing negotiations on ambitious and legally binding agreements, the EU is often seen both as a leader and a mediator (*a leadiator*) in this endeavour (Delreux & Ohler, 2019).

The literature shows how the EU has established the world's most comprehensive climate policy framework, based on an economic incentive scheme with emission allowances in the framework of the Emission Trading System, and binding commitments for Member States to reduce emissions. These measures have also been successful internationally, in some cases reaching far beyond the EU's borders (Ferenczy, 2019). However, the literature points out that this is not enough to achieve the EU's own long-term goals. To do so, more fundamental shifts in a range of EU policy areas—from energy production and consumption, to transport, agriculture and industry—are required (Delreux & Ohler, 2019).

While an incentive-based logic of consequentiality, in the form of emission allowances, thus has reaped some success both within the EU and beyond, the literature suggests that the EU is most successful in the global arena if and when it succeeds in persuading/convincing its international partners through diplomatic negotiations (Delreux & Ohler, 2019; Ferenczy, 2019; Oberthür & Groen, 2017). A socialisation-based approach thus seems more likely to succeed. The low point in Copenhagen in 2009, when the EU failed to achieve its objectives and no agreement was reached, is regarded as resulting from the EU having set too high targets, which were poorly anchored with other states, and paid too little attention to the interests of its partners. In particular, the partners' insistence that their right to economic development had to have consequences for the climate, as the EU and the rest of the industrialised world already had largely used their rights in this regard, was taken too lightly by the EU (Delreux & Ohler, 2019; Oberthür & Groen, 2017). Thus, along with the argument pursued here, it was the lack of common orientation, local ownership and mutual dialogue in relation to the norms that led to the failure in Copenhagen.

This lesson was however not lost on the EU. In the run-up to the 2015 Paris meeting, the EU worked hard to ensure that the agreement was genuinely anchored, through active diplomacy and coalition- and bridge-building with partners, a strategy which paid off in the agreement reached (Oberthür & Groen, 2017). This agreement was certainly less ambitious from a climate point of view than the EU's previous targets, but also more realistic (Delreux & Ohler, 2019). Most agree that the Paris Agreement was a great success for the EU—it is better to have a less ambitious agreement where the parties agree on their commitments than either no agreement at all or a divisive one, even if the agreement is not really considered sufficient to save the climate (Delreux & Ohler, 2019; Oberthür & Groen, 2017).

After Paris, the socialisation-based anchoring process has been further refined, with even more focus on common orientation towards the goals, genuine local ownership both in the setting of goals and of processes and true mutual dialogue. The literature points out that actors in the global arena need partners to support an ambitious, comprehensive agenda and that the EU's active climate diplomacy provides such support (Oberthür & Groen, 2017).

Central to the Paris Agreement is the recognition that conditions matter and that the states with the most favourable conditions have the greatest responsibility. Part of this responsibility is the various forms of support that industrialised countries provide to developing countries. In the 2021 COP meeting in Glasgow, the EU pledged even more financial support for climate action in developing countries. The Paris Agreement also introduced common rules for how climate action should be carried out in its different phases. In Glasgow, this rulebook was completed, and it was decided that the ambition of climate action should be further increased (United Nations, 2023). In Sharm el-Sheikh in 2022, the EU contributed to securing the final agreement and putting in place new funding to help vulnerable communities face the loss and damage caused by climate change (European Commission, 2022).

Analysing the international climate action of the EU from the perspective put forth here reveals that this action is conducted mainly along a socialisation-based logic of appropriateness, based on the fundamental idea that we are all in this together, even if more short-term, interest-based material incentives also are present (cp. Jurgelaitytė, 2023). This socialisation-based approach is underscored by the fact that the Paris Agreement stipulates that the action to address climate change should take into account crucial societal aspects like human rights and gender equality, thus addressing the more fundamental social contract (United Nations, 2015). The developments from Copenhagen to Paris and beyond also show that climate action is only successful to the extent that it is based on a common orientation, local ownership and mutual dialogue. Unlike in democracy promotion, there is furthermore a genuine willingness on the part of all parties to work towards common goals to combat climate change, even if it comes at a cost. The EU has thus been more successful in promoting norms on climate change, both because it has worked actively on securing socialisation and because all parties are genuinely interested in the common goals.

The EU emphasises that climate action is also important in relation with the southern neighbourhood. The European External Action Service stresses that the EU supports its neighbours in reaching their nationally determined contributions to the Paris Agreement through the external dimension of the Green Deal and that the EU will increase its support for the climate transition (EEAS, 2021). The 2021 New Agenda for the Mediterranean underlines that action to address the global climate challenge is a fundamental pillar of the EU's policy in the region (Council of the European Union, 2021). It is emphasised that the EU is convinced that it, by working together with the southern neighbourhood partners, will contribute to a just and inclusive green transition. In line with the external dimension of the Green Deal, the EU will also work to increase the climate ambitions of the partners. It is stressed that the southern neighbourhood plays an important role in attaining the objective of a climate-neutral world and supplying green energy to Europe.

Thus, at level of policy, the EU sets out to cooperate with its southern neighbourhood partners in climate action, based on common orientation, local ownership and dialogue. The question is how this works out in practice. In the run-up to the 2021 COP meeting in Glasgow, a review showed that there are major difficulties for the southern Mediterranean states to fulfil their commitments under the Paris Agreement, not least because of domestic political instability (The National, 2021). While important achievements have been made, particularly in Egypt and Morocco, limited progress was recorded in Israel and Lebanon. Countries, like Jordan and Tunisia, have developed ambitious visions, but with little concrete action to show for it. Achieving success on the ground obviously has its challenges. Most southern neighbours however showed a positive development in their environmental performance, including performance on climate change, ranking among the top half of countries worldwide in terms of positive climate change mitigation over the last ten years (Wolf et al., 2022).

Despite the challenges, and even though the EU's climate cooperation with the southern neighbourhood is relatively new, the prospects for success seem relatively bright. Not least because it is in the interest of the authoritarian states themselves—to a greater extent than in other issues—to cooperate with the EU in climate action, to secure their own survival as they are located in a region that is among the most vulnerable to climate change globally (Bremberg, 2022). The EU's interest in achieving success is also obvious, not least because climate change in the southern Mediterranean is driving migration towards the EU, in a way that it regards as highly undesirable. Many different diplomatic and technical initiatives have been taken by the EU to support national measures to strengthen climate action in the southern Mediterranean. For example, at the 2022 COP in Sharm El-Sheikh, a partly EU-sponsored Mediterranean pavilion was set up for the first time, with the aim of bringing together different regional actors—from Europe and the Mediterranean—in the fight against regional climate change (Union for the Mediterranean, 2022). While it is still early to judge the success of these initiatives, and while political leaders in the southern neighbourhood have shown some reluctance in this respect, a common orientation to shared goals, local ownership and mutual dialogue appear to be emerging in regard to climate change cooperation—all important factors for success in the EU's climate action globally as well as in its cooperation with the partner countries in the southern neighbourhood.

Can the EU Promote Norms Beyond its Borders in a Conflictual World?

This chapter shows that the EU's efforts to promote norms seem to work better in some areas than in others. It is argued that this is because both the EU and its partners are not as interested in the diffusion of some value-based norms, as they are in the diffusion of others. While the EU and the Mediterranean partners seem to have a genuine common interest in addressing rampant climate change, not least for the sake of their own survival, a similar interest is not at hand in the furthering of democracy. Even if the EU argues that democracy leads to stability and security, which is desired in the long run, and the neighbouring states in the South sometimes talk about democracy, both parties seem to agree that democracy is not desirable in the southern neighbourhood at present. Instead, a process of democratisation seems likely to lead, at least in the short-term, to the kind of instability and insecurity that both parties want to avoid. The EU has no interest in the migration flows that such a situation would generate, and the authoritarian regimes are not interested in undermining themselves.

For value-based norms to be successfully diffused, there needs to be a genuine political will on all sides. Furthermore, the diffusion of a value-based norm requires that both the EU and the partner state are oriented towards the norm in question and that there is local ownership in the implementation and mutual dialogue between the EU and the partner state. If these prerequisites do not exist, the prospects for norm diffusion are poor. This chapter has shown that these prerequisites seem to be present in the EU's work on climate change mitigation to a much greater extent than in its promotion of democracy, especially in relation to the southern neighbourhood. The chances for success in the battle against climate change thus seem far greater than the chances for success in the promotion of democracy.

How, then, can the EU work to promote value-based norms globally, especially with regard to democracy? Along with the argument pursued here, it is particularly important to focus on two things. First, it is crucial that the EU does not claim to promote value-based norms if this is not genuinely meant. The EU's promotion of democracy is an important example of how such an approach is not likely to succeed. Furthermore, such an approach risks undermining faith in democracy itself. If the EU believes that democracy is the best political system at hand for safeguarding human rights and ensuring stability and security in the long term—as it indeed has good reasons to think—the EU needs to prioritise democratisation, not stability and security, even if it comes at a cost. The EU must stand up for democratic principles in practice, even in difficult circumstances. The EU's discourse needs be followed in practice, and support to non-democratic partner states should be reconsidered.

Secondly, the EU needs to base its policies on the research that unequivocally shows that democracy has to be locally rooted in order for it to take hold and flourish. Democracy cannot be imposed from the outside, but help can be offered to promote a domestic dialogue about democracy and what democracy means in the local context. The EU can contribute to such a discussion by addressing what democracy could mean locally in its dialogue with both partner states and other local actors, and by showing what benefits the EU itself has reaped from democracy in practice. By encouraging such a locally rooted discussion, which includes all parts of society, societal pressure for democratisation may grow.

In order to promote value-based norms beyond its borders in this era of geopolitical conflict, the EU needs to promote a local orientation towards these norms, to ensure that the work on these norms is locally owned and that there is a genuine dialogue. In the work to promote democracy, the EU can learn from the work against climate change and genuinely contribute to a local, contextualised development of democratic objectives and of the local approaches to meet them, by using inclusive dialogues.

At a time when the global order is at stake, and democracy is being challenged worldwide, the EU needs to reconsider its discourse, and, above all, its actions. To promote a global order based on democracy and human rights, the EU needs to honour its stated aims, both in discourse and in practice. The EU cannot afford to undermine democratic norms by claiming to act in accordance with them, when in fact it does not. The EU needs to stand up for its values, even if this may counteract interests in the short term, as the erosion of these values risks undermining the EU's long-term interests. In the inevitable conflict between interests and values, the latter needs to be prioritised over short-term interests. The EU needs to genuinely stand by its own values in the norm promotion and work to ensure that the norm-takers also embrace them. This is vital if the EU does not want to risk undermining the value-based norms themselves as well as its legitimacy and thus its influence worldwide, all of which are crucial to its own survival.

References

Alizada, N. et al. (2022). *Case for Democracy: Conference Report*. Gothenburg: V-Dem Institute.

Barbé, E., & Morillas, P. (2019). The EU global strategy: The dynamics of a more politicized and politically integrated foreign policy. *Cambridge Review of International Affairs, 32*, 6.

Bremberg, N. (2022). Climate Security in the Mediterranean: What Prospects for Regional Cooperation? In Dessì, A. & Fusco, F. (eds.), *Climate Change and Security in the Mediterranean*. IAI Research Studies 9. Rome: Istituto Affari Internazionali.

Chaban, N. & Elgström, O. (2021). Theorizing External Perceptions of the EU. In Gstöhl, S. & Schunz, S. (eds.) *The External Action of the European Union: Concepts, Approaches, Theories*. London: Red Globe Press.

Checkel, J. (1998). *Norms, institutions and national identity in contemporary Europe*. ARENA Working papers, WP 98/16. Oslo: ARENA.

Council of the European Union. (2021). *Council conclusions on a renewed Partnership with the Southern Neighbourhood - A new agenda for the Mediterranean*. Brussels, 19 April 2021 (OR. en) 7931/21. 2021.

Dandashly A. & Noutcheva, G. (2022). Conceptualizing norm diffusion and norm contestation in the European neighbourhood: Introduction to the special issue. *Democratization, 29*(3).

Dandashly, A., & Noutcheva, G. (2019). Unintended consequences of EU democracy support in the European neighbourhood. *The International Spectator, 54*, 1.

Delreux, T., & Ohler, F. (2019). Climate policy in European union politics. *Oxford Research Encyclopedia of Politics*. https://doi.org/10.1093/acrefore/9780190228637.013.1097

Directorate-General for Neighbourhood and Enlargement Negotiations, (2023). *The European Union and Tunisia agreed to work together on a comprehensive partnership package*. News Article. June, 2023. https://neighbourhood-enlargement.ec.europa.eu/news/european-union-and-tunisia-agreed-work-together-comprehensive-partnership-package-2023-06-11_en Accessed 26 September, 2023.

Duchêne, F. (1972). Europe's role in world peace. In R. Mayne (ed.), *Europe Tomorrow: Sixteen Europeans Look Ahead*. London: Fontana.

EUR-Lex. (2023). *Accession Criteria (Copenhagen Criteria)*. EU Publications Office. https://eur-lex.europa.eu/EN/legal-content/glossary/accession-criteria-copenhagen-criteria.html. Accessed 18 August, 2023.

European Commission. (2004). *European Neighbourhood Policy*. Brussels, 12.5.2004. COM(2004) 373 final.

European Commission/High Representative of the Union for Foreign Affairs and Security Policy. (2015). *Review of the European Neighbourhood Policy*. Brussels, 18.11.2015 JOIN(2015) 50 final.

European Commission. (2022). *EU agrees to COP27 compromise to keep Paris Agreement alive and protect those most vulnerable to climate change*. Press release, 21 November 2022. Brussels. https://ec.europa.eu/commission/presscorner/detail/en/ip_22_7064. Accessed 18 August, 2023.

European External Action Service (EEAS). (2016). *Shared Vision, Common Action: A Stronger Europe. A Global Strategy for the European Union's Foreign and Security Policy*. EU Publications Office, 2016.

European External Action Service (EEAS). (2021). *European Neighbourhood Policy. 29.07.2021.* www.eeas.europa.eu/eeas/european-neighbourhood-policy_en#7135. Accessed 18 August, 2023.

European Neighbourhood Policy and Enlargement Negotiations (DG NEAR). (2021). EU external action budget: European Commission welcomes the final adoption of the EU's new long-term external action budget for 2021–2027. *News Article. 9 June 2021. EU external action budget: European Commission welcomes the final adoption of the EU's new long-term external action budget for 2021–2027 (europa.eu)*. Accessed 25 September, 2023.

European Union. (2020). *Official Journal of the European Union*, Vol. 63, 7 December, 2020.

Ferenczy, Z. A. (2019). Green power? European normative influence on Chinese environmental policy. *Australian and New Zealand Journal of European Studies, 11*, 1.

Füle, Š. (2011). *Speech on the recent events in North Africa Committee on Foreign Affairs (AFET), European Parliament*. Reference: SPEECH/11/130. Brussels, 28 February 2011.

Galtung, J. (1973). *The European community: A superpower in the making*. Oslo: Universitetsforlaget.

Grimm, S. (2019). Democracy promotion in EU enlargement negotiations: More interaction less hierarchy. *Democratization, 26*, 5.

Hyde-Price, A. (2006). "Normative" Power Europe: A Realist Critique. *Journal of European Public Policy, 13*, 2.

Jonasson, A. (2013). *The EU's democracy promotion and the mediterranean neighbours*. London: Routledge.

Jurgelaitytė, A. (2023). *The EU as a normative power in climate change negotiations. A Study of External Perceptions*. Gothenburg: University of Gothenburg, Master thesis.

Kelley, J. (2004). International actors on the domestic scene: Membership conditionality and socialization by international institutions. *International Organization, 58*, 3.

Khakee, A. (2022). EU democracy promotion cannot continue to remain silent on colonial crimes. *The Loop*. European Consortium for Political Research. https://theloop.ecpr.eu/eu-democracy-promotion-cannot-continue-to-remain-silent-on-colonial-crimes/. Accessed 18 August, 2023.

Lucarelli, S. (2018). The EU and the crisis of liberal order at home and abroad. *Globus Research Papers*, 12/2018.

Manners, I. (2002). Normative power Europe: A contradiction in terms? *Journal of Common Market Studies, 40*, 2.

March, J. & Olsen, J. (2004). The logic of appropriateness. *Arena Working Papers*, 04/09. Oslo: Arena.

The National. (2021). *Paris Climate Agreement: What have Middle East Countries done Five Years On?* https://www.thenationalnews.com/mena/2021/11/04/paris-accords-five-years-on-what-have-mena-countries-done-lately/. Accessed 18 August, 2023.

Oberthür, S., & Groen, L. (2017). The European union and the paris agreement: Leader, mediator, or bystander? *Wires Climate Change, 2017*(8), e445.

Risse, T., & Sikkink, K. (1999). *The power of human rights: International norms and domestic change*. Cambridge: Cambridge University Press.

Schimmelfennig, F., & Sedelmeier, U. (Eds.). (2005). *The Europeanization of central and Eastern Europe*. New York: Cornell University Press.

Silander, D. (2022). Utvidgad, men urholkad demokrati: en union i existentiell kris. In Bakardjieva Engelbrekt, A., Michalski, A. & Oxelheim, L. (eds). *EU mellan federalism och flexibel integration*. Stockholm: Santérus Förlag.

Sjursen, H. (2006). The EU as a "Normative" power: How can this be? *Journal of European Public Policy, 13*, 2.

Treaty on European Union. (2012) consolidated version. Official Journal of the European Union. 26.10.2012. C 326/13 https://eur-lex.europa.eu/resource.html?uri=cellar:2bf140bf-a3f8-4ab2-b506-fd71826e6da6.0023.02/DOC_1&format=PDF. Accessed on 29 September 2023.

Union for the Mediterranean. (2022). *COP 27. Mediterranean Pavilion*. https://ufmsecretariat.org/cop27-mediterranean-pavilion/. Accessed 18 August, 2023.

United Nations. (2015). *Paris Agreement*. https://unfccc.int/sites/default/files/english_paris_agreement.pdf. Accessed 18 August, 2023.

United Nations. (2023). *The Glasgow Climate Pact—Key Outcomes from COP26. United Nations Climate Change*. https://unfccc.int/process-and-meetings/the-paris-agreement/the-glasgow-climate-pact-key-outcomes-from-cop26. Accessed 18 August, 2023.

Wolf, M. J. et al. (2022). Environmental Performance Index. *New Haven, CT: Yale Center for Environmental Law & Policy*. epi.yale.edu. Accessed 21 August, 2023.

Youngs, R. (2004). Normative dynamics and strategic interests in the EU's external identity. *Journal of Common Market Studies, 42*, 2.

Youngs, R. & Ventura, E. et al. (2022). *European Democracy Support Annual Review 2022*. Brussels: Carnegie Europe and European Partnership for Democracy. https://carnegieeurope.eu/2023/01/30/european-democracy-support-annual-review-2022-pub-88818. Accessed 26 September, 2023.

CHAPTER 6

The Ability of the EU to Extend Its Model of a Social Market Economy Beyond Its Borders

Pär Hallström

February 24 2022 is history. In the spirit of nineteenth-century nationalism, the leadership of an authoritarian and capitalist Russia decided to use military aggression in order to fulfil its aims, and crosses the borders of a state associated with the European Union (EU), a Union based upon the fundamental trust that violence between European states is nowadays unlikely. Two views on international relations and the role of law are confronted, one political view based on power, scantly limited by public international law, and another, where the rule of law, liberalism and human rights serve as a guarantee for peace and cooperation between states.

Russia's war against Ukraine can be seen at once as a military assault on the role of the EU in Europe and constitutes as such the most direct and clear challenge to the Union's ability to act in accordance with its

P. Hallström (✉)
Umeå University, Umeå, Sweden
e-mail: par.hallstrom@umu.se

A. Bakardjieva Engelbrekt et al. (eds.), *The Borders of the European Union in a Conflictual World*,
https://doi.org/10.1007/978-3-031-54200-8_6

values. However, this ability is also challenged by other purely material circumstances. Ever since the Renaissance, the demography, the aptitude for industrial innovation and the advancement of arts and culture have made it possible for the European countries to exercise their influence on the rest of the world. Notably since the end of World War II, the Western European ideas of how a democratic state, characterised by human rights and social aims, is to be realised within a liberal market economy have prevailed. However, during the twenty-first century, the global trend is in the direction of a new pluralism where the role of Europe is diminishing. To be sure, Europe, organised within the EU, is still the world's biggest economy measured in GDP per capita, and its largest trading bloc. The EU is the most important trading partner for 80 countries of the world and ranks first in both inward and outward-bound international investments (European Commission, 2023). At the same time, this leading position is declining as a result of the fact that the EU population in relation to the world population is diminishing, and so is its part of the world's economy and trade. This trend is occurring parallel to the increase of importance of countries that do not share the European view of the ideal society. In 2021, one-third of the world's population lived under authoritarian rule, and only 6.4% lived in full-fledged democracies according to the Democracy Index of the Economist (The Economist, 2022).

This chapter explores the questions to what extent, and how, the EU and its member states influence other countries to adopt domestic rules as well as international cooperation mechanisms comparable to the democratic and liberal social market economy model and international policy aims of the EU. Such ability seems, to this author, being of great importance for a harmonious future development of political and trade cooperation on a world level, as well as for cooperation between the EU and its partners in their bilateral relations. And it is of relevance for the survival of the foundational ideology of the Union itself.

The chapter does not purport to provide an exact answer to the questions outlined above, nor does it draw the contours of their future implications. Instead, it points out and systematises the most relevant circumstances that condition the EU's ability to extend its values beyond its borders, and it does so from seven aspects. First, it provides a background in consideration of theories of power in international relations. Second, it gives a historical explanation of the influence of European legal thinking in the world, and why European-inspired law meets resistance for particularly cultural reasons in Asian and African countries. The third aspect relates to how the EU's soft and economic power influences its commercial partners to introduce EU market rules in their jurisdictions. The fourth aspect illuminates how the EU model, in its quality of an economic as well as a political project, has inspired countries in Latin America as well as in Africa to establish economic communities with political aims. The fifth one is directed towards the economic power that the EU exercises in the bilateral trade agreements that the EU has established with most countries in the world. The sixth aspect focuses on the influence that the EU exercises in multinational economic organisations, foremost the WTO; and the seventh aspect puts the EU model for cooperation in relation to future alternatives, in particular to those led by China. The chapter ends with final reflections on Europe in the present world disorder.

Geo- and Real Politics Meet Liberal and Value-Based Politics—A Theoretic Background to EU Powers

One way of analysing Europe's place in a multipolar world is to depart from the teachings of the Swedish political scientist Rudolf Kjellén (1864–1922). He was partly inspired by the German legal philosopher von Savigny, the principal member of the historical school, which was critical of the opinions of the liberals about the possibility to couching abstractly framed rules of universal application (von Savigny, 1831). Contrary to the liberals, he meant that law is created by tradition and results from how legal rules have been shaped over time within a national culture. He consequently meant that law should reflect the national spirit. Kjellén understood the development within a state to be a political and dialectical struggle for power between progress, attached to liberalism, and reaction, attached to the traditional values of a country, expressed as conservatism. When it comes to international relations, Kjellén introduced the concept of geopolitics, and in a spirit of real politics (*Realpolitik*) he meant that the will to expand is part of the nature of the great resourceful powers as well as their reasoning in terms of spheres of interest (Kjellén, 1911, 1916). It is not without merit to use his theories for explaining the causes of the present authoritarian military/police rule of Russia as well as of

Russia's will for re-establishing the Russian/Soviet empire. His theories can also serve as a tool for explaining the EU's value-driven foreign policy as well as the resistance to it from non-European cultures.

The comprehension of international relations by Kjellén, that rational interests and not ideas are the decisive factors behind the foreign policy of nations, is also close to the theory of real politics, but it is Hans J. Morgenthau who stands as the Nestor of the theory of real politics and its application on international relations. In his quality of an international lawyer as well as a political scientist, he was well aware of the relation between law and politics in international relations.

Morgenthau meant that states are acting rationally in conformity with their interests and that international politics is a struggle for power in which states use international law but even more their political resources for attaining maximal power and thereby national security (Morgenthau, 1948). He divides the concept of power into three parts: political power, economic power and charismatic power. Political power includes unilateral decisions about military force towards another state, economic power is exercised by a state when using its economic resources for compelling another state, charismatic power, that Morgenthau also calls the power over the minds of men, relates most of all to the cultural influence that a state may enjoy in relation to other states. The United States since long possess all three types of power while South Korea may be referred to as an example of a country that has got charismatic power since the 2010's via its music, films and technological achievements.

The power of the EU vis-à-vis third states is based on its economic power, but maybe even more on its charismatic attraction. The EU itself is arguably better explained by the liberal theories within the academic subject of international relations than by the real political ones. In its quality of an organisation, it constitutes an institutionalised peaceful area of international cooperation that is built upon binding rules of law, democracy and free trade. This organisation has an influence on third states both as an example of successful cooperation and of being the hub of a net of cooperation organised around free trade agreements between the EU and third states. These agreements do not only comprise rules on trade, creating economic interdependence but they also include legal obligations on matters of, e.g., protection of human rights and the environment.

The theory about charismatic power to influence the action of others has been further developed by the political scientist Joseph Nye, who named it "soft power". When speaking about the soft power of the EU, we must not forget the importance of the culture of its member states for creating the power of attraction of the EU. Again, the EU rather serves as a hub or as an umbrella assembling the member states.

Nye makes a distinction between hard power on the one side, consisting of political and economic power, and soft power on the other. He means that soft power cannot be very well created by governments but is the result of non-state actors in an open society. It is influenced by culture and political values concerning democracy and human rights like a free press and the right to demonstrate (Nye, 1990). But decisions on foreign policy may also be important like the will to cooperate with treaty partners and being favourable to multilateralism (Nye, 2004). The observations by Nye may very well have had the case of Europe and the European Union in mind.

European circumstances are the focus of the study by the legal scholar Anu Bradford. With her book *The Brussels Effect—How the European Union Rules the World* she demonstrates concretely how the EU by adopting internal legislation and regulatory standards in areas such as product safety, competition and data protection, exercises economic and mainly soft international power resulting in rules and norms voluntarily taken over and followed by the world at large (Bradford, 2020).

A Historical Background to the Present EU Influence in the World

In order to understand the power of the EU and of its member states, not the least the importance of law as a soft power, it is difficult to ignore the history of Europe's relations with the world and its colonial heritage. This heritage still negatively affects the minds of those peoples that were subjects of the British, French and Russian Empires, as well as of those of the Belgian and Portuguese systems. The since long ended Spanish one has less impact today. At the same time, the colonial systems contributed to modernisation of those societies in the European sense, in determining geographical borders, in setting up an administrative apparatus, school systems and legal systems moulded after European prototypes.

The British and French Empires reached their largest extension after the First World War and the Peace of Versailles, but simultaneously the resistance to colonialism took off. However, it would take until the end of World War II for an almost forty-year-long decolonisation period to get started. The Russian Empire, on the contrary, together with the Austrian and German Empires, was split up after World War I, but it was re-established after World War II in the form of the Soviet Empire based on political, ideological and military power. It collapsed with the Soviet Union in 1991, but the present war in Ukraine is part of the political ambition of a re-established Russian Empire.

The decolonisation of the British Empire proceeded fairly peacefully, i.e., without major resistance from the British government, yet not from British people in Kenya and former Southern Rhodesia, and the newly sovereign states could be assembled with the United Kingdom in the informal "conversation club", the British Commonwealth of Nations. The decolonisation of the French Empire, by contrast, could only be achieved through crises, in Tunisia and Morocco, and through war, in Indochina and Algeria. The efforts by France to establish institutionalised cooperation with former colonies within firstly the French Union and thereafter through the French Community, *la Communauté française,* failed because of the domineering role of France. Neither could the Portuguese system be ended without wars. The strongest resistance movements in some of the French and Portuguese colonies were of communist ideology and after those countries had reached independence they were declared people's republics and initiated economic systems inspired by the Soviet model.

In particular, during the 1960s and 1970s, the belief in a planned economy, nationalisation, and state-owned companies was strong, in Europe as well as in the newly independent states, and many former colonies considered themselves to be threatened by imperialism in all its four dimensions: political, economic, cultural and ideological. Despite the fact that the Soviet Union displayed three of these dimensions in relation to its neighbourhood, the newly independent states positioned themselves against the former Western colonial powers and the United States. Together with the Soviet Union and its puppet states, they formed a majority in the United Nations General Assembly and could carry through resolutions against what they considered to be economic imperialism from the West: 1962 on Permanent Sovereignty of States over their Natural Resources (UN, 1962); on a New International Economic Order (1972) and the Charter of Economic Rights and Duties of States (1974). These resolutions confirmed the principle of state sovereignty and non-interference in internal affairs, including the choice of economic system, the right to expropriate foreign property in application of the national law of the expropriating state and to claim access to new technologies.

However, the major part of international trade was between the richer OECD countries, and in order not to be further marginalised the developing countries chose to find compatible arrangements with the established Western order. The former colonies could keep their traditional duty-free trade between them and the metropolis by entering into the large non-reciprocal free trade arrangements with the EEC/EU, the Yaoundé (1963) and Lomé conventions (1975, 1979), giving free access to the common market of the EU for the former colonies, while at the same time allowing them to keep their markets protected. In addition, these agreements contained parts on economic and technical cooperation and aid, e.g., on advanced legal and administrative training. The developing countries furthermore entered into bilateral agreements on investments and investment protection with many European countries individually, conditioning the right to expropriation, and a majority of the developing countries acceded to the World Bank International Centre for Settlement of Investment Disputes, giving multinational companies the right to have their disputes with the investing state settled by an international arbitration court, which decides on the basis of international law. The developing countries also participated actively in the negotiations leading up to the establishment of the World Trade Organisation (WTO) and became members with special status granting them favourable rights and exceptions. WTO membership encroaches somewhat upon domestic sovereignty, as it entails obligations about ensuring competent administration and independent courts; obligations that are patent when it comes to the protection of intellectual property rights.

In 1992, after the foremost challenger of the European view on society, the Soviet Union, had collapsed, its command economy system was recognised as inefficient, and the states that had been part of the Soviet system had started transforming themselves into liberal states in the Western sense of the concept, with democracy, the rule of law, market economy and respect for human rights. Many of them were aiming towards membership of the European Union and liberal democracy seemed to be the only important ideology in the world. The political scientist Francis Fukuyama (1992) formulated his winning thesis that history had reached its end. He based his thesis on the fact that parliamentary democracy and market economy had become the norm also in Eastern Europe, Latin America and Asia.

Fukuyama's thesis was disputed by his colleague, the political scientist Samuel Huntington (1996). According to his opinion, history continues, but conflicts in the world will not take place between states separated by political ideology. They will rather occur as a result of differences of cultures or civilisations that are not bound by national borders. He defined seven such world views: (1) Western, (2) Latin American, (3) Islamic, (4) Chinese, (5) Hindu, (6) Japanese and (7) African. The Western belief in universal values would be shared by a shrinking part of humanity and they would lose their global convincing power.

This classification of world views coincides in broad terms with the one drawn up by the legal scientist René David (1950), when he analysed the major legal systems of the world later described extensively by Konrad Zweigert and Hein Kötz (1995). However, analyses from legal science are more directed towards the coexistence of legal cultures than what is the case in political science, where pointing at conflicts is frequent in order to illuminate essential differences. Legal science may explain how in some countries, parts of life like marriage and penal law may be regulated for instance by Muslim law, on the basis of traditional religious values, while administrative and business life is mainly regulated by law of European origin. In the fields of constitutional and administrative law, a great part of the principles expressed in the constitutions of the European countries have been included in the constitutions of the former colonies. In some cases, this has been effectuated in a very concrete way, for example, in respect of human rights, the constitution of Gabon refers directly to the French Declaration of Human Rights of 1789.

In the same line as Huntington, the legal scientist Patrick Glenn (2000) emphasises that, from a legal point of view, many legal systems of the world are not pure but represent commixtures of traditions from various origins. He stresses that law is influenced and adapted depending on the social context of local societies. He points to the fact that legal traditions are conservative by nature and that they are connected to a view of society as being static. This entails that societies do only change very gradually, often as a result of new traditions being gradually consolidated, many of those originating from other traditional cultures (Cf. Kjellén, supra, on dialectic progress). The legal historian Alan Watson (1974) has underlined the importance for social change that new law is imported, and transplanted, but that this reformation of law can fail in countries with strong legal traditions by the fact that the transplanted law is repelled.

In order to explain how and why local law that has been shaped after European models is being actually applied, both in the private and the public law fields, it is consequently necessary to investigate the role of cultural traditions. Within the public law field this may explain the strengthening of presidential power, or, regarding human rights in Africa, that the African Charter puts equal emphasis on individual and collective rights and it also emphasises the duties of the individual towards country and family.

Today, not only the UK and France but also other European countries and the EU play a role as sources of inspiration for law reform in the partner countries. Furthermore, the EU is financing vast programmes on legal cooperation. They are often carried out in cooperation with EU member states or non-governmental organisations. Worth to mention is also the cooperation within the legal field that takes place between French-speaking supreme courts within *l'Association des Cours suprêmes judiciaires francophones* and that courts in countries with ties to Europe not seldom refer to French or English case law when interpreting their own law. The EU is also the only non-African representative at the sessions of the African Commission for human and peoples' rights.

In this admittedly brief historical overview of European/EU influence in the world it is also appropriate to mention a positive heritage of the colonial past, namely languages. English, French, Spanish and Portuguese have united nations within states and united states in cooperation between themselves and with Europe. As these languages are also official languages of the EU, all its legal acts are easily accessible and ready to be transformed into the legal systems of the EU partner countries.

Social Market Economy—A Soft Power Asset for the EU's Global Influence

For Germany, having been dominated since the beginning of the 1950s by a moderate ordoliberal thinking (Gerber, 1998), i.e., permitting social aims within a liberal economy, it has been a condition for transferring power to the EU in order to create a Common European Market, that such transfer would not result in making it difficult to reach national social aims. Such aims were therefore also to be part of EU policy. This view has been consistently shared by all the member states of the EU. Already in 1951, when the first European Community, the European Coal and Steel Community, was created, liberalisation was therefore complemented by financial means allowing ECSC to provide support for professional training, expected to be needed as a result of the industrial transformation. This capacity increased when a social fund was created simultaneously with the establishment of the European Economic Community (EEC) in 1957. The EEC also received competence to make politics with social contents, e.g., concerning the prohibition of sexual discrimination related to working life, part-time work, and parental leave. Already in the 1970s the EEC set out the objective of becoming a social community, *eine Sozialgemeinschaft*, according to the German social democratic chancellor Willy Brandt (Brandt, 2019; Leibfried, 1992). Environmental policy was officially recognised as an EU policy with the Single European Act in 1986 and the social quality of EU policy was manifested by the EC Social Charter 1989, and written into the Lisbon Treaty Article 3(3) confirming that the EU shall be based on a social market economy.

In the 1970s and 1980s, considerations of welfare politics were inherent in many EU rules that were introduced in order to establish the common market. In the field of agricultural policy, heavily regulated by the EEC, prices should be reasonable to consumers (EEC Article 39(1,e)). EEC rules were issued on product liability, consumer credit and prohibition of misleading advertising. Considerations of environmental or social nature were taken into account when EEC technical standards were introduced, e.g., about exhaust gas cleaning and security regulations for cars, sulphur in fuel oil, industrial discharge of dangerous substances, norms for air quality, sound level for machines, procedures for control of chemical substances before they are marketed, classification, marketing and norms for dangerous substances, limits to the use of hormones for animal breeding, limits to the use of pesticides and other poisonous substances for protecting plants, regulation on additives and packaging materials for food products, on the contents of marketing and packaging of cosmetics, classification marking and prohibition of textile substances, rules on approval of pharmaceutical substances, security norms for toys etc.

EU legislation on the quality of products and production processes is an ever-ongoing activity, the resulting rules being compulsory both for goods produced in the EU, as well as for those imported into the EU. Therefore, all companies wanting to sell their products in the common market need to make them in conformity with EU standards. In fact, as convincingly shown by Bradford (2020), many international companies tend to adapt all their production to EU standards. They do so because of the giant size of the EU market, the biggest consumer market in the world, and as it is cheaper to follow one standard than to produce different products for different markets, companies chose EU standards for all their markets, and as EU standards mostly are the strictest of the world such products are admitted everywhere. Hence, EU standards become world standards.

It is worth noting that adapting products to EU standards is not merely a technical matter, but that the social aims of the standards are simultaneously being marketed abroad. Anu Bradford mentions in this respect in particular the EU regulation on Registration, Evaluation, Authorisation and Restriction of Chemical Products (REACH) (Bradford, 2020, p.193). It does not put the responsibility on the state but on producers and importers for collecting and assessing information on the properties and hazards of substances. The regulation has not only had an impact on companies but it has also led to legislation in most countries with a large chemical industry, e.g., China, Japan, South Korea, India and Turkey.

Bradford points at EU legislation in one field that is particularly illustrative of EU soft power influence on not only commercial conditions but also on human rights in the digital economy, namely the EU General Data Protection Regulation (GDPR) from 2016 about personal data (Bradford, 2020, p.133 et seq.). It is applicable to all companies collecting data on people in the EU, irrespective of whether they are being established on EU territory or outside of it. Bradford found that national legislation corresponding to EU law has been introduced by 120 countries worldwide. The USA is an exception while the Chinese legislation resembles it on paper.

The social aims of the EU are not absent even in the most typical ordoliberal field, competition policy. According to the original Article 86(b) EEC Treaty, current Article 102 (b) TFEU companies with a dominant position are not allowed to act in ways leading to the prejudice of consumers. In a similar manner, the original Article 85 (1) EEC Treaty and present Article 101(1) TFEU prohibiting restrictive agreements may, according to the third paragraph of the same article, allow exceptions to the rule in certain cases, provided consumers get a fair share of the resulting benefits. Still, from a power perspective, the EU's external actions in the field of EU competition policy are of mainly economic nature.

If a company, regardless of its nationality, acts in a way that is contrary to the EU's competition rules, and its conduct has effects on the internal market of the Union, the European Commission has the right to open infringement proceedings and may decide to impose very high fines, of up to 10 per cent of the annual turnover of the infringing undertakings. The Commission also has the power to prohibit the acquisition or merger of undertaking, the decisions of the Commission being subject to judicial review before the Court of Justice of the European Union (CJEU). Such decisions of the Commission and of the CJEU have legal effects worldwide. What is more, not only has EU competition law produced worldwide effects through its application by EU institutions, but it has, according to Bradford, served as a model for the competition laws of the major part of the 130 states of the world (Bradford, 2020, p.115). Not only have its substantive provisions been almost literally transferred but also its administrative set up with an independent competition authority whose decisions may be controlled by a court of law.

The European social market economy has evidently a charismatic soft power, mixed with some economic power instruments encouraging countries all over the world to undertake legal reforms in the direction of the European model. The reasons can be explained by economic and objective factors as well as by cultural and ideological circumstances. The need for companies to export to the European market can be considered an economic factor, and objective factors are the circumstance that laws of purely commercial and technical nature are neutral to cultural traditions and are therefore easily integrated into legal systems of non-European countries. As cultural and ideological factors can be considered the fact that the elites of many countries are well acquainted with European languages and culture, and they are positive to European ideology concerning the government being active in assuring consumer and environmental interests in a market economy. Regarding competition law, they share, according to Bradford (2020, p.122), the European view that it should express a compromise between the free market and the will of governments to interfere in order to take consumer interests, small- and medium-sized companies, and market structure into consideration. Moreover, as European competition law also includes control of state aid and market structure it could inspire countries like China, India and Russia.

The European Union Inspiring the Establishment of Regional Organisations With Economic as well as Political Aims and Objectives in Latin America and Africa

The EU serves as an inspiration for countries not willing to go as far as to establish a federation, but yet wanting to have intimate regional cooperation in the economic area and to coordinate their policies generally. Organisations having the European Community/European Union as a model have been established in Latin America and Africa. This occurrence can be understood as a result of the soft power of the EU. One such organisation was created already in 1969 when the Andean Community, *La Communidad Andina* (CAN), was established by its members Bolivia, Colombia, Ecuador and Peru. Among these novel organisations, it is CAN that is the copy following most truly the original EEC and the EU, and having the most efficient legal system. The institutions of CAN correspond to those of the EU with a Council consisting of the heads of states, agreeing about the larger policy questions and settling political disputes between the member states, a Council of Ministers taking supranational norms, decisions, a Commission making proposals, a Parliament, and a Court of Justice having the power to control that the CAN-Treaty, the economic constitution, is respected by the member states (Alter & Helfer, 2017). Important for the efficiency of the organisation, and for assuring that persons can rely on the economic rights of the constitution, is the fact that it has been given direct effect in the national legal orders of the member states and that their courts may submit to the CAN Court of Justice requests for preliminary rulings, that are binding for the national courts.

The Central American Community (SICA), *Sistema de integración centroamericana,* corresponds as well, grosso modo, to the EC/EU, and its Court of Justice quotes cases decided by the European Court of Justice, but the other community organisations in Latin America do not live up to the original. The southern common market, Mercosur, which comprises Argentina, Brazil, Paraguay and Uruguay, still lacks an efficient tribunal; the Caribbean Community (Caricom) lacks efficient political institutions, but on the other hand it has an efficient tribunal having wide competences. The tribunal is part of the judicial systems of the member states, and it serves as an appellate tribunal in even private- and penal law cases.

On the African continent, the EU model has most clearly inspired the creation of the West African economic and monetary union, *l'Union Économique et Monétaire Ouest Africaine*, consisting of seven French-speaking and one Portuguese-speaking country. Its institutions, including its Court of Justice with vast competences, correspond fully to those of the EU, but unfortunately the work of the court has come to a standstill during the last years. The Central African Economic and Monetary Community, *la Communauté Économique et Monétaire de l'Afrique Central*, (CEMAC), consisting of six member states, is worth mentioning. It has the same institutional structure as the EU, including a Court of Justice which has, at least on paper, the same competences as the EU court. As these organisations are aiming to establish common markets with free movement for goods, services, persons and capital, it is logical that they find inspiration in the EU.

The EU has actively supported these countries in Africa, Latin America and the Caribbean to cooperate within their community organisations and to have rules corresponding to those of the EU, but the EU has also concluded agreements with other countries of these regions encouraging regional cooperation and taking rules corresponding to those of the EU. Among such organisations are the wide-encompassing African Union (AU) established in 2000, and the Southern African Development Community (SADC), established in 1992. Both of them have ambitious aims, corresponding to those of the EU, but only the future will show how the communities in this important continent may develop.

The EU Bilateral Trade and Cooperation Agreements—Means to Influence Partner States to Follow the EU Model of Social Market Economy

The EU has concluded trade and partnership agreements with most of the countries of the world and can be considered to use its economic power in the Morgenthau sense in its relations with its partners. This power is strengthened in EU relations with developing countries by the fact that trade agreements with them are often accompanied by technical and financial aid and loans from the EU.

An active EU trade policy started some 50 years ago as a result of legal and political necessity. With the establishment of the customs union, the power of deciding tariffs and concluding tariff and trade agreements was transferred from the EU member states to the EU institutions. The 1957 EEC Treaty Article 113 stated that commercial policy was a domain where the EEC (EU) had exclusive competence. By concluding free trade agreements between the EEC and former colonies interruption of privileged trade between them and their respective metropolis was prevented. Instead, it was extended to all EEC member states, allowing non-discrimination between them.

Exclusive EU competence means power to the EU but at the same time loss of important external policy tools for individual member states. Consequently, the latter have been cautious to put limits to its expansion. With Article 207 TFEU, member states agreed that the common commercial policy encompasses tariff rates, the conclusion of tariff and trade agreements relating to trade in goods and services, commercial aspects of intellectual property, foreign direct investment, export policy measures and protective measures such as antidumping duties or countervailing duties in the event of subsidies.

However, the Court of Justice of the European Union (CJEU) has made a wide interpretation of the concept of commercial policy. The leading case is still the opinion 2/15 (CJEU, 2017) on the EU agreement with Singapore (EUSFTA). The CJEU interpretation departs from the words of Article 207 that the commercial policy shall be conducted in the context of the principles and objectives of the Union's external action. Those aims are enumerated in Article 21 (a) to (h) of the Treaty on European Union (TEU). They relate to a wide array of matters from peace, democracy and human rights to the environment. An agreement can be classified as a commercial agreement even if it affects such non-commercial matters under the condition that it relates specifically to international trade in that it is essentially intended to promote, facilitate or govern such trade and has direct and immediate effects on it (CJEU, 2017). A second condition is that a commercial agreement may not have a legislative effect. The EU legislative procedure must be followed to create binding internal law.

In the Opinion EUSFTA the Court affirmed that sustainable development may be included in the New Generation Free Trade Agreements as it is relevant or essential to trade, as it is an objective of the EU mentioned in Article 21(2)(f) TEU and as Articles 9 and 11 TFEU contain guarantees concerning the protection of workers and the environment. Such guarantees must consequently be an integral part of EU commercial policy. Trade agreements may make liberalisation of trade subject to the condition that the parties comply with their international obligations concerning the protection of workers and the environment (CJEU, 2017). It may also contain provisions compelling parties to combat illegal actions in the environmental and social fields.

EU external exclusive competence, however, is not limited to commercial policy. According to the early case law of the CJEU (1971 and 1977), and to Article 3(2) TFEU, it may concern any area where the EU has competence to legislate. In fact, member state competence is pre-empted as soon as the EU has issued a legislative act, and the competence in the matter is transferred to the EU institutions. The EU may thereafter use this exclusive competence to conclude international agreements.

Still, some trade agreements contain matters under member state competence, but all EU agreements are prepared and negotiated by the Commission and reflect its view on EU international relations. It may have a clear value-driven trade policy. As expressed by the former Trade Commissioner Cecilia Malmström in 2015: "The new approach will safeguard the European social and regulatory model at home [...] the new approach also involves using trade agreements and trade preference programmes as levers to promote, around the world, values like sustainable development, human rights, fair and equitable trade and the fight against corruption. We will use future EU agreements to improve the responsibility of supply chains" (EU Commission/Trade, 2015).

EU international cooperation agreements can best be described as circles consisting of groups of countries. A first inner one comprises the European countries that live up to the conditions of EU membership but have chosen to abstain: the EFTA countries Island, Liechtenstein and Norway. They are parties together with the EU in the European Economic Area (EEA) establishing a free trade area between the parties. Moreover, the EEA agreement obliges the EU partner states to swiftly adopt all new EU internal market rules except those regulating agriculture and fishery. By doing so, the partners are recognised as members of the internal market.

A second circle consists of European states fulfilling the so-called Copenhagen criteria, i.e., having institutions guaranteeing democracy, the rule of law, human rights including the protection of minorities, having a functioning market economy and an ability to take on the obligations of membership including adherence to the aims of political, economic and monetary union (European Council, 1993). European countries living up to those criteria may apply for membership of the European Union. They obtain the status of candidate state. The association agreements that they conclude with the EU foresee that they successively adopt EU compulsory as well as non-compulsory rules. Türkiye since long, Ukraine, Georgia, Moldova, Albania, Montenegro and North Macedonia are among those countries together with Serbia.

An especially comprehensive dialogue based on European values takes place with African countries south of the Sahara and with Caribbean and Pacific states. (cf. Article 208 TFEU). They have had association agreements with the EU for almost 60 years establishing free trade and economic and technical cooperation. The early Yaoundé-Convention and its successors the Lomé Conventions as well as the present Cotonou agreement are not only aiming at contributing to economic and political development but also, contrary to a *devide et impera* strategy, to facilitate for the EU partner states to cooperate between themselves. These are bilateral agreements between the EU on the one side and the partner states on the other, but they also establish common bodies where decisions are taken by consensus between the EU, as one part, and all the partner countries as the other part. The agreements do not only set up governmental bodies but they also contain a democratic element, namely a parliamentary assembly. As a consequence of this cooperation with the EU, the EU partner countries have established the Organisation of African, Caribbean and Pacific States (OACP), which is the largest organisation of developing countries.

The new post-Cotonou agreement, the EU-OACP Partnership agreement, initiated in 2021, resembles a development strategy with welfare state aims for the cooperation of the EU and its 79 partner states covering actions in all areas of the society. It lays down six priority areas: (1) human rights, democracy and governance, accommodating the African concept of peoples and rights with the rule of law and gender equality, good administration and combating corruption, (2) peace and security, including non-spreading of nuclear weapons, (3) human and social development, (4) environmental sustainability and climate change, (5) inclusive sustainable economic growth and development and (6) migration and mobility. It continues with a part about global alliances and international cooperation aiming to make the EU and OACS privileged political partners. This new partnership agreement is combined with three specific, action-oriented regional protocols (Africa, Caribbean, Pacific) with a focus on regional needs.

Similar provisions have been included in trade- and partnership agreements with other overseas countries, e.g., the agreement with the CAN-countries, Colombia, Ecuador and Peru. Except for rules establishing free trade areas, they also have provisions about respect for the human rights of the UN Charter, political cooperation aiming at disarmament and to prevent the spread of nuclear weapons, transparency, respect of international conventions in the social and environmental fields as well as to promote biological diversity and to counteract climate change.

All free trade agreements of the EU nowadays include obligations about democracy and human rights, respect of ILO-conventions on labour law and of environmental conventions and to counteract climate change. A clause about democracy and human rights being essential elements of the agreement is to be found in many agreements, e.g., the neighbourhood agreements with the countries on the southern and eastern sides of the Mediterranean. This clause justifies a party to retaliate by suspending the economic parts of the agreement in case of non-fulfilment of the human rights obligation. However, in more recent agreements with stronger economies like Singapore, Vietnam, Canada, Japan and New Zealand, the obligation is only expressed in the preamble, without mentioning that it constitutes an essential part of the agreement. In the agreement about trade and cooperation between the EU and the UK it is framed in its more obligatory form as an article of the agreement.

In fact, the EU has only decided about sanctions in very flagrant cases, on less than 30 occasions. Such decisions are taken by the member states according to the procedure of political cooperation. It is to be noted that, except for member countries of the European Convention on Human Rights, human rights obligations refer to those of the UN conventions permitting a wide scope of interpretation taking consideration of as many legal cultures as there are members of the UN Council of Human Rights.

Like other international treaties, those of the EU lay down reciprocal obligations. However, most developing countries enjoy exceptions. Retaliatory measures by one party, e.g., the EU, may be taken only after negotiations between the parties and after an arbitral tribunal has established the existence of a breach. Suspension of obligations shall be proportionate and that is easiest to determine if the breach has caused economic damage. Infringement of the obligation of sustainable development is to be settled through a dialogue between the parties.

The EU agreements with third states also refer to economic human rights that are better sanctioned than the classic ones. Intellectual property rights belong to them. They concern copyright, patents and designs and are nowadays part of all EU free trade agreements. They oblige the parties to have adequate intellectual property legislation giving right to individuals and enterprises to access competent national courts in order to have their rights tried. Protection of investments is another economic right. It is included in the more recent free trade agreements or added to them in a separate part. In case of expropriation contrary to the agreement, the investor, i.e., an individual or an enterprise from the EU or its partner country, has the right to sue the expropriating state in an impartial arbitration tribunal.

The Court of Justice of the European Union has accorded many individuals and companies a further important right by recognising direct effect of most free trade- and partnership agreements in the EU. This effect was first accorded the EU/EFTA states' free trade agreements (CJEU, 1982), thereafter the Europe Agreements of the candidate countries (CJEU, 1987), the partnership agreements of East European countries (CJEU, 2005), and association agreements with developing countries (CJEU, 2016). If a person considers that such a free trade agreement gives more rights than national law, that same person may rely on the agreement in a national court, and the court may ask the CJEU for an interpretative ruling. If national law is incompatible with the agreement, the rules of the agreement prevail. This direct effect is granted by the EU on a unilateral and non-reciprocal basis.

The Influence of the EU in Multinational Economic Organisations

On the multilateral level, for example in the UN, the International Monetary Fund (IMF), the World Bank, the Food and Agriculture Organization (FAO) and the World Trade Organisation (WTO), the EU takes part in various forms. In organisations dealing with questions that are under the exclusive competence of the EU, the EU is represented by the European Commission; in some organisations the EU is a member together with its member states, such as the WTO; in organisations limiting membership to states, only the EU member states have membership, but the European Commission coordinates their positions. Multilateral organisations and bodies may be active in various domains.

Some bodies develop product standards, others—health and environmental norms, and some UN bodies deal with human rights, where the EU has taken an active role.

However, it is the WTO that is the central organisation for global economic governance and for EU efforts to prioritise an international multilateral trade system bound by law. The crisis of the WTO and its diminished importance to the advantage of new protectionism is a blow to EU policy.

The policy of the EU and its member states can be analysed as an effort to attain multilateral economic governance characterised by a constitutional three-level system consisting of states, regional organisations and the WTO at the top. WTO and regional organisations mostly regulate the same questions: trade with goods and services, dumping, subsidies, intellectual property rights, investments etc. The regional organisations mostly follow the legal interpretations made by the WTO and its dispute settlement bodies.

This is true also for regional free trade agreements concluded by the EU. The system for settlement of disputes of these free trade agreements is moreover intimately tied to the one of the WTO. If a conflict concerns issues common to a trade agreement and the WTO, the parties may choose to have their conflict settled by the WTO settlement system. In this way, the free trade agreements and the WTO belong to the same system. Settlement of investment disputes of recent EU free trade agreements also reflects multilevel constitutionalism (Petersmann, 2012). They establish investment tribunals on two levels that could easily be integrated into a future system of investment tribunals of the WTO.

The crises that the WTO has gone through since the year 2017 should be considered in relation to three circumstances. Firstly, when the WTO was established in 1995, it corresponded fairly well with what its members wanted in the areas of reduction of obstacles to trade in goods and services, and of better protection of intellectual property. Since then, new conditions for trade have come into existence, but, because unanimity of all 164 members is required for making decisions, needed reform of the WTO has not been attained. Reform is urgent for subsidies, state trading enterprises, trade in services, compulsory technology transfer, investment issues, e-commerce and environmental and labour law. Furthermore, developing countries have the right to protectionist measures, and, as each country may qualify itself as a developing country, two-thirds of the WTO members have opted for that privileged status.

Among them are countries with highly competitive industrial sectors, like China.

The second circumstance concerns the impracticability of dispute settlement to cure decisional inability. Dispute settlement consists of two steps, quasi-judicial panels and a permanent Appellate Body (Hallström, 1994). During its life period, this Appellate Body has been the most successful of all international courts, and used, to about the same extent, by rich as well as by poor countries. However, the lack of WTO reform has forced the Appellate Body to apply principles of law and thereby widen the application of WTO written rules. Such practice may be understood as legislating rather than strictly applying law.

Already before the Trump presidency, the United States had manifested its annoyance by court decisions in international economic questions, but President Trump decided in 2017 to cripple the WTO dispute settlement procedure by blocking the appointment of new judges of the Appellate Body. At present, the Appellate Body exists only on paper. A party that has lost a case in the Panel may still appeal to the Appellate Body, but it remains pending, and the decision of the Panel becomes non-effective. This makes the law less compulsory and gives more room to bilateral negotiations, where the parties may fully profit from their economic and political power.

Another reason for the United States to weaken the WTO was that China, the third strongest trading unit of the world, did not sufficiently live up to the requirements of free and fair trade. The state capitalist system of China, granting subsidies, other state aid, and having important state-owned enterprises, combined with a lack of transparency, resulted in a situation where competition conditions for foreign companies were being distorted in contradiction to the aim and objectives of the WTO. Such policy involves no challenges to Chinese communist party doctrine and economic success to China but is adverse to EU multilevel constitutionalism.

Future Alternatives or the European Model

It is an old saying that the future is in Africa, and so is the case when looking at the demography and the resources of raw materials, but the highest economic growth in the world takes place in the countries belonging to the large regional free trade organisations in Asia

(Hsieh, 2021; Rolland & Trubek, 2019), in particular in the Comprehensive and Progressive Agreement for Trans-Pacific Partnership (CCTPP), comprising a great number of states in South East Asia, Latin American states bordering the Pacific and Australia and New Zeeland. China, because of its insufficient rules on state-owned enterprises and intellectual property, is not a member of CCTPP but of the second important organisation, the Regional Comprehensive Economic Partnership (RCEP), comprising the Southeast Asian ASEAN-countries and China, Australia and New Zealand. Both organisations have provisions on environmental protection and labour law but not on human rights. It is possible to consider that these organisations, together with the trade agreements referred to above, form a multilevel system together with the WTO. They regulate many common issues, they comprise dispute settlement systems with panels, copied from that of the WTO, and these panels shall pay regard to interpretations made by the WTO panels and its Appellate Body. Furthermore, if a dispute concerns an issue that is regulated by both the organisation concerned and the WTO, the complainant may choose to file its complaint to the WTO.

The EU has negotiated agreements with most of the member states of the ASEAN, and many of them have entered into force. Their long-term aim is to establish a vast inter-regional EU/ASEAN free trade agreement. As far as trade relations between the EU and China are concerned a comprehensive agreement on investments has been negotiated. It refers in its preamble to the UN Charter of Human Rights and includes an extensive chapter on environmental protection, labour law, and social responsibility of companies. It is not in force as yet, and the parties intend to add an agreement on investment protection to it.

Both China and the parties to the great Asian free trade organisations are dependent on global trade. They therefore actively participate in the WTO, and loyally use its dispute settlement mechanism, but China also makes global trade politics via its Belt and Road Initiative (BRI). This project leads to the expansion of Chinese political power and its legal tradition building on the old Confucian idea that settlement of disputes by courts should be avoided as it is confrontational. Conflicts should instead be settled by negotiations in a spirit of due respect to the position of the stronger and the weaker party in a hierarchical system (Bogdan, 1994). From a legal point of view this way of settling disputes results in weak case law and ad hoc outcomes of the settlements.

BRI is a well-elaborated strategy for tying countries to China, and at present, it comprises more than 140 states. It is built as a global network coordinated by a light advisory forum. Being very flexible when it comes to institutions and legal norms does not correspond to an international organisation, neither does it live up to the WTO requirements of transparency and predictability of trade rules and their application. Its activity consists of carrying out specific projects based on international agreements and private law contracts. Those projects are financed with Chinese capital, and they mostly concern investments in raw material extraction and infrastructure like roads and ports. The agreements are primarily in the form of non-binding memoranda of understanding and binding agreements are concluded at the time when individual projects are to be carried out. In case of a conflict about the obligations of an agreement or of a contract, China wants Chinese to be the court language. It is expected that China will also increase the number of its free trade agreements and act to make Chinese norms global ones in fields like technical standards, information technology and e-trade.

Only China offers a viable alternative to the multilateralism of the present global economic governance. A political dimension to the economic BRI was formulated by China at the XIV BRICS Summit 2022, assembling Brazil, Russia, India, China and South Africa. It concerned a Global Security Initiative (GSI) based on Chinese values. It is to be understood as part of a scheme to take over global leadership from the USA, comprising economy as well as security policy. It is still vaguely formulated but is to be seen in relation to BRI, China's efforts to replace the US dollar with the Chinese Yuan as the main trading currency, to make Beijing the main depositary of reserve currencies and to replace the present digital system for international transactions with a Chinese one. Furthermore, the establishment of Chinese arbitration tribunals for international commerce in Beijing, Shenzhen and Xi'an can be understood as a Chinese desire to promote Chinese legal thinking in private law matters.

As far as Russia is concerned, it could have increased its general influence by democratising, strengthening the rule of law, developing its partnership agreement with the EU and simultaneously strengthening cooperation with Ukraine via its free trade agreement and completing it with agreements on cultural cooperation, but the Russian leadership chose the way of violence. The result is that the only direction for Russia is now to be integrated into the Chinese alternative.

Of the three great economic powers, the EU, the United States and China, it is today only the EU that expresses a clear voice for multilateralism in international trade, compulsory trade rules efficiently supervised, and for including human rights in trade agreements. The United States has not shared the EU's positive view of multilateralism since almost ten years back; neither has the United States concluded as many free trade agreements as the EU and the US free trade agreements also differ from the EU ones regarding human rights. The US endeavours to uphold human rights outside of its trade agreements. It is also a US priority to sustain the very strong position of its multinational companies in the world economy.

It is clear, however, that the EU's optimism about multilateralism stands in contrast with present realities. Mercantilism, pluralism and bilateral agreements have been the order of the day for more than 15 years. At the same time, the WTO and multilateralism are needed. All countries, as well as companies engaged in international trade, still need global WTO rules. This fact is demonstrated by the frequent use of its dispute settlement system by rich as well as poor countries, including China. The problem is the difficulty to adapt the WTO rules to new forms of protectionism.

Concluding Reflections

At the time of writing in 2023, two years had passed since the Court of Justice of the European Union celebrated the 50 years anniversary of one of its most important cases, ERTA, decided in 1971 (Case 22/70). It caused a considerable transfer of power from the EU member states to the EU institutions in the domain of external relations. It made clear that the external competence of the EU equals its internal, the so-called parallel doctrine, meaning that the EU may have exclusive competence not only in the field of commercial policy but in other fields of EU activity as well, and that competence in such fields become exclusive at the same time as the EU legislates in that field. Thanks to this ruling, the coordinated policy of the EU member states could be united into a forceful common EU external policy focusing on trade but carrying out the EU values and ideology about a social market economy (TEU Article 3(5)).

A motto of the external policy of the EU has been "*Wandel duch Handel*", i.e., change by trade, meaning that trade with the EU would result in the partner countries approaching the EU ideological model. Belief in this credo was strongest in relation to Eastern Europe.

In 2022, the hope for a successful policy under this motto was partly frustrated. Russia did not develop towards democracy but in the contrary direction; the congress of the Chinese Communist Party in October 2022 decided to strengthen China's centralised system and to retain its discriminating protectionism; the US administration under Joe Biden proved not to be more inclined than the former Trump administration to favour multilateralism; and the UN climate conference in November, touching upon areas under EU competence, made it evident that inability of national policy and the anarchy of the international system would lead to climate catastrophe.

Waiting for Godot, the EU is still influencing global neighbours through its soft and economic powers and with law as an instrument in order to make them approach the EU ideals.

References

Alter, K. & Helfer, L.R. (2017). *Transplanting international courts: The law and politics of the Andean tribunal of justice*. Oxford University Press.

Bogdan, M. (1994). *Comparative Law*. Kluwer Law and Taxation, Deventer.

Bradford, A. (2020). *The Brussels effect—How the European union rules the world*. Oxford University Press.

Brandt, W. (2019). *Rede des Bundeskanzlers Willy Brandt vor dem Europäischen Parlament in Strassburg 13 November 1973*. Available at https://willy-brandt-biografie.de.

CJEU. (1971). Court of justice of the European Union. Case 22/70 *ERTA*, ECLI:EU:C:1971:32.

CJEU. (1977). Court of justice of the European union. Opinion 1/76. *Laying up Fund for Inland Waterway Vessels*. ECLI:EU:C:1977:63.

CJEU. (1982). Court of justice of the European union. Case 104/81. *Kupferberg*. ECLI:C:1982:362.

CJEU. (1987). Court of justice of the European union. Case 12/86. *Demirel*. ECLI:EU:C:1987:400.

CJEU. (2005). Court of justice of the European union. Case 265/03. *Simurenkov*. ECLI:EU:C:2005:213.

CJEU. (2016): Court of justice of the European union, Case 464, *Secil*, ECLI:EU:C:2016:896.

CJEU. (2017). Court of justice of the European union. Opinion 2/15, *EU-Singapore Free Trade Agreement*, para. 36, 166, ECLI:EU:C:2017:376.

David, R. (1950). *Traité élémentaire de droit civil compare—introduction à l'étude des Droits étrangers et à la methode comparative*. Librerie Génerale de Droit et de Jusprudence.

The Economist. (2022). *Democracy Index*. 9 February. Available at: https://www.eiu.com/n/campaigns/democracy-index-2022/

European Commission/Trade. (2015). *Towards a more responsible trade and investment policy*. Available at: www.trade.ec.europa.eu/doclib/docs/2015/october/tradoc_153846.pdf. The trade strategy formulated in 2021 is on the surface more interest than value-oriented.

European Commission. (2023). *EU trade relationships by country/region*. Available at: https://policy.trade.ec.europa.eu/eu-trade-relationships-country-and-region_en

European Council. (1993). *Presidency conclusion, copenhagen European Council – 21–22 June 1993*. SN 180/1/93 REV1.

Fukuyama, F. (1992). *The end of history and the Last Man*. Free Press.

Gerber, D. (1998). *Law and competition in twentieth century Europe: Protecting prometheus 1998*. Clarendon Press.

Glenn, P. (2000). *Legal traditions of the world*. Oxford University Press.

Hallström, P. (1994), *The GATT panels and the formation of international trade law*. Juristförlaget, Stockholm.

Hsieh, P. (2021). *New Asian regionalism in international economic law*. Cambridge University Press.

Huntington, S. (1996). *The clash of civilizations and the remaking of world order*. Simon & Schuster.

Kjellén, R. (1911). *Stormakterna. Konturer kring samtidens storpolitik*. H. Gebers, Stockholm.

Kjellén, R. (1916). *Die Grossmächte der Gegenwart*. Salzwasser Verlag, 2012, Paderborn.

Leibfried, S. (1992). *Social Europe. Welfare Trajectories of the European Community*. In Stephan Leibfried. *How to Organize Prevention*. De Gruyter, Berlin.

Morgenthau, H. J. (1948). *Politics among nations*. Alfred Knopf.

Nye, J. (1990). *Bound to lead: The changing nature of American Power*. Basic Books.

Nye, J. (2004). *Soft Power: The Means to Success in World Politics*. Public Affairs.

Petersmann, E.-U. (2012). *International Law in the 21st Century: Constitutional Pluralism and Multilevel Governance of International Public Goods*. Hart Publishing.

Rolland, S. E., & Trubek, D. M. (2019). *Emerging powers in the international economic order—cooperation*. Cambridge University Press, Cambridge.

von Savigny F. K. (1831). *Of the Vocation of our Age for Legislation and Jurisprudence*. In Halsted, J.B. (eds) (1969). *Romanticism. The Documentary History of Western Civilization*. Palgrave Macmillan, London.

United Nations. (1962). *A/RES, 1803(XVII).*
United Nations. (1972). *A/RES//S-6/3201.*
United Nations. (1974). *A/RES/3281(XXIX).*
Watson, A. (1974). *Legal Transplants.* University of Georgia Press, Athens, Georgia, US.
Zweigert, K., & Kötz, H. (1995). *An introduction to comparative law.* Oxford University Press.

CHAPTER 7

The EU's Dependence on Russian Energy—A Force that Divides or Unites the Union?

Torbjörn Becker and Anders Åslund

Russia has long been an important energy exporter to Europe and other parts of the world. The European energy imports from Russia have largely been based on the giant oil and gas fields in Western Siberia that were developed in the 1970s. In the beginning of the 1980s, a great battle arose between West Germany, which wanted to build large gas pipelines from Western Siberia to Germany, and the United States who under President Ronald Reagan wanted to stop them. Germany won that time. Gradually, the Russian export of oil and gas to Western Europe expanded. Russia's war on Ukraine and the ensuing discussion about sanctions have focused attention on the mutual energy dependence of the European Union (EU) and Russia.

T. Becker (✉)
Stockholm School of Economics, Stockholm, Sweden
e-mail: Torbjorn.Becker@hhs.se

A. Åslund
Georgetown University, Washington, USA

A. Bakardjieva Engelbrekt et al. (eds.), *The Borders of the European Union in a Conflictual World*,
https://doi.org/10.1007/978-3-031-54200-8_7

When the Soviet Union collapsed in December 1991, Russia's oil production was halved, while its gas production remained almost constant. Russia repeatedly cut off both oil and gas supplies to former Soviet republics such as the Baltic States, Ukraine, Moldova, and Georgia, while it did its utmost to maintain steady supplies to the West, above all to Germany and Finland. Despite persistent Russian proposals that Sweden should buy Russian gas, Sweden always declined for security policy reasons. This is an example of an EU country that made another choice than Germany, which turned out to be far-sighted. The varying European countries' experiences of Russia as an energy supplier led to completely different attitudes. The Baltic States, Poland, and Sweden thus sought to minimize their dependence on Russian energy while Germany, Italy, the Netherlands, and Austria considered Russian energy to be cheap and safe. A few countries that imported a lot of Russian energy—the Czech Republic, Slovakia, Hungary, and Bulgaria—appeared to have no real energy policy but just carried on as before. Balmaceda (2013) discusses in more detail how countries in Europe handled the politics of Russian energy dependence while Gustafson (2012) focuses more specifically on the role of gas.

During the 1990s, the EU's electricity and gas sectors were state monopolies, while oil trading took place on an international market. Gradually, the EU began to develop an.

energy policy as part of the creation of the internal market. The key words were privatization, liberalization and "unbundling", i.e. that individual actors would not own all parts of energy supply from production, network, and distribution. While the intention was to liberalize the European energy market, this had important consequences for Russia as its major gas company Gazprom, with majority state ownership wanted to control all parts of the energy supply, endeavouring monopoly. Gazprom represented the antithesis of the new European liberal market policy. Since the 1990s the EU has adopted four energy packages, which have liberalized the electricity and gas sectors. In this context, the EU's gas policy is important. The first two gas packages were adopted in 1998 and 2003, but they did little to develop the gas market, though they stimulated market economic thinking in the gas sector.

Gazprom's main pipeline to Europe passed through Ukraine. In January 2006, Gazprom cut off all gas transit through Ukraine to Europe for four days, which disturbed the Europeans. In January 2009, Russia stopped all gas transit through Ukraine for two weeks, affecting sixteen

European countries. The myth of Russia as a reliable energy supplier had been shattered. The result was the EU's third energy package, which the Union adopted in 2009 (Commission of the European Communities, 2009). It was a real breakthrough for the market in the European gas sector. Gas producers would no longer be allowed to own pipelines, forcing Gazprom to sell its pipelines in the Baltics. The crucial role of Gazprom is further detailed in Stern (2005) while Nemtsov and Milov (2008) discuss the links between Gazprom and Russia's President Vladimir Putin.

However, the conflict between Gazprom's friends in Europe and its enemies had not been resolved. Germany, Austria, and the Netherlands insisted that Russian gas was the best and safest option. Therefore, Gazprom was allowed to maintain its ownership of Nord Stream 1, which supplied gas from Russia to Germany through the Baltic Sea. Curiously, Russia and Germany also pushed through Nord Stream 2, although it was clearly against all the EU's market principles. In 2019, the "Clean energy for all Europeans" package was adopted, that aims to reduce the dependence of fossil fuels (European Commission, Directorate-General for Energy, 2019). This package changed the rules for electricity markets but for the gas market the third package still applied.

This chapter discusses the differences in Russian energy dependence between different EU countries and how these differences made it difficult to reach a consensus regarding sanctions against Russia in the EU before Russia started its full-scale invasion of Ukraine in February 2022. Even after the EU unanimously adopted several sanctions packages, tensions remain within the union, which in many cases are directly linked to the extent to which the various countries import Russian energy. These tensions risk leading to such great contradictions within the Union that individual member states may in the future reject important collaborations. A first sign of this was that both the Netherlands and Germany opposed proposals to introduce price caps on gas, but in May 2022, German Chancellor Scholz stated that the country will stop all imports of Russian energy, including gas. Hungary is in 2023 a far more difficult case. Its government has a much more positive view of Russia. It has pursued massive campaigns within the country to depict sanctions against Russia as a threat to Hungary. At the same time, the energy crisis has created a debate about how the EU should cooperate better and develop systems to reduce the risks of its external energy dependence. The research question addressed in this chapter is therefore whether the break from Russian energy dependence may persuade countries to leave the Union or whether it can instead act as a unifying force, leading to deepened cooperation within the Union.

We approach this question by first considering the EU countries' energy balances and which types of energy they have imported from Russia. The other issue is Russia's dependence on energy exports in general and exports to the EU in particular. An account of EU sanctions against Russia follows, first after Russia's 2014 Crimean and east Ukrainian invasion and then the EU sanctions imposed after Russia launched a full-scale war of aggression on Ukraine on 24 February 2022. Next, we briefly outline Russia's counter-sanctions before discussing their impact on the EU and then on Russia. The chapter concludes with our recommendations on how the EU can manage the energy transition to create cohesion within the Union and, at the same time, security at the external border.

The EU's Dependence on Russian Energy

The EU's 27 member states have energy balances that differ significantly (see Fig. 7.1). If we look at the main energy sources in order of the carbon dioxide emissions they generate, the average EU country has about 10 percent of its energy supply from coal. Poland stands out receiving 40 percent of its energy from coal in 2020. Yet, several countries use no coal as an energy source, and roughly two-thirds of the EU countries use coal for less than 10 percent of their energy supply.

Oil accounts for about 35% of the energy balance in the Union. Here, too, there are large variations between the member states, although oil in the 2020s is mainly used for transport. Cyprus tops the list in terms of oil dependence with a share of almost 90%, while for several countries in the eastern part of the Union oil account for less than 20% of their energy balances.

The next source of energy is natural gas, which accounts for about 25% of the EU's overall energy balance. Sweden is at the bottom of the list with about 3 percent of its energy from gas, while the Netherlands tops the list with 40 percent. Like coal, gas is mainly used to generate electricity and for heating.

With regard to nuclear power, roughly half of the EU countries have no nuclear power, while the share of nuclear power in France is the

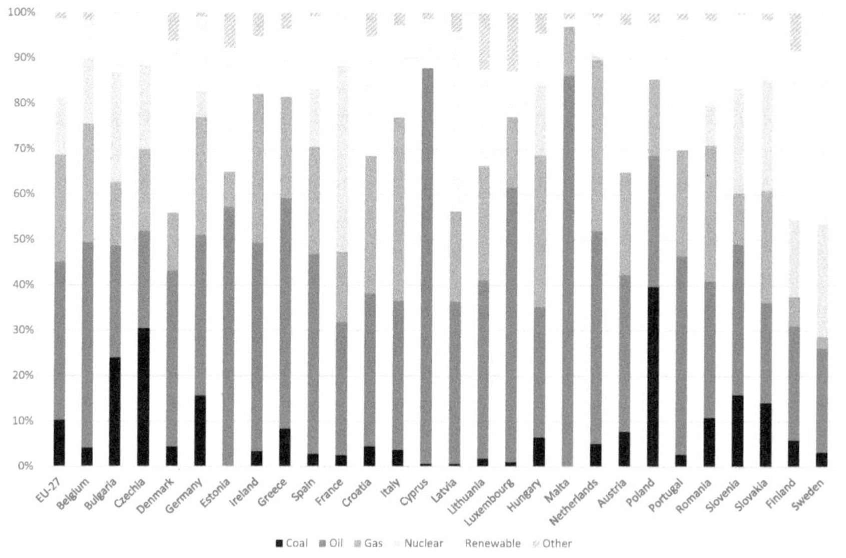

Fig. 7.1 Energy balances of EU countries in 2020. *Source* Eurostat

highest at around 40% of the energy balance. The EU as a whole gets roughly 10 percent of its energy from nuclear power.

Finally, renewable energy supplies just under 20% of the Union's energy. Sweden tops the ranking with renewable energy amounting to almost 50% of the energy balance, while Malta receives only 2 percent of its energy from renewable energy.

To conclude, the differences in the member states' energy balances are a perfect breeding ground for political disagreements within the Union regarding everything from climate goals, taxonomy, and the relationship with Russia, including sanctions that we discuss below.

The Russian component in the EU countries' energy balance is summarized in Fig. 7.2, which shows how much of the countries' energy comes from Russia, broken down into different types of energy. First, before the war in 2022 the EU received about 30% of its energy from Russia. Of this 30%, gas accounted for one-third, while oil and some coal historically accounted for two-thirds of energy imports from Russia. The EU average hid large variations within the Union. Lithuania topped among importers of Russian energy, but it did not use all itself. Among the Baltic countries, Latvia was instead most dependent on Russian gas, which accounted for about 20 percent of its energy balance. Hungary is otherwise at the top in terms of dependence on Russian gas, which has been reflected in the Hungarian advertising campaigns against Russian sanctions. Several countries obtained about 15% of their energy from Russian gas, notably Germany, Italy, and the Netherlands. Yet, a handful of countries, such as Sweden, are not at all dependent on Russian gas. However, the most valuable Russian energy exports are crude oil and oil products. Finland received nearly two-thirds of its energy from there. Oil and oil products can be replaced more easily than gas which overwhelmingly comes in gas pipelines, but some oil is supplied through pipelines, causing logistical and technical challenges to changing suppliers, but as we discuss below, many of these challenges were overcome in 2023.

Source: Eurostat.

Already in 2008, Le Coq and Paltseva (2008) created an index that describes the security of EU countries in terms of energy supply. The index summarizes the risks in relation to how diversified countries are with regard to suppliers of energy, political risk in supplier countries,

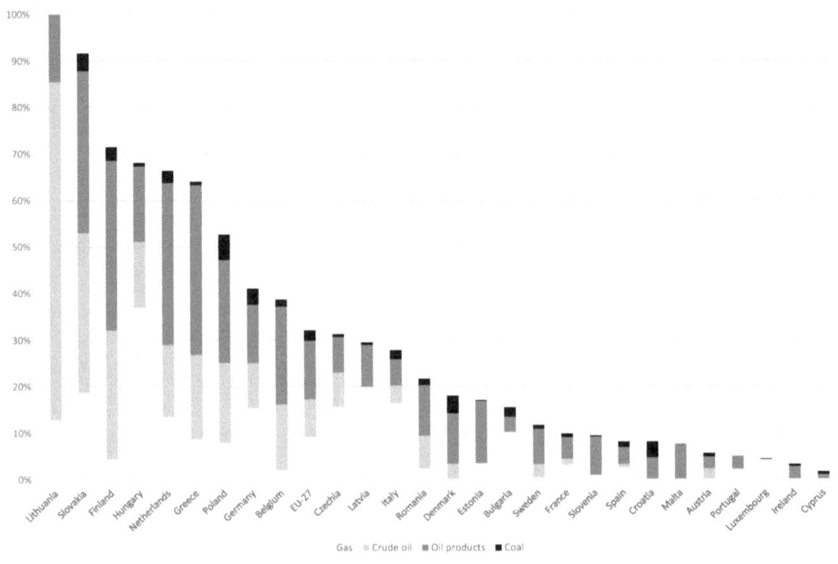

Fig. 7.2 Sources of the dependence on Russian energy for EU countries

supply risks, and the economic consequences of non-delivery. This index is calculated for each type of energy and not aggregated like many previous indices. Unsurprisingly, their calculations show major risks for Germany and Italy in terms of gas but also for France and Spain in terms of crude oil. One conclusion of their study is that the risk profiles of the various EU countries make it more difficult to arrive at a common energy policy in the EU. Although this was written back in 2008, this index is an important analytical tool for the time of Russia's invasion of Ukraine.

Russia's Dependence on Energy Exports in General and to the EU in Particular

Russia's economy is heavily dependent on energy exports, mainly oil and gas, while coal exports are much smaller. Although the volume of energy exports has been relatively stable, its value varies significantly with market prices. When energy prices were high in 2011–13, oil and gas accounted for two-thirds of Russia's merchandise exports by value. In 2021, oil and gas exports accounted for approximately half of the value of Russia's goods exports. Revenues from oil exports are in the order of 10% of Russian GDP, while the value of gas exports is around 4 percent. For Russia's GDP, it is evident that this export is crucial for economic growth.

Russia used to sell its oil on the spot market at the current market price which made it dependent on what happens to the world market price of oil. Admittedly, as the producer of 11% of the world's oil, Russia might marginally influence the international oil price in the short term, not least since it became a more active part of the negotiations of the Organization for the Petroleum Exporting Countries, OPEC+. But by and large, Russia is a price taker in the international commodity market and sells its oil at the price offered. Therefore, the Russian macroeconomic development is not controlled by the leaders in the Kremlin or anyone else in Russia, but by what is happening on the world market.

There are few countries where so much of the growth is dependent on a single exogenous variable as is the case of Russia and international oil price. Since the mid-1990s until 2021, 70 percent of Russian growth can be derived from changes in international oil prices. Since the Crimean invasion in 2014, this percentage has risen to 90 percent (see Becker, 2016 and 2017). This concentration has been maintained despite repeated discussions of diversification and modernization of the Russian economy and a move to a floating exchange rate when oil prices plummeted in 2014 (which was not a function of Russia's illegal annexation of Crimea but the level of global demand). From 2020 to 2021, dollar earnings for oil exports rose by 50% and for gas earnings by more than 100% even though volumes were almost unchanged, i.e. the entire change was due to rising international prices. This leads to some problems regarding how to interpret Russia's real economic development (Becker, 2021a).

The Russian state budget is also heavily dependent on raw material exploitation and exports and thus on what happens with international oil prices. Between 2020 and 2021, government revenues increased by 90 percent in nominal ruble terms or 65 percent in real terms. Given how difficult it is to forecast changes in oil prices, this creates great uncertainty regarding the state's income, whose revenues from extraction and export taxes on oil and gas varied from just under 30% to 50 % between 2017 and 2021. Changes in oil prices also affect the exchange rate and inflation which in turn affect the work both of the Central Bank and the Ministry of Finance.

The state's income is strongly associated with exports to the EU countries, which is why the EU's dependence on Russian energy has a clear counterpart in Russia's dependence on the EU as an export market; at least in the short and medium term. In 2020, EU countries bought a total of three-quarters of Russia's gas exports, half of Russia's crude oil exports, and basically all Russian exports of oil products. Russian statistics are not always consistent with those reported for the EU by Eurostat, so the numbers must be interpreted with some caution.

The Russian oil and coal companies act as individual sellers on the European market, while Gazprom has a monopoly on the sale of gas delivered through pipelines to Europe. This has led to gas sales being far more politicized than Russia's oil and coal exports. Since the EU does not act as a common buyer towards Russia (see Le Coq & Paltseva, 2012a) it is important to understand which EU countries are important buyers from the Russian perspective. Le Coq and Paltseva (2012b) also analyzed the risk with gas transits from Russia to the EU. Not unexpectedly, Germany is by a good margin Russia's most important customer in the EU. Figure 7.3 shows how much the EU countries paid for Russian energy divided into crude oil, oil products, and gas. In 2020, the estimated value of Germany's imports of Russian energy was $28 billion, or almost double that of the Netherlands in second place with imports worth about $15 billion. Since available statistics are only for quantities, dollar values are estimates based on average prices for different types of energy for corresponding periods. However, the Netherlands also exports a large part of its energy imports. In total, the EU imported energy from Russia to a value of almost $115 billion in 2020, while the corresponding figure for 2021 would have been about $185 billion if the EU's share of Russian exports was unchanged, i.e. an increase of more than 60% due to price increases. In other words, it is not only the Russian state budget and the economy that are exposed to the development of international energy prices, but also EU countries. With these large swings in energy prices it is not surprising that the European Central Bank and the central banks of the other EU countries are having difficulties to keep inflation within their target ranges.

Source: Eurostat, Central bank of Russia (cbr.ru), and authors' calculations.

A few EU countries made up a significant part of Russia's market in the EU. Figure 7.4 shows how large a share of Russia's total exports of various types of energy individual EU countries accounted for. The four largest importers of Russian energy in the EU, Germany, Italy, the

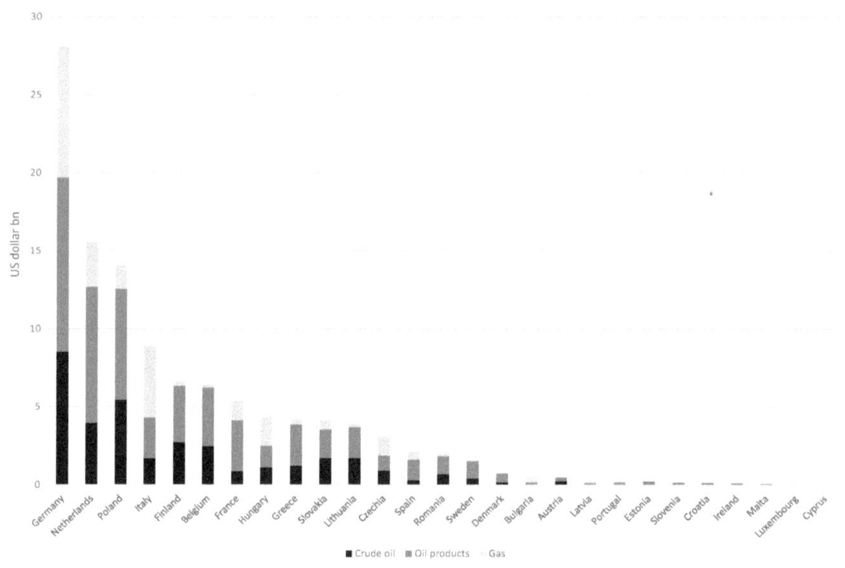

Fig. 7.3 Estimate of what EU countries paid Russia for energy in 2020

Netherlands, and Poland, accounted for more than half of the EU's Russian energy bill in 2020. Meanwhile, a dozen EU countries bought energy from Russia for less than a billion dollars. These large differences mean that the economic interests among EU countries and from the Russian side can create divisions in the EU and give Russia opportunities for bilateral negotiations with a few important EU countries that will not always focus on what is best for the EU as a collective. It was not only Hungary that contributed to division within the EU in terms of sanctions against Russia. Large countries such as Germany and the Netherlands were doubtful about a joint price ceiling for gas in 2022. In addition, Italy's government, headed by Prime Minister Georgia Meloni who took office in October 2022, had coalition partners that considered themselves personal friends of Vladimir Putin, while she did not. Writing about European energy cooperation at this time may seem like an afterthought, but Le Coq and Paltseva (2008) have argued for this for a very long time and it is high time that the EU countries make this a reality for the good of the Union. After Russia's invasion of Ukraine also Germany, the Netherlands and Italy have joined a broad EU consensus, while Hungary has remained a pro-Russian outlier.

Sanctions Against Russia After the 2014 Crimean Invasion

Russia had hardly expected such a strong and coordinated response to its renewed war of aggression against Ukraine in February 2022 from the EU, the United States, and many other countries. This was based on the Russian experience after the illegal annexation of Crimea and the subsequent war in Donbass in eastern Ukraine. The February 2014 invasion had indeed led to sanctions, but on a much more limited level. However, even these limited sanctions influenced Russian growth through increased uncertainty and lower investments (Becker, 2019 and 2021b). After the first EU meeting on March 3, 2014 after Russia's invasion of Crimea, EU leaders did indeed condemn Russia but emphasized that they would seek a peaceful solution that respected international laws with proposals that the OSCE should launch a "fact-finding mission" in Ukraine. The EU also declared that it would not participate in the planned G8 meeting in Sochi, Russia. Yet, this was not a forceful response to a Russian invasion of a European neighbour. At an extraordinary meeting for EU heads of

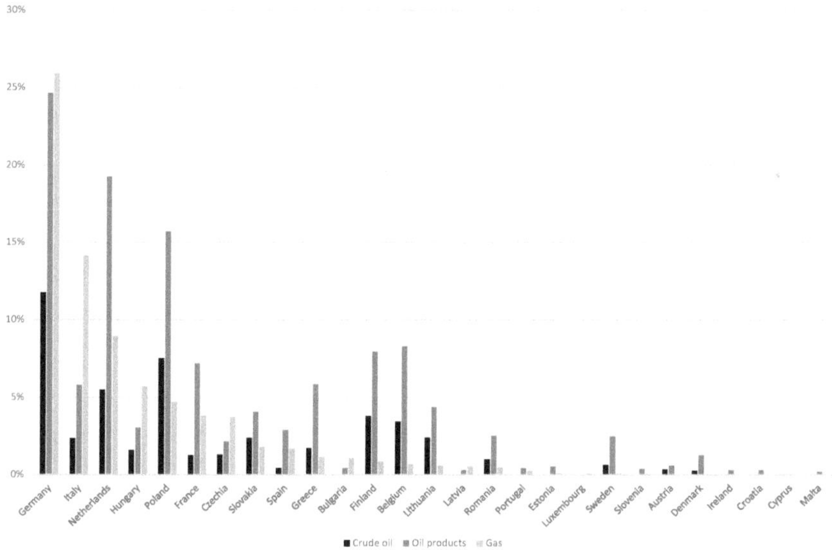

Fig. 7.4 EU countries' shares of total Russian energy exports in 2020. *Source* Eurostat, Central bank of Russia (cbr.ru), and authors' calculations

government, the Prime Minister of Ukraine participated, but the conclusions were still that there would be an attempt at a dialogue between Russia and Ukraine in where the EU could participate.

Only at a meeting on March 17, 2014, the EU imposed sanctions against 21 individuals who were involved in the illegal referendum in Crimea (EU Foreign Affairs Council, 2014a). On March 20, a few more individuals were added to the EU's sanctions list and the planned EU-Russia summit was canceled. The EU announced that member states would also not hold any bilateral summits. The EU also put on the table that if Russia continued to "destabilise" Ukraine, there may be economic sanctions against Russia. After further meetings on sanctions, it took until June 23 for the EU to ban imports of goods from occupied Crimea and a few days later to sign the Association Agreement with Ukraine (EU Foreign Affairs Council, 2014b). In mid-July, the European Investment Bank (EIB) was stopped from further investments in Russia and the European Development Bank (EBRD) as well as bilateral financiers were called on to stop implementing projects in Russia.

On July 17, 2014, the Malaysia Airlines flight MH17 was shot down by Russia over eastern Ukraine—which resulted in nearly 300 deaths (of which roughly 200 from EU countries). Then, the tone regarding the need for EU sanctions was sharpened. On July 29, the first more extensive economic sanctions from the EU against Russia were launched (European Council, 2014). They had been coordinated with US sanctioned two weeks earlier and targeted three sectors—finance, military technology, and oil technology. They included certain restrictions on the maturity with which Russian state financial institutions could finance themselves on the EU's capital markets, bans on the import and export of military equipment, and bans on the export of other technology that can be used for military purposes ("dual-use goods"). Technology for the oil sector focused on deep sea, arctic, and shale extraction was also limited. These sanctions were slightly tightened in September 2014, but no more extensive financial sanctions were launched. In the years leading up to Russia's full-scale attack on Ukraine in 2022, some individuals and companies were added to the sanctions lists and the (very limited) economic sanctions were extended but no more extensive sanctions were added during the period.

Sanctions Against Russia, 2022

In late 2021, Russia built up a large military force on the border with Ukraine (Congressional Research Service, 2022). The US and allied intelligence services stated openly that this was a preparation of another attack on Ukraine. Discussions in the West started about potential sanctions against Russia, including stopping Nord Stream 2, if Russia went further in its war preparations. In January 2022, the United States stated that it, together with partner countries, was ready to impose comprehensive sanctions on Russia, far beyond what it had done in 2014 and that this time there would be no question of an escalation of sanctions, but comprehensive sanctions would immediately follow a Russian attack (The New York Times, 2022). However, many in the West as well as in Russia and Ukraine did not believe that Russia would carry out a full-scale attack on Ukraine, and several Western leaders went to Moscow to hold talks with Putin in order to avoid a war. Apparently, the Kremlin did not take the threat of far greater Western sanctions seriously and launched its invasion on February 24, 2022.

Some did see the war coming; for example, Gudrun Persson, a researcher at the Swedish Defence Research Agency (FOI), announced at the People and Defense conference on February 3, 2022 that "no one can say that we didn't know anything". In December 2021, Russia had escalated its political demands, insisting that the West should accommodate Russian interests not only to stop NATO enlargement but to reduce NATO (Reuters, 2021).

On February 21, Putin recognized the so-called People's Republics of Donetsk and Luhansk. Germany responded by halting the certification of Nord Stream 2. The next day, on February 23, the EU agreed on a first package of sanctions that targeted Duma parliamentarians and economic relations with Donetsk and Luhansk.[1] But on February 24, Russia nevertheless launched its full-scale assault on Ukraine.

On February 25, the EU immediately responded with a second package of sanctions which, among other things, froze Putin and Lavrov's assets in the EU and included personal sanctions against Russia's Security Council. Sanctions were introduced against financial transactions with Russian counterparties, against the oil sector, against the aviation industry and the sale of spare parts for Russian aircraft, extended sanctions against "dual-use" technological exports, as well as aggravating visa rules for Russian officials and business persons.

Already on February 28, the EU introduced a third package of sanctions, which, among other things, prevented transactions with Russia's central bank and froze its foreign exchange reserves within the EU. All Russian aircraft were banned from taking off, landing, and flying over the EU, and the EU funded lethal military equipment to Ukraine for the first time. It might appear a bit late as the sanctions after the Crimean invasion, but these sanctions were far more serious. They were welcomed by Ukraine and probably came as a surprise to the Russian leadership. A few days later, the EU added new sanctions to the third sanctions package that excluded seven Russian banks from SWIFT, the international messaging system for financial transactions, further financial restrictions, and stopped Russia Today (RT) and Sputnik, Russian state-funded propaganda channels in the EU. Sanctions were added against Belarus because it allowed Russia to use its territory for the attack against Ukraine and against a

[1] For a timeline of sanctions imposed by the EU, see https://www.consilium.europa.eu/en/policies/sanctions/restrictive-measures-against-russia-over-ukraine/history-restrictive-measures-against-russia-over-ukraine/.

number of so-called oligarchs and politicians in Russia. The severe EU sanctions against Russia's central bank and the exclusion of Russian banks from SWIFT came as a surprise to most.

On March 15, the EU delivered a fourth package of sanctions. It targeted Russian state-owned enterprises, the financial sector via credit rating agencies, and investments in the Russian energy sector. In addition, more people classified as oligarchs and lobbyists were sanctioned. The EU also initiated processes within the World Trade Organization (WTO) to remove rules that favour Russia's foreign trade and pause Belarus' application for membership in the organization.

Barely a month later, on April 8, the EU delivered its fifth package of sanctions against Russia. For the first time, the EU sanctions targeted Russian energy exports to the EU through an EU import ban on Russian coal. However, this ban was of little economic importance as coal can be imported from many other countries. The EU also banned shipments by land and sea from Russia and Belarus to the EU and added a number of other goods to the import ban list (cement, wood, seafood, and spirits). The export ban to Russia was extended and several Russian banks were shut out of the EU and had their assets in the EU frozen. More individuals who were considered complicit in the war or who may be involved in circumventing the sanctions imposed were also added to the sanctions lists.

In early June 2022, the sixth EU package of sanctions against Russia arrived with a significant energy component, namely an EU embargo on the import of crude oil and refined oil products from Russia. This is the part of Russia's foreign trade that has the greatest economic value of all products traded between Russia and the EU. It has an annual trade of about 100 billion dollars, depending on the year's international oil prices. But the process of shutting off the Russian oil takes time and a phase-out period of 6–8 months was part of the package with additional exceptions for countries that received their oil via pipelines. Thus, at the beginning of 2023, the EU's oil embargo was still a threat rather than a reality for Russia. This round of sanctions also added Russia's largest bank, Sberbank, to the list of Russian banks suspended from SWIFT.

The seventh sanctions package from the EU on July 21, 2022 was officially called a "maintenance and alignment package". It focused on transactions in gold (and precious stones) from Russia to limit another source of income that could generate international currency. The EU also made clear that it did not target Russian food exports as food exports from both Ukraine and Russia had become an important part of the global discourse among poorer countries outside the EU, not least in Africa. This package indicated that the EU had lost momentum. Everyone knows that oil and gas are the most important subjects, but the EU had failed to agree on such sanctions. Hungary, in particular, opposed any sanctions against oil and gas, but it also received support from Germany and other central European countries heavily dependent on Russian energy exports. The US had already banned all imports of Russian energy to the US on March 8, 2022, but it was easier for the US because it had not imported much Russian energy.

At the beginning of October 2022, Russia annexed additional parts of Ukraine in violation of international law, which led to a new package of sanctions on October 6. The EU laid the foundation for a price ceiling for the export of Russian oil to countries outside the EU together with restrictions on maritime transport of Russian oil. It added new goods that the EU should not import or export to Russia and more individuals directly involved in the illegal Russian activities in Ukraine were also sanctioned. With this, the sanctions work within the EU gained new momentum after a few months of silence. However, it took until December 3 before a price cap of 60 dollars per barrel for Russian seaborn oil was agreed upon with the so-called Price Cap Coalition (PCC) that includes G7 countries, the EU, and Australia. The reinforcement mechanism is tied to maritime services, in particular insurance and reinsurance, provided by companies in the PCC.

A ninth sanctions package was then announced on December 16, which focused on four areas. First, several individuals and organizations were added to the list subject to freezing of assets. Many directly connected to the Russian armed forces and military-industrial complex. Then the package introduced additional export bans on dual-use and other technologies and services that are used in the production of drones and other military equipment and also the export of drone engines through third countries such as Iran. More banks were also added to the list of entities with transaction bans and four additional media channels were also sanctioned.

Sanctions package ten followed on February 25, 2023, exactly one year after the second package that was introduced on the first day after Russia's full-scale attack on Ukraine. The first part of the package listed more Russian individuals and entities focusing on politicians, government officials, and military leaders but also individuals from Iran and members of the Wagner mercenary group. The list of sensitive and dual-use goods with export bans to Russian was also extended to trucks and various industrial goods. At the same time, more Russian high-value goods were banned from import to the EU. The packages also focused on limiting circumvention possibilities and a reporting requirement on Russian central bank assets, which is an important first step in not only freezing but later transferring central bank assets to Ukraine.

On June 23, the eleventh package was adopted by the EU. The focus was on reducing the possibilities to circumvent trade sanctions and the packages included restrictions on Russian transports by land and sea. The package also ended the possibility to import oil via pipeline to Germany and Poland, further underlining the EU's move away from Russian energy. Later in August, additional sanctions were introduced to make it harder to circumvent sanctions via Belarus.

EU's sanctions against Russia are coordinated and largely in line with the sanctions imposed by the US and other G7 countries. Yet, many countries, not least China and India, have not imposed sanctions against Russia but instead take advantage of the sanctions imposed by the EU and other countries. These countries have bought Russian oil at deep discounts and continued to do so after the formal price cap was introduced. This is in line with the PCC sanction and helps preserve stability on the international oil market. However, when it comes to exports to Russia, these countries together with Turkey and Central Asian countries clearly help Russia buy some of the high-tech and dual-use goods they cannot produce at home.

If the Russian war of aggression continues, we can expect more sanctions packages against Russia. An important part of the work on developing effective sanctions is done by the group coordinated by the former American ambassador to Moscow Michael McFaul, who is now a Professor at the Stanford University, and the head of the presidential administration of Ukraine, Andriy Yermak, and goes under the guise of The International Working Group on Russian Sanctions.[2] The group is now working on several proposals for more specific areas and with the aim of closing various loopholes in the sanctions that have already been introduced.

[2] Both authors of this chapter participate in the group's discussions and have contributed to various working papers.

The EU is determined to reduce its consumption of Russian oil and gas in the medium term. The European Commission set a target to reduce gas imports from Russia by two-thirds by the end of 2022, which was achieved. By the second quarter of 2023, EU had made significant progress in weaning itself off Russian energy; only 2.7 percent of EU imports of petroleum oil came from Russia compared with almost 16 percent in the second quarter of 2022. For pipeline gas, the import share from Russia declined from 28.3 percent in the second quarter of 2022 to 13.8 percent by the second quarter of 2023 and for LNG from 15.2 to 12.4 percent. Finally, for coal, the share of imports to the EU from Russia went from 32.8 percent to zero over the same period (Eurostat, 2023a).

Russia's Response to EU Sanctions

Russia's response to EU sanctions has varied in strength and clarity. One response to Western sanctions is that Russia has prevented trade and financial transactions with individuals and companies from "unfriendly" countries, i.e. countries that have imposed sanctions against Russia, which includes the member states of the EU, the US, and other countries in the West as well as Japan.[3]

In terms of energy transactions, the most notable counter-sanction is that on March 31, 2022, Russia required payments for gas to be made in rubles.[4] When countries like Poland and Bulgaria refused to pay in rubles, their gas supplies were cut off, and the same happened to Finland, Denmark, the Netherlands, and Latvia. Russia also imposed sanctions on a number of companies in the energy sector in the EU, the US, and other countries, including Gazprom's former subsidiary in Germany. Energy companies from Germany, Hungary, France, and Italy instead chose to carry out transactions in rubles via Gazprom's bank, which was not sanctioned by the EU, and the European Commission did not get involved - presumably because these countries were too influential in the Union.

All major European energy companies operating in Russia have declared that they intend to leave Russia and have done so to varying

[3] Russian Government's Order No. 430-r of March 5, 2022, and Russian President's Decree No. 95 of March 5, 2022.

[4] Russian President's Decree No. 172 of March 31, 2022.

degrees. Putin threatened to nationalize abandoned energy resources, and he has done so with Shell's gas extraction on the Russian island of Sakhalin, UNIPER, and Fortnum. Russia will presumably continue to nationalize all major abandoned energy companies.

Initially, Russia did not try to reduce its oil exports, but in October 2022, OPEC+, which includes Russia, concluded that their combined production should decrease by 2 million barrels per day due to "economic factors" (OPEC, 2022). The US has so far unsuccessfully pressured Saudi Arabia and other countries to prevent this from happening, as it drives up the world market price of oil, but with little or no success.

Although OPEC+ negotiations are political, Russian oil exports beyond these negotiations have taken place in a relatively free market, while Russian gas exports have been much more politicized. For years, Russia has limited its gas supplies via the large pipeline through Ukraine. Now Gazprom has also stopped its deliveries through Belarus and Poland. After Germany blocked the newly built pipeline Nord Stream 2, Gazprom also cut its deliveries through Nord Stream 1. In a situation when no more gas was delivered through these pipelines, several of Nord Stream 1 and 2's pipelines burst just off the coast of Sweden in September 2022. The Nord Stream pipes will most likely not deliver any Russian gas for the foreseeable future even if they were repaired. Russian gas can be imported through Turkstream and the Ukrainian transit line, but this is a fraction of what Russia exported to the EU in previous years. Russian gas has become toxic as too political and too unreliable. To the surprise of many, the EU has succeeded to replenish its gas reserves from alternative sources, such as Norway and through a greatly increased import of liquefied natural gas, mainly from the US. It may seem strange that Russia is much more aggressive with gas than with oil, but gas deliveries are almost exclusively via pipelines and by state-controlled Gazprom, which has a long tradition of cutting off supplies for political reasons.

What is Happening in the EU?

For many years, the EU has discussed and planned its green energy transition and to simultaneously reduce its dependence on Russian fossil-based energy. This had no impact on the energy prices the EU paid. Gas prices were relatively constant and predictable, while oil prices fluctuated with global economic fluctuations and occasionally due to conflicts in the Middle East. As a result of the global COVID-19 pandemic, both oil and gas prices fell sharply in Europe in 2020. With the global economic recovery in 2021, prices turned upwards again. Oil prices followed their historical pattern, while gas prices in Europe skyrocketed towards previously unimagined heights. Just as other forces had set energy markets in motion before Russia invaded Crimea in 2014, other factors had been affecting energy markets even before Russia invaded all of Ukraine in February 2022.

In 2014, several factors coincided to cause the price of oil to drop like a stone; America's shale oil had made the country self-sufficient in oil, which created an oversupply in the market. When OPEC led by Saudi Arabia did not want to reduce its supply and lose market share at the same time as demand in Europe and China decreased, the prices of crude oil were depressed. The price drop was further reinforced by the fact that the dollar strengthened by 15–20 percent against other important currencies in the world. This matters as the oil market is priced in dollars but the consumers are in countries that use other currencies that have become less valuable.

In 2021, gas prices had already started to rise due to structural factors in the gas markets both in Europe and other parts of the world. Demand in Asia was high coming out of the COVID-19 pandemic, while gas deals in Europe had moved towards shorter contracts with prices based on spot prices. This led to a complicated market dynamic where Gazprom, thanks to its strong market position, was able to reduce supply and drive up spot prices. When customers in Europe turned to the market for liquefied natural gas, LNG, they faced competition from buyers in Asia. The reduced gas deliveries from Gazprom coincided with discussions about Nord Stream 2, which created further incentives for Russia to hold down deliveries.

Superficially, this can be explained by Gazprom's business interests, but this was also a way to reduce Ukraine's transit income and hurting Europe's economy with high gas prices, when Russia was preparing to invade Ukraine. Yet, it was not Western sanctions that drove up prices before the war started.

Gas prices in Europe have fluctuated greatly in recent years. In 2022, this drove the price of electricity to multiples of prior heights that led to support packages, tax adjustments, and subsidies around Europe. Gas contracts in Europe were traded in 2022 between 100 and 340 euros/MWh, which should be compared to the years before the pandemic when they were around 25 euros/MWh. Le Coq and Paltseva (2022) discuss what the gas crisis reveals more generally about energy security in the EU. The increased gas prices affected households as well as industry, not least in Germany, where large parts of the economy have been dependent on relatively cheap energy for their competitiveness at the same time as many households get their heat from gas. In 2023, European gas prices fell by 90 percent to a normal level as storage of gas before the winter season reached record levels in the EU (Reuters, 2023a).

Oil prices also rose sharply in 2022, but that trend started long before Russia's attack on Ukraine. The oil price bottom occurred during the 2020 pandemic when certain types of contracts briefly produced negative prices for oil but more generally only generated very low oil prices seen in our near term. From lows around $20 for Brent oil in 2020, oil prices rose to over $80 per barrel in early 2022. With Russia's invasion and subsequent sanctions, the price of oil skyrocketed further, passing $120 per barrel before oil prices turned downward. During the autumn of 2022 and afterwards, the oil price dropped to a level that was lower than before the outbreak of the war at about $80 per barrel. Nevertheless, many voices are heard in the EU that this is too high an oil price and the question is what it means for consumers and companies in the EU? Obviously, many motorists and transport companies in the EU pay a lot for their petrol and diesel, but the price of crude oil was at the same level in 2013 and even higher before the global financial crisis in 2008 when the price of crude oil was more than $140 per barrel. After the period of declining international oil prices in the second half of 2022 prices then started to increase again in the summer of 2023 after output cuts by OPEC. Later in the fall, the prices again fell and instead of surpassing $100 per barrel as some feared it reversed back to $85 per barrel but with significant uncertainty remaining about the longer-term trend as OPEC did not manage to agree on further cuts in production and there are worries about a global recession (Reuters, 2023b).

EU leaders and member states have tried in different ways to deal with the price increases for energy and have made plans for how reduced flows from Russia can be replaced with other suppliers and a changed energy mix. On March 8, 2022, the EU held a meeting where the President of the European Commission, Ursula von der Leyen, said that EU member states must become independent from Russian oil, gas, and coal, diversify energy sources and speed up the green transition. Given the way Russia has behaved, this seems to be the natural outcome. Who dares to trust Russian energy anymore?

The European Commission was tasked with drawing up a plan to achieve it which was presented on 18 May 2022 and goes by the name REPowerEU (European Union, 2022). The goal is to phase-out dependence on Russian fossil energy through a combination of measures: saving energy, accelerating the transition to clean energy, and diversifying the EU's energy sources. The plan places great emphasis on justice and solidarity and on faster achievement of the climate goals the EU has set. The phasing out of Russian energy and the transition to renewable energy enjoys great popular support within the EU; and according to the European Commission's REPowerEU report, 85 percent of the respondents supported this change in an opinion poll (Eurobarometer, 2022).

Energy saving is the fastest measure, and much money can be saved according to the European Commission, which claims that the EU countries can save around 100 billion euros by stopping importing Russian energy. The EU Commission wants to achieve energy savings by raising the binding targets for energy efficiency. In addition, the EU must focus on changing consumer behaviour, which could reduce the consumption of oil and gas by 5 percent. This can be done by information and "nudging" (Le Coq, 2022).

Energy saving targets have been further tightened with the plan from July 2022 to reduce the EU's gas use by 15 percent. Given the differences that exist in terms of gas use in the EU countries, this plan met resistance from several countries, which led to several exceptions and compromises to get the proposal adopted. An important part of the plan is solidarity and coordination between the countries to cope with the reduction. Le Coq (2022) also discusses how market mechanisms can be used to reduce gas use, but this could in turn lead to further price increases for some consumers. If market solutions are also introduced nationally, it can affect solidarity within the EU to deal with reduced gas flows.

The European Commission intends to set aside an additional 200 billion euros until 2027 for investments to achieve the goals of the plan for alternative energy, but it will take time before these investments are implemented. Di Bella et al (2022) focused on what could happen at the macro level if natural gas deliveries from Russia decrease in various EU countries. For many countries in the EU, the estimated GDP loss was less than in connection with the COVID-19 pandemic and other crises the EU has gone through in recent decades. The study concluded that the EU could manage a 70 percent reduction in Russian gas supplies in the short term through a combination of other suppliers, switching gas to other energy sources, and reduced demand as a result of previously high prices. However, there would be major challenges if the gas from Russia is shut off completely. Yet, that was what happened in 2023, and the European spot market price of gas fell by some 90 percent from the peak of August 2022. This was due to a combination of factors that included a mild winter and a successful switch away from Russian gas to gas delivered by other countries, notably Norway and Algeria.

What Will the Effects Be for Russia?

The Russian economy has always been driven by international energy prices via export earnings and state budget revenues. With energy prices rising sharply in 2022 the Russian economy without sanctions could have flourished, with GDP growth returning to the levels of around 7–8 percent (based on calculations from a model in Becker, 2017) that Putin enjoyed in his first eight years as president before the global financial crisis hit in 2008.

The IMF's forecast for Russia in October 2022 (IMF, 2022) projected a decline of 3.4 percent for 2022 which later was revised to a 2.1 percent drop in GDP. In light of this, what is a realistic assessment of the immediate effect of sanctions? Any assessment of this need to start with a realistic counterfactual, which in this case is growth of 7 percent, so a 2 percent decline of GDP in 2022 means that the effect of sanctions that year was a 9 percentage point reduction in GDP.

In 2023, Russia's GDP is projected to grow by between 1 and 2 percent due to the massive fiscal stimulus the war implies. This can be funded in the short run by savings, but in the longer run, President Putin faces the challenges that savings will run out at the same time as capital, foreign companies, and highly productive people are leaving the country. Again, this is a very poor growth number in a normal year and a sign that sanctions are having a real (but perhaps too small) effect on Russian GDP.

Since 2009, Russia has faced major challenges to generate growth without support from rising international oil prices. In several reform programs, modernization and diversification have been discussed, but with the lack of fundamental reforms of legal certainty and property rights since 2002, the investments needed for a new growth model have not been generated. Åslund (2019) discusses how the Russian economy has transformed into a kleptocracy that lacks the law enforcement institutions that are so central for secure property rights in a market economy. Instead, many talented and successful Russian scientists and entrepreneurs have left the country to build businesses and fortunes in the West. Russia has tried to attract companies from the West to modernize its economy, but the war against Ukraine has effectively thwarted all these efforts and instead turned the flow of knowledge and capital out of Russia at breakneck speed. The start of the war on Ukraine and the mobilization in September 2022 are likely to have scared around 1 million highly qualified Russians to leave their country (The Economist, 2023).

The near stagnation that the IMF and others predict for the Russian economy for the coming years is likely to be a permanent deterioration of the Russian economy as long as the current leadership remains in power. It becomes clear once again that the economic prosperity of citizens is not at the top of the agenda of the Kremlin, although this is important for Putin's popularity in more normal times (Becker, 2019). The uncertainty that the Russian leadership already created after the invasion of Crimea in 2014 left its mark on the Moscow stock market, on investments and on the economic growth discussed above. When in the future we can analyze the full economic effect of the war, the economic costs will prove to be enormous.

In the fall of 2022, important changes occurred. First, Russian statistics-producing authorities became more restrictive about publishing data, which arouses the question of whether the data published is correct. This is a question that the much-paraphrased paper by Sonnenfeld et al (2022) addresses. Russia recorded an extraordinary current account surplus of $236 billion in 2022, but this was the result of very high prices for energy exports. Since the start of the war, exports from EU countries to Russia fell sharply, from €8.4 billion in January 2022 to €2.9 billion in June 2023, i.e., two-thirds of EU exports to Russia have gone over this period (Eurostat, 2023b). Thanks to the extremely high energy prices and maintained export volumes in 2022, Russia was not much hurt by the financial sanctions. The price cap for oil and the end of most gas exports to Europe in 2023 sharply changed the situation for the worse for Russia. The Kyiv School of Economics (2023) estimates that Russia lost 140 billion dollars in revenue due to sanctions on oil and gas.

In February 2022, Russia ended up in financial panic. For a month, the exchange rate of the freely floating ruble collapsed from 73 rubles per dollar to 135 rubles per dollar. The Central Bank of Russia reacted by shock-hiking the interest rate from 9.5 percent to 20 percent, and it worked. The ruble rose to some 55 rubles per dollar. In August 2023, however, the ruble has sunk again reaching 102 rubles per dollar. The causes are multiple. Russia has increased its budget deficit to increase military expenditures; the capital flight has been enormous, and it is still legal; the credibility of the Russian state has decreased. The Central Bank once again responded by raising the interest rate, but the outcome is not clear as yet. Thus, Russia's macroeconomic situation is unstable, but it cannot be excluded that the authorities manage to salvage the situation once again. However, using savings to wage a war while capital and people leave the country does not bode well for Russia's longer-term economic development and strength.

How the EU Can Manage the Energy Transition to Create Cohesion Within the Union and Security at the External Border

Russia's full-scale war compelled the EU to impose extensive sanctions against Russia. Although sanctions have not been able to immediately stop the Russian aggression, they have certainly weakened the Russian economy.

Perotta Berlin (2022) notes that when sanctions are introduced, the deterrent effects of threatened sanctions have by definition not worked. Studies of sanctions thus risk underestimating the effect of sanctions because their possible deterrent effect is often missed. In addition, if it is uncertain what sanctions may be imposed, a country's leaders may implement a policy that they will later regret but not be able to undo, which can again make sanctions look ineffective. When evaluating the effects of sanctions against Russia, the signalling effect they have had on other countries need to be included to provide a more complete evaluation of these sanctions.

When policymakers try to predict future sanctions on the basis of their past experiences, the lack of strong sanctions by the EU and other countries against Russia after the 2014 Crimean invasion may have contributed to Russia's full-scale attack on Ukraine in 2022. That Russia's military forces are not withdrawing when comprehensive sanctions are being implemented is hardly a sign that sanctions are ineffective but that Putin and his supporters realize that it would be a domestic political disaster to admit their miscalculations about both EU and Western collective sanctions as well as Ukraine's resistance. The EU response must be to stick to the current sanctions and prevent that they are being circumvented. How this could and should be done is a central part of the current policy discussion in the EU and other sanctions coalition partners and it is clear that it will involve a close dialogue with some of the countries that are currently part of rerouting trade to Russia.

As long as the war in Ukraine continues, Europe's sanctions against Russia and its energy sector have to become stricter. Although an outlier such as Hungary does not appreciate sanctions, the EU has more generally steered clear away from Russian energy. Through its countermeasures, Russia has reinforced EU unity by discrediting itself as a reliable energy supplier to Europe. Politically, this means that the Baltic States and Poland have won over Germany and Austria, who previously believed in Russia as an energy supplier. Therefore, it is likely that Europe will come closer together in its energy policy vis-à-vis Russia. It seems clear that Europe will reduce its imports of both Russian oil and gas over the next few years. Such a development is consistent with the EU's policy to gradually abandon fossil fuels. High energy prices push the EU in the same direction.

A strong cohesion within the EU is required to once and for all end the dependence on Russian energy and together convert the entire EU to green energy. In order for all member states to move in the same direction, financial transfers within the Union may be needed so that the transition does not become financially unmanageable for poorer countries or those countries that cannot easily become independent of Russian energy. This is an investment that will yield returns for generations to come in terms of both safety and environmental and climate goals and adds to the credibility of continued sanctions on Russian hydrocarbon-based energy.

The mutual energy dependence between the EU and Russia has created economic and political problems for both sides after Russia's renewed war on Ukraine. But the EU can deal with these problems by switching suppliers and energy types in a few years, which is in line with a necessary switch to fossil-free energy to meet the EU climate goals. Russia's transition, on the other hand, is much more complicated and deeply structural, and may take decades to implement with great financial costs for the Russian population. Russia's current leadership will find it difficult to manage the transition and Russia's dependence on the EU as a market for its energy could be the beginning of the end for Putin's regime. If it turns out that this leads to the fall of the Russian regime, the EU must be ready to support all the liberal and democratic forces that after all exist inside and outside of Russia and that in the future can work for a peaceful Russia at the EU's external border.

References

Åslund, A. (2019). *Russia's Crony Capitalism: The Path from Market Economy to Kleptocracy*. Yale University Press.

Åslund, A. (2022). "How to Win Friends and Drain Russia's War Machine," *Project Syndicate*, August 4.

Available at: https://ec.europa.eu/eurostat/statistics-explained/SEPDF/cache/46126.pdf

Balmaceda, M. M. (2013). *The Politics of Energy Dependency: Ukraine, Belarus, and Lithuania between Domestic Oligarchs and Russian Pressure*. University of Toronto Press.

Becker, T. (2016). "Russia and Oil — Out of Control", FREE policy brief, October 31.

Becker, T. (2017). "Russia: Macroeconomic challenges", Chapter 8 in *The Unwinding of the Globalist Dream: EU, Russia and China*. Reds. S. Rosefielde, M. Kuboniwa, S. Mizobata, K. Haba, World Scientific, Singapore.

Becker, T. (2019). "Russia's Real Cost of Crimean Uncertainty", FREE policy brief, June 10.

Becker, T. (2021a). "Understanding Russia's GDP Numbers in the COVID-19 Crisis", FREE policy brief, March 9.

Becker, T. (2021b). "Russia's Macroeconomy — A Closer Look at Growth, Investment and Uncertainty", Chapter 2 in *Putin's Russia—Economy, Defence and Foreign Policy*, Red. S. Rosefielde, World Scientific, Singapore.

Di Bella, G., M. Flanagan, K. Foda, S. Maslova, A. Pienkowski, M. Stuermer and F. Toscani (2022). "Natural Gas in Europe: The Potential Impact of Disruptions to Supply", IMF Working paper, 22/145, July, IMF, Washington D.C.

European Commission, Directorate-General for Energy (2019). *Clean energy for all Europeans*. Publications Office. https://data.europa.eu/doi/https://doi.org/10.2833/9937

Commission of the European Communities, (2009). " Commission staff working document on Article 22 of Directive 2003/55/EC concerning common rules for the internal market in natural gas and Article 7 of Regulation (EC) No 1228/2003 on conditions for access to the network for cross-border exchanges in electricity", Commission Staff Working Paper, SEC(2009)642 final, Brussels.

Congressional Research Service. (2022). Russian Military Buildup Along the Ukrainian Border. 7 February. CRS Insight Report. Available at: https://crsreports.congress.gov/product/pdf/IN/IN11806

Le Coq, C. and E. Paltseva (2012). "Buyer Power as a Tool for EU Energy Security", FREE policy brief, June 7.

Le Coq, C. and E. Paltseva (2022). "What does the Gas Crisis Reveal About European Energy Security?" FREE Policy Brief, January 24.

Le Coq, C. (2022). "Hedging EU's "Winter Risk" by Curbing Gas Demand: Solidarity, Nudge, and Market Solutions", FREE policy brief, July 27.

Council, E. (2014). *"Statement by the President of the European Council Herman Van Rompuy and the President of the European Commission in the name of the European Union on the agreed additional restrictive measures against Russia", Statement EUCO 158/14, July 29.*

The Economist. (2023). "Russians have emigrated in huge numbers since the war in Ukraine", August 23.

EU Foreign Affairs Council. (2014a). "Council condemns the illegal referendum in Crimea". 17 March. Available at: https://www.consilium.europa.eu/en/meetings/fac/2014/03/17/

EU Foreign Affairs Council. (2014b). "Council supports Kiev efforts for a peace plan". 23 June. Available at: https://www.consilium.europa.eu/en/meetings/fac/2014/06/23/

Eurobarometer. (2022). "EU's Response to the War in Ukraine". May 5.

Eurostat. (2023a). "EU Imports of Energy Products - Latest Developments". September.

Eurostat. (2023b). "EU Trade With Russia – Latest Developments". Eurostat Statistic Explained. Available at: https://ec.europa.eu/eurostat/statistics-explained/index.php?title=EU_trade_with_Russia_-_latest_developments#Main_product_groups_in_EU_exports_to_Russia

Gustafson, T. (2012). *The Bridge: Natural Gas in a Redivided Europe.* MA, Harvard University Press.

https://ec.europa.eu/info/strategy/priorities-2019-2024/european-green-deal/repowereu-affordable-secure-and-sustainable-energy-europe_en#:~:text=REPowerEU%20is%20the%20European%20Commission's%20plan%20to%20make%20Europe%20independent,as%20possible%20to%20support%20Ukraine

https://freepolicybriefs.org/2012/06/07/buyer-power-as-a-tool-for-eu-energy-security/

https://freepolicybriefs.org/2022/07/27/eu-winter-risk-gas-demand/

Le Coq, C., & Paltseva, E. (2008). Common Energy Policy in the EU: The Moral Hazard of the Security of External Supply. *SIEPS Report, 2008*, 1.

Le Coq, C., & Paltseva, E. (2012b). Assessing Gas Transit Risks: Russia vs. the EU. *Energy Policy, 4*, 642–650.

Nemtsov, B., & Milov, V. (2008). *Putin i Gazprom (Putin and Gazprom)*. Novaya Gazeta.

OPEC. (2022). "33rd OPEC and Non-OPEC Ministerial Meeting". Press Release. 5 October. Available at: https://www.opec.org/opec_web/en/press_room/7021.htm

Reuters. (2021). "Russia demands NATO roll back from East Europe and stay out of Ukraine". 17 December. Available at: https://www.reuters.com/world/russia-unveils-security-guarantees-says-western-response-not-encouraging-2021-12-17

Reuters. (2023a). "Europe's record gas inventories cap prices." 9 August. Available at: https://www.reuters.com/markets/commodities/europes-record-gas-inventories-cap-prices-2023-08-08/

Reuters. (2023b). "Oil settles down more than $5 as US data shows weak demand for gasoline". 4 October. Available at: https://www.reuters.com/markets/commodities/oil-rises-tightening-crude-supply-2023-10-04/

Sonnenfeld, J., S. Tian, F. Sokolowski, M. Wyrebkowski and M. Kasprowicz (2022). "Business Retreats and Sanctions Are Crippling the Russian Economy", July 19. Available at SSRN: https://ssrn.com/abstract=4167193 or https://doi.org/10.2139/ssrn.4167193

Stern, J. P. (2005). *The Future of Russian Gas and Gazprom*. Oxford University Press.

The Kyiv School of Economics. (2023). "Sanctions Impact Exports and the Ruble, but Continued Effectiveness Needs to Be Ensured". 21 September. Available at: https://kse.ua/about-the-school/news/kse-institute-s-russia-chartbook-sanctions-impact-exports-and-the-ruble-but-continued-effectiveness-needs-to-be-ensured/

The New York Times. (2022). "U.S. Sanctions Aimed at Russia Could Take a Wide Toll". 29 January. Available at: https://www.nytimes.com/2022/01/29/us/politics/russia-sanctions-economy.html

Union, E. (2022). *REPowerEU: Affordable, Secure and Sustainable Energy for Europe*. European Commission.

CHAPTER 8

The EU's Fight against Money Laundering and Terrorist Financing in a Digital and Fragmented World

Maria Bergström

Introduction

Money laundering (ML) poses a clear and present threat to citizens, democratic institutions and the financial system. The rules to prevent dirty money from being laundered through the financial system have today grown into an extensive regulatory framework, and do not only apply to European Union (EU) Member States, as similar regulations exist at both global and regional level in many other parts of the world.

There is no accepted international definition of ML and the term has only existed for about 40 years. However, what is typically understood by ML is the handling of money derived from crime, which is often the result of or prerequisite for illicit trafficking or other transnational criminal activities.

M. Bergström (✉)
Faculty of Law, Uppsala University, Uppsala, Sweden
e-mail: maria.bergstrom@jur.uu.se

A. Bakardjieva Engelbrekt et al. (eds.), *The Borders of the European Union in a Conflictual World*,
https://doi.org/10.1007/978-3-031-54200-8_8

The fight against ML and terrorist financing (TF) is crucial for ensuring financial stability and security in Europe. The complex issue of dealing with dirty money flows is not new. Within the EU, anti-money laundering (AML) rules were introduced as compensatory measures when the borders between EU Member States were removed and the internal market began to be realised from the early 1980s onwards. The free movement of capital and financial services and increased cross-border trade also brought new opportunities for criminal actors and networks.

In order to protect the EU's financial interests and maintain sound financial systems, the EU AML framework has been closely linked to the Union's efforts to combat the financing of terrorism. The EU regulatory framework is today a central part of the EU's security policy, and the EU's AML rules are now among the toughest in the world (European Commission, 2021b). Despite this, we have also seen a number of recent examples of ML scandals. With the increased digitalisation and fragmentation of key parts of our modern world, newly updated regulatory frameworks are facing rapidly accelerating challenges.

In sum, ML constitutes a 'chameleon threat', as Valsamis Mitsilegas so aptly described it (Mitsilegas, 2003a), which must be constantly combated, because ML facilitates new forms of illegal and criminal activity, such as drug trafficking in the 1980s, organised crime in the 1990s, and after 11 September 2001, also terrorism.

This chapter, which builds on my previous research in the field,[1] is based on a historical and contextual presentation where the development of the EU regulatory framework against ML and TF is placed in its historical context and is described in terms of the different threats, interests and actors involved. A selection of analytical and partly overlapping perspectives with specific challenges for the emerging regulatory framework is continuously identified and presented: Firstly, the increase in private–public cooperation where private actors have been involved in shaping the regulatory framework and been assigned "policing" tasks. Secondly,

[1] There is an extensive body of literature and public sources dealing with the fight against money laundering and terrorist financing. Using the author's previous publications in the field, this chapter takes the underlying aims, the development of the regulatory framework at different levels, as well as the interests and actors involved, as a starting point for a historical and contextual analysis. For this reason, reference is made to these partially overlapping sources for further reading. Additional sources can be found in these publications.

the exchange of information and the specific challenges posed by digitalisation. Thirdly, the interaction between administrative law and criminal law and different types of sanctions. Fourthly, the increased focus on EU security policy and the long-standing so-called securitisation of ML and TF, which has led, among other things, to an increased competence for the EU institutions to regulate this area.

The questions this chapter asks and tries to answer are thus: How has the regulatory framework against ML and TF evolved in relation to globalisation, as well as the theme of this volume, the renewed importance of borders and a consequential real or apparent regulatory fragmentation? What analytical perspectives and legal challenges can be identified when studying this development? What shortcomings and legal challenges remain, and are they addressed by the existing and recently updated instruments as well as recent legislative proposals, or is there room for further reform?

These analytical and partly overlapping perspectives will be addressed in the historical and contextual presentation of this chapter after a brief presentation of the EU acquis in a global context, describing parallel developments at the EU level, followed by current reform proposals, and finally, the new EU legislative package and remaining challenges.

The EU Regulatory Framework in a Global Context

Although ML is an international phenomenon that has been a major problem around the world for a long time, the phenomenon and the concept have only come to prominence in the last 40 years. Although the term ML was used in the past, it was introduced into legislation only in 1986 in the US ML Control Act. In the beginning, ML was mainly recognised as a domestic problem, but the dirty money laundered often came, and still comes today, from drug trafficking, human trafficking and other cross-border criminal activities.

At the same time, ML is a crime that hinders the proper functioning of financial systems. As the International Monetary Fund has pointed out, possible consequences of ML and TF include risks to the soundness and stability of financial institutions and systems, increased volatility of international capital flows and a dampening effect on foreign direct investment (International Monetary Fund, 2023). In this respect, ML poses a particular threat as a sound financial infrastructure is one of the fundamental elements of a stable society. With increased economic globalisation, national borders became less relevant also for financial transactions. Taken together, the threats of ML and the emerging AML Regulation have gradually become transnational and global, which also has a significant impact on the regional and national levels.

In 1988, ML was recognised as a global problem with the prohibition of laundering of drug proceeds in the UN Convention against Illicit Traffic in Narcotic Drugs and Psychotropic Substances (Vienna Convention, 1988). However, the Vienna Convention was limited to drugs and did not refer specifically to the concept of ML. In the same year, principles on ML were also adopted by the Basel Committee on Banking Supervision (BCBS, 1988). This body is made up of banking supervisory authorities in a number of states and aims to develop common standards for the supervision of banking and financial institutions. The 1990 Council of Europe Convention on Laundering, Search, Seizure and Confiscation of the Proceeds from Crime (Strasbourg Convention, 1990) is the first multilateral treaty dealing with ML offences in general (Kersten, 2002). The Strasbourg Convention also extended the so-called predicate offences, i.e., the types of offences that can form the basis of ML offences, to go beyond drug trafficking. In 1998, the Organisation of Economic Cooperation and Development (OECD, 1998) presented a series of recommendations on harmful tax practices. In 1999, the UN International Convention for the Suppression of the Financing of Terrorism was adopted (UN Convention, 1999), and in 2000 the UN General Assembly adopted the UN Convention against Transnational Organized Crime (UN Convention, 2000).

The Council of Europe Convention on Laundering, Search, Seizure and Confiscation of the Proceeds from Crime and on the Financing of Terrorism (Warsaw Convention, 2005) builds on and updates the 1990 Strasbourg Convention and is the most comprehensive international convention on ML. It aims to facilitate international cooperation and mutual assistance in criminal investigations. The Convention contains not only provisions on the criminalisation of ML but also provisions on the freezing and confiscation of assets. The Warsaw Convention is the first international convention covering both the prevention and control of ML and TF. The adoption of the Warsaw Convention reflects the importance of timely access to financial information or information on assets held by criminal organisations.

Today, the Financial Action Task Force (FATF) is the most important international standard-setter for combating ML and TF. FATF was established in response to the G7's recognition of the threat that ML poses to banks and other financial institutions (Winer, 2002). FATF is thus a part, albeit independent, of the OECD (Bergström, 2013). The FATF currently consists of 38 member jurisdictions and two regional organisations, representing most major financial centres in all parts of the world including Hong Kong, Japan, Singapore, the United Kingdom and the United States. Members include the European Commission and fourteen Member States, but also, up until 24 February 2023, Russia, when membership was suspended after the Russian Federation's "illegal, unprovoked and unjustified full-scale military invasion of Ukraine" (FATF, 2023a). The remaining thirteen Member States, which have been part of the EU since 2004 onwards, are members of Moneyval, which is a FATF-type regional body that carries out self-assessments and mutual assessments of the measures taken in the Member States of the Council of Europe. The members of Moneyval also include, for example, Ukraine (MONEYVAL, 2023).

The FATF recommendations on ML were first issued in 1990, and the current version from 2012 was last amended in November 2023 (FATF, 2023b). They cover both administrative and criminal law measures to combat ML. With the first revisions in 1996, the 40 FATF recommendations were extended beyond the laundering of drug proceeds, and after 9/11, 2001, FATF explicitly extended its recommendations to TF. As a result, FATF's preventive measures now include not only the use of money derived from crime, but also the collection of money or property for terrorist purposes.

The method of mutual evaluation used is that FATF sets standards, model rules, or recommendations, and then evaluates Member States against these. The FATF methodology was adopted in February 2013 and last updated in June 2023 (FATF, 2023c). It operates through peer-review: panels of national legal and banking experts are set up, which then regularly evaluate the laws and practices of other states. FATF applies sanctions in the form of warnings to states deemed not to comply with the non-binding FATF standards. This results in significantly higher transaction costs for financial institutions in the blacklisted state, as financial institutions in other FATF states require greater security when dealing with them. This type of blacklisting partly explains a relatively high level of compliance with FATF standards. As far as EU Member States are concerned, the standards are binding, as they have been transposed into EU law by a wide range of directives and regulations concerning ML (Bergström, 2013).

Compensatory Measures when Borders were Removed

In a European context, the justification for introducing the first AML Directive (1AMLD, 1991) in 1991 was that the emergence of the European internal market, with European rules on financial transactions and the abolition of national borders, required compensatory measures to curb cross-border financial crime (Bergström, 2016). The purpose of the 1AMLD was therefore to prevent an open and liberal financial market, including the free movement of capital and the freedom to provide financial services, from being used for ML purposes.

The 1AMLD was strongly influenced by international rules and was based on the 40 original FATF recommendations and influenced by UN conventions and the recommendations and principles adopted by the Council of Europe and the BCBS. The definition of ML was taken from the Vienna Convention. The preamble to the 1AMLD stated that ML must be combated mainly by means of criminal law and within the framework of international cooperation between judicial and law enforcement authorities. Despite this, as the EU lacked criminal law competence at the time, it adopted the directive invoking as legal bases the right of establishment, and the establishment and functioning of the internal market.

The preamble further stated that ML has a clear impact on the emergence of organised crime in general and drug trafficking in particular and that there is a growing awareness that combating ML is one of the most effective means of combating this form of crime, which constitutes a particular danger to society in the Member States. According to the Directive, a criminal law approach should not be the only way to combat ML, as the financial system can play a highly effective role.

In 2001, the Second AML Directive (2AMLD, 2001) was adopted, amending the first. The 2AMLD referred in particular to the extended definition of ML, beyond drug offences as predicate offences. The Directive identified the fight against organised crime as an objective particularly closely linked to AML measures. The directive contained a long list of acts to be considered criminal offences when committed intentionally, which has since been extended to also prevent TF.

Extension towards Terrorist Financing and Enhancing the Role of Private Actors

In order to protect the EU's financial interests and maintain sound financial systems, the EU AML framework has been closely linked to the Union's efforts to counter TF. After 9/11, 2001, the FATF explicitly extended its recommendations to TF and in October 2001 adopted eight specific recommendations to this end (FATF, 2023b, p. 7). According to these, each country should take immediate steps to ratify and implement the 1999 UN International Convention for the Suppression of the Financing of Terrorism, and to implement the UN Resolutions on the Prevention and Suppression of the Financing of Terrorist Acts. Each country should criminalise the financing of terrorism, terrorist acts and terrorist organisations, and ensure that such offences are classified as predicate offences for ML. FATF also agreed on rules on freezing and confiscation of terrorist assets, reporting suspicious transactions related to terrorism, international cooperation, alternative remittance, wire transfers, and non-profit organisations. In 2004, a ninth specific recommendation on cash couriers was drawn up to ensure that terrorists and other criminals cannot finance their activities or launder the proceeds of crime through the physical cross-border transport of currency and bearer-negotiable instruments (FATF, 2023b, p. 7 and 25).

The adoption of the Third AML Directive (3AMLD, 2005) in 2005 brought regional EU rules into line with FATF's comprehensive, revised and extended recommendations. As a result, the preventive measures in the directive now covered not only the handling of money derived from crime, but also the collection of money or property for terrorist purposes. In addition to extending the provisions to all financial transactions that may be linked to terrorist activities, the biggest change in the 3AMLD and the solution to the problem of ML was to establish a standard for risk analysis (Herlin-Karnell, 2011). The starting point was that the risks differ between countries, customers and business areas as well as over time. The operators themselves are the best analysts of where the risk areas are, or may arise, because they know their business and their customers best. Under a risk-based approach, companies are expected to carry out risk assessments of their customers and divide them into low- and high-risk categories. As a result, the concept of "know your customer", used in the financial sector, became de facto applicable to everyone covered by the directive.

One of the reasons for more actively involving the private sector in AML was to gain better access to knowledge about the activities of actors who may be involved in illegal behaviour. It is for the private sector to collect appropriate information and decide when suspicious transaction reports should be made. At the beginning of AML regulations, private actors were only part of the public sector in preventing ML offences. However, the shift to the risk-based approach had major consequences for the relationship between private and public actors. A natural part of this change was the expansion of the "policing" tasks of private actors, which have always played an important role in crime prevention. Focusing on this shift of responsibility to the private sector and on the consequent increase in private–public partnerships is therefore an important perspective in the analysis of EU policy against ML and TF (Bergström, 2011; Bergström et al., 2011).

Private actors are not only expected to work against money launderers and report suspicious transactions under threat of administrative and criminal sanctions. They are also actively involved in shaping the underlying rules and procedures at different levels. In addition to the public initiatives of the international and regional supervisors, banking organisations have been involved in the regulation. The current Basel III is a comprehensive set of reform measures developed by the Basel Committee to strengthen the regulation, supervision and risk management of the banking sector. One of the most striking features of the EU AML framework is therefore the intensified multi-level cooperation between public and private actors, where traditional public tasks are shared by public and private actors. As a result, this area of law is extremely complex, involving international, EU-based and national actors and regulations, covering public, private and criminal law rules as well as enforcement mechanisms (Bergström, 2018a).

The risk-based approach introduced by the revised FATF Recommendations and 3AMLD was further developed in 2015 in the Fourth AML Directive (4AMLD, 2015) towards a more targeted and focused risk-based approach with evidence-based decision-making, to better target risk. It further provided guidance from European supervisory authorities, with their increased focus on the effectiveness of AML/CFT (Countering the Financing of Terrorism) systems, and addressed the shortcomings of the 3AMLD identified by the European Commission (European Commission, 2012). According to the Council, the strengthened rules reflected the need for the EU to adapt its legislation to take account of technological developments and other means at the disposal of criminals.

In February 2016 the European Commission adopted an Action Plan (European Commission, 2016a) to better counter TF and to ensure greater transparency of financial transactions following the revelations in the so-called Panama Papers. This was a coordinated action with the G20 and the OECD aimed at directly and vigorously combating tax evasion by both legal and natural persons in order to create a fairer and more efficient tax system. In this respect, it is part of a broader EU effort to improve tax transparency and tackle tax evasion (European Commission, 2016b).

In December 2016, the Council adopted a compromise text aimed at amending the 4AMLD. Although the objective of combating tax evasion was no longer explicitly mentioned, tools designed to achieve this aim remained, albeit slightly modified. The previous directives were repealed on 26 June 2017, when the 4AMLD was to be implemented by Member States. The scope of the directive was extended in several ways: by lowering the threshold for cash payments, which triggers reporting obligations, from EUR 15,000 to EUR 10,000, by including providers of gambling services in the scope of the directive and by including tax crimes as a new predicate offence. In addition, the 4AMLD incorporated new data protection provisions and clarified how AML supervisory powers are applied in cross-border situations.

At this time, the Transfer of Funds Regulation (European Parliament & Council of the European Union, 2015) adopted in 2015 also entered into force. This Regulation sets out rules based on the FATF regulations on the information on payers and payees accompanying transfer of funds in order to help prevent, detect and investigate ML and TF.

Subsequently, in May 2018, after almost two years of negotiations and counter-proposals, the European Parliament and the Council adopted the Fifth AML Directive (5AMLD, 2018) amending the 4AMLD. By 23 June 2020, five months after the transposition deadline (10 January 2020), all 27 Member States except Cyprus, Portugal, Romania and Spain, including the United Kingdom, had reported that they had transposed the new provisions.

As the UK has now left the EU and the post-Brexit transition period has expired, UK-EU security and criminal justice relations are governed by the EU-UK Trade and Cooperation Agreement (Trade & Cooperation Agreement, 2021), which entered into force on 1 May 2021. The EU-UK Trade and Cooperation Agreement includes a title on AML and CFT, largely devoted to prevention, as well as detailed provisions on EU-UK cooperation on freezing and confiscation. The provisions of this Title and the relevant definitions take precedence over the relevant provisions of the 2005 Warsaw Convention and the 1990 Strasbourg Convention (Mitsilegas, 2022).

Exchange of Information and Digitalisation

Another important perspective in the analysis of the Union's AML policy, which is closely linked to the above-discussed intensification of private–public partnerships, is the specific challenges associated with increased information exchange and digitalisation. The processing and exchange of personal data to detect a criminal who may be hiding behind the customer of a person subject to AMLD's monitoring obligations, such as financial institutions and lawyers, involves a delicate balancing act between security and protection of fundamental rights. As customers' personal data is used to report and investigate suspicious financial transactions, customers should be assured that decisions are not based on data that should not have been collected, that has been stored without permission, or is not, or is no longer, accurate.

The proposed amendments to the 4AMLD, and the 2015 Regulation, were criticised by the European Data Protection Supervisor (EDPS), an independent supervisory authority within the EU tasked with monitoring compliance with Union rules on the protection of personal data by the Union's own institutions, bodies, offices and agencies. The criticism concerned the proposals to introduce policy objectives other than countering ML and TF without these being clearly identified. The processing of personal data collected for one legitimate purpose for another, completely unrelated purpose violates the data protection principle of purpose limitation and risks violating the principle of proportionality. Thus, certain forms of processing of personal data that are acceptable in the context of AML and the fight against terrorism need not be necessary and proportionate in other contexts (EDPS, 2017).

A similar problem arises when it comes to client loyalty and client confidentiality, which is central for example to the legal profession and crucial for an effective representation of clients. Despite concerns within the legal profession, the CJEU (2007) has ruled in Case C-305/05 *Ordre des barreaux francophones* that the obligations of the AML Directives do not infringe the right to a fair trial guaranteed by Article 6 of the European Convention on Human Rights (ECHR) and Article 6(3) TEU, so the provisions must therefore be upheld also against lawyers. Similarly, in *Michaud v. France*, Application No 12323/11, the European Court of Human Rights (ECtHR, 2012) has held that the obligation for French lawyers to report suspicious transactions made by their clients does not disproportionately interfere with confidential lawyer-client relations or with the rights under Article 8 of the ECHR.

As has been pointed out, the fact that there are few appeals or complaints about the financial penalties, possibly due to the "name and shame" risk associated with AML and TF, may raise concerns about procedural guarantees, the effectiveness of sanctions and whether or not the penalties imposed are actually effective in preventing crime (Bergström, 2016). It has also been argued that AML measures have little effect in preventing TF, which, on the other hand, involves comparatively little money that does not have to be the proceeds of crime, but often comes from perfectly legitimate sources, as underlined, among other things, in a book on EU sanctions from 2013 (Cameron, 2013).

In addition to the above-mentioned examples of privacy and data protection challenges, there are a number of specific challenges linked to the increasing reliance on electronic reports, e-evidence and other digitisation themes. Not least, can it be difficult to identify who is responsible, where certain information including evidence is located, and which rules should apply at different stages of the various processes planned to deal with such issues. This may have a greater impact on inter-agency cooperation, the free movement of information and the wider protection of fundamental rights.

However, cooperation between police and judicial authorities, and companies providing information and communication services, is nothing new. In addition to the involvement of private actors in the financial sector, including AML, police and judicial authorities have been cooperating with telecom operators and providers for decades. However, there is an increased use of online services and new information and communication technologies (ICT) that are usually addressed by private companies as technology companies or service providers (Franssen, 2018). Such data is often processed, transferred and/or stored by foreign companies or service providers. This poses particular challenges for police and judicial authorities collecting electronic evidence to fight crime committed using or involving the use of ICT. This is because the information that criminals share or store using new ICT, thus processed by private companies, is not accessible to public authorities without cooperation with these private actors (Bergström, 2020; Franssen, 2018).

Administrative Law Measures and the EU Criminal Law Directive

In the same way that the previous section highlighted the importance of private–public collaboration and the challenge of information exchange and digitalisation, our third analytical perspective, focuses on another key element in the fight against ML and TF, namely the interaction between administrative law and criminal law and between different types of sanctions. As is well known, the EU originally, and for a long time, lacked competence to adopt legislative measures in the area of criminal law. This changed with the Treaty of Lisbon, whereby the TFEU paid attention to a number of particularly serious crimes with a cross-border dimension, such as ML, and made it possible for the Union to adopt minimum rules on the definition of criminal offences and sanctions for these crimes. Thus, Article 83(1) TFEU allowed the European Parliament and the Council to lay down minimum rules concerning ML by means of directives adopted in accordance with the ordinary legislative procedure.

Still, this new competence did not immediately lead to legislation. Instead, for a long time, the regulatory framework continued to consist mainly of two administrative instruments, the already mentioned 4AMLD and a Transfer of Funds Regulation, both of which were based on Article 114 TFEU on the internal market. The main aim of this regulatory framework was to improve the conditions for the establishment and functioning of the internal market by setting up common rules for the financial systems that could otherwise be used for ML purposes. The main focus of the EU AML measures based on the risk-based approach remained on prevention, while AML in terms of control and sanctioning was still a matter for national law and the emerging regulatory framework for international cooperation between judicial and law enforcement authorities. The EU AML Criminal Law Directive (European Parliament and Council of the European Union, 2018a) later extended the EU's focus from the prevention to the control of ML and TF.

But despite all the assumptions that the EU's framework for combating ML and TF is mainly of an administrative nature, there is a blurred and not at all clear line between administrative law, criminal law and sanctions in each area (Bergström, 2018a, 2018b). Not least because the provisions of national and EU law are intertwined and interlinked. This may have negative effects in terms of procedural safeguards and the protection of fundamental rights—for example, if sanctions are in fact criminal rather than administrative in nature, or if the different solutions chosen in different Member States lead to variations in the level of protection of fundamental rights across the EU.

Although the 4AMLD already provided for an EU definition of ML and thereby harmonised national criminal law on AML measures, it did not require Member States to introduce certain criminal law provisions setting out certain specific minimum and maximum sanctions for infringements (Herlin-Karnell, 2016). In other words, the regulatory framework laid down harmonised rules with regard to the definition of ML, i.e., the rules specifying which conduct was considered to constitute a criminal offence, but it did not specify the type and level of sanctions applicable to such conduct.

Instead, the 4AMLD stressed that sanctions or measures for infringements of national provisions transposing the directive must be effective, proportionate and dissuasive. Member States may thereby decide not to lay down rules for administrative sanctions or measures for breaches which are subject to criminal sanctions in their national law. In that case, Member States must communicate to the European Commission the relevant criminal law provisions. As the President of the Court of Justice of the European Union, Koen Lenaerts, and Legal Secretary José Gutiérrez-Fons pointed out in their chapter (Lenaerts & Gutiérrez-Fons, 2016), the CJEU (2013) recalled in Case C-617/10 *Åkerberg Fransson* that where EU law does not specifically provide for a sanction for an infringement of EU law or refers to national laws and regulations, Member States are free to choose the applicable sanctions; i.e. administrative, criminal or a combination of these. However, the resulting penalties must comply with the EU Charter of Fundamental Rights and be effective, proportionate and dissuasive. On the other hand, a measure based on Article 83(1) TFEU does not leave Member States any such freedom.

Therefore, probably unsurprisingly, on 21 December 2016, only two days after the Council adopted the compromise proposal amending the 4AMLD, the European Commission proposed a directive aimed at combating ML by criminal law. Furthermore, the explanatory memorandum stated that terrorists often use criminal proceeds to finance their activities and use ML in that process. The underlying idea was thus that criminalising ML would help CFT. The first EU directive on combating ML by criminal law was adopted on 23 October 2018 and had to be implemented by Member States by 3 December 2020 (Bergström, 2019).

Prior to the implementation of this directive, it was the responsibility of Member States to ensure that administrative sanctions and measures in accordance with the Internal Market Directive, and criminal sanctions in accordance with national law in compliance with international and other relevant Union law, had been put in place. Although the AML Directive by criminal law changed this situation, the line between administrative law and criminal law and sanctions in the AML system is not clear. On the one hand, the new directive reinforces the existing measures to detect and prevent abuse of the financial system for ML and TF. On the other hand, the EU's current focus is being extended from prevention to control. The new directive covers the definitions, scope and sanctions of ML offences and affects cross-border police and judicial cooperation between national authorities and the exchange of information. It is part of the global fight against ML and TF. The directive implements international commitments in this area, including the Warsaw Convention and FATF Recommendation 3, which in turn calls on countries to criminalise ML on the basis of the Vienna Convention and the Palermo Convention.

The EU AML Acquis in the Context of EU Security Policy

From having been extended to the collection of money or property for terrorist purposes, the AML regulatory instruments are now included in an even broader security context. According to the so-called Copenhagen School, the word security in international relations refers to a perceived existential threat, usually to the state, a region or a society, which justifies extraordinary measures (Emmers, 2018). A classic example is then US President George W. Bush's speech about the war on terror after 9/11 (Bush, 2001). An issue is securitised when an actor claims that the issue constitutes a security threat. If this threat is not taken seriously, the state risks going under. If the securitisation is successful, it means that an actor can justify extreme measures that are not accepted under normal circumstances.

In the context of the securitisation of cross-border crime the EU AML framework represents a new paradigm for security governance (Mitsilegas, 2003b). The securitisation of cross-border organised crime and TF have been used to increase the EU's powers, or at least have resulted in such an increase (Bergström, 2020). This is most evident in the area of EU judicial and police cooperation. In particular, the terrorist attacks of 9/11, 2001, accelerated the decision-making process in the European Union. In addition to the adoption of measures such as the framework decision on the European arrest warrant, the securitisation of cross-border crime, and more recently the securitisation of terrorism as such, has resulted in intensified AML rules. Both of these threats require action at the global level, and at the EU regional level. AML and asset freezing measures thus exemplify the shift towards the securitisation of threats to the financial sector in general and cross-border organised crime and TF in particular.

Similar to the securitisation process, the concept of risk and risk management signals that an issue is placed high on both the business agenda and the political agenda (Bergström et al., 2011). To call something a risk is to require action, risk assessment and risk management. The risk-based approach introduced by the revised FATF Recommendations and the 3AMLD has been further developed towards a more targeted and focused risk-based approach using evidence-based policy-making as well as guidance from European supervisory authorities.

In parallel with these developments, the EU became more active in the area of security policy, where AML has taken on an increasing role in recent years. In 2015, the European Commission presented the European Agenda on Security for the period 2015–2020 (European Commission, 2015). It stressed that the primary objective of organised crime is profit and that international criminal networks use legitimate business structures to conceal the source of their profits. The European Commission called for strengthening the capacity of law enforcement authorities to tackle the financing of organised crime, cybercrime, the prevention of terrorism and countering radicalisation. Key actions include effective measures to follow the money and reduce the financing of criminals, where cooperation between competent authorities, in particular the national FIUs to be connected to Europol, will be strengthened. In addition, Eurojust can offer more expertise and support to national authorities in financial investigations. Cross-border cooperation between FIUs and national asset recovery offices (AROs) is intended to help fight ML and gain access to the illicit proceeds of crime. The powers of FIUs will thus be strengthened to better track the activities of organised crime networks and their financial activities and to strengthen the powers of the competent national authorities to freeze and confiscate illicit assets. The EU further contributes to the prevention of TF through the network of EU FIUs and EU-US Terrorist Finance Tracking Programmes. The European Agenda on Security supports Member States' cooperation in addressing these security threats, and called for further action in the area of TF and ML.

In February 2016, the European Commission presented an action plan to further step up the fight against TF, in brief with two main objectives (European Commission, 2016a). The first objective was to prevent the movement of funds and identify TF. Key issues included ensuring that virtual currency exchange platforms are covered by the AML Directive, CFT through anonymous prepaid instruments such as prepaid cards, improving access to information and cooperation between EU FIUs. Furthermore, to ensure a high level of protection of financial flows from high-risk third countries and to provide EU FIUs with access to centralised bank and payment account registries and central data retrieval systems. The second main objective was to disrupt sources of income for terrorist organisations, including addressing sources of TF, and to work with third countries to ensure global mobilisation with the same aim. The European Commission's Action Plan stressed the need to combat ML through criminal law and the need to ensure that criminals who finance terrorism are deprived of their assets.

On 24 July 2019, the European Commission adopted the Communication "Towards better implementation of the EU's anti-money laundering and countering the financing of terrorism framework" (European Commission, 2019a), together with four reports aimed at helping European and national authorities better manage risks (European Commission, 2019b, 2019c, 2019d, 2019e). These reports provide an update on sectoral risks related to ML and TF, analyse the shortcomings in current supervision and cooperation and identify ways to address them. The four reports stress the need for full implementation, while underlining that a number of structural weaknesses in the implementation of Union rules in this area still need to be addressed.

Although the incorporation and entry into force of the 5AMLD was expected to address some of these issues, other issues remain. In particular, the 5AMLD increases the transparency of beneficial ownership information, gives FIUs greater access to information, improves cooperation between supervisors and regulates virtual currencies and prepaid cards to better prevent TF.

Current Reform Proposals

On 7 May 2020, the European Commission adopted an Action Plan for a comprehensive Union policy preventing money laundering and terrorist financing (European Commission, 2020a). This is based on six pillars, which aim to improve the EU's overall fight against ML and TF and strengthen the EU's global role in this area. They include effective implementation of existing rules, a common EU regulatory framework, supervision at the EU level, a support and cooperation mechanism for FIUs, better use of information to maintain criminal law and a stronger Europe in the world. As a result, EU rules will become more harmonised and thus, according to the European Commission, more effective. The rules will be better monitored and coordination between Member States' authorities will be improved. These measures build on the results of the 2019 AML package, which highlighted in particular regulatory fragmentation, uneven supervision and limitations in cooperation between FIUs across the EU, which can be said to be partly consistent with the analytical perspectives of this chapter.

Six months earlier, in November 2019, the finance ministers of France, Germany, Italy, Latvia, the Netherlands and Spain published a joint document on a joint monitoring mechanism in the field of ML and TF, *Towards a European Supervisory Mechanism for Money Laundering and Terrorist Financing* (Joint Paper, 2020). In the conclusions of the ECOFIN meeting on 5 December 2019, the finance ministers of all EU Member States addressed the European Commission. The European Commission was asked to explore the possibility of conferring certain responsibilities and powers for AML supervision on a Union body with an independent structure and direct powers over certain obliged entities selected by the Union body in accordance with a risk-based approach. The European Commission was invited to make legislative proposals in this regard in parallel with efforts to achieve a higher level of harmonisation through AML legislation.

Building on the progress made under the European Commission's European Agenda on Security 2015–2020 and President von der Leyen's Political Guidelines, on 24 July 2020 the Commission presented its new EU Security Union Strategy for the period 2020–2025 (European Commission, 2020b). The strategy underlined that strengthening the EU AML/CFT framework will also help curbing terrorism and organised crime. It also identified four strategic priorities for action at the EU level. Firstly, "Ensuring a future-proof security environment for individuals"; secondly, "Tackling evolving threats"; thirdly, and of greatest interest in this context; "Protecting Europeans from terrorism and organised crime" including work on countering radicalisation, prosecuting terrorists, border security, better use of existing databases and cooperation with non-EU countries. It also includes an agenda to fight organised crime, specific actions against trafficking in human beings, an agenda on drugs, an agenda on illicit trafficking in firearms and a new EU action plan against migrant smuggling, among others. Fourthly, 'Developing a strong European security ecosystem', specifically mentions cooperation and information exchange and important measures to strengthen Europol's mandate, further develop Eurojust and better connect judicial and law enforcement authorities, as well as cooperation with Interpol.

The New EU Legislative Package and Remaining Challenges

Eventually, on 20 July 2021, the European Commission presented its legislative package to strengthen EU AML and CFT rules (European Commission, 2021a). The package contains four legislative proposals, considered to be a coherent whole, creating a new and stricter enforcement framework for AML and CFT in the Union: a new regulation establishing a new EU authority; A new regulation establishing a single rulebook including rules on customer due diligence and beneficial ownership measures; A sixth directive complementing the regulation and replacing the 5AMLD and containing provisions that will be implemented in national law, such as provisions on national supervisory authorities and FIUs, and; A recast of the Transfer of Funds Regulation to track the transfer of crypto-assets. The underlying aim is to improve the detection of suspicious transactions and activities and to close loopholes used by criminals to launder illicit proceeds or finance terrorist activities through the financial system. The new regulatory framework increases coordination and cooperation between Member States' authorities, while the creation of a new EU agency forms the core of the legislative package.

The regulation establishing the new EU AML and CFT Authority (AMLA) aims to create control at EU level and to bring about a support and cooperation mechanism for FIUs. Like the current legal framework, the proposal is based on Article 114 TFEU. Within the framework of that provision, according to settled case-law (CJEU, 2006, 2014), the EU legislature may consider it necessary to establish an EU body responsible for contributing to the implementation of a harmonisation process.

The new legislative package introduces far-reaching changes. Having directly applicable rules in a regulation, with more detail than in the existing directive, will both promote consistency in supervisory and enforcement practices in the Member States, as well as provide rules for the new EU authority to apply itself as a direct supervisor for selected obliged entities. AMLA will directly supervise some of the most risky financial institutions operating in a large number of Member States or require immediate action to address imminent risks.

In the area of indirect supervision and coordination and support for FIUs, the proposal contains various provisions empowering AMLA to develop technical supervisory- and implementing standards and to adopt guidelines and recommendations, thus determining a defined role and function for the Authority. AMLA will thus establish a single integrated AML/CFT supervision system across the EU.

AMLA's coordination of national authorities aims to ensure that the private sector correctly and consistently applies EU rules. AMLA will monitor and coordinate national supervisors responsible for other financial entities and coordinate supervisors for non-financial entities. AMLA will further support cooperation between national FIUs and facilitate communication and joint analysis between them to better detect illicit flows of a cross-border nature. AMLA's support to supervisors and FIUs in risk assessment and analysis will be an important function of the new enforcement structure. AMLA will help FIUs improve their analytical capacity on illicit flows and make financial intelligence an important source for law enforcement agencies.

AMLA should be operational in 2024 and will start its direct supervisory work somewhat later, once the new directive has been transposed and the new regulatory framework becomes applicable. According to the European Commission, a more harmonised framework will facilitate compliance for the bodies covered by the rules, not least for those operating across borders. The EU regulatory framework will harmonise rules across the EU, for example through more detailed rules on customer due diligence, beneficial ownership and the powers and tasks of supervisory bodies and FIUs. Existing national registers of bank accounts will be interconnected, which will give FIUs faster access to information on bank accounts and safe-deposit boxes. The European Commission will also make this system available to law enforcement authorities, which will speed up financial investigations and the recovery of criminal assets in cross-border cases. Access to financial information will be subject to strong safeguards in the proposed Financial Information Exchange Directive that would allow designated competent authorities responsible for the prevention, investigation, detection or prosecution of criminal offences to access and search Member States' centralised bank account registers through a single access point.

The legislative package includes an EU-wide limit of EUR 10,000 for large cash payments. Restrictions already exist in around two-thirds of Member States, but the amounts vary. National ceilings below EUR 10,000 may remain. In addition, it will be forbidden to provide or own anonymous wallets for crypto assets, just as anonymous bank accounts are already banned. Currently, only certain categories of crypto-asset service providers are subject to EU rules. The proposed reform will extend these rules to the entire crypto sector and force all service providers to make checks on their customers. These changes are intended to ensure full traceability of transfers of crypto-assets, such as bitcoin, and will make it possible to prevent and detect their possible use for ML or TF.

The EU legislative package thus strengthens the existing regulatory framework by taking into account new and emerging challenges related to technological innovation, such as virtual currencies, more integrated financial flows in the internal market and the global nature of terrorist organisations. ML is a global phenomenon that requires strong international cooperation. AMLA will support the Union's policy towards third countries with regard to ML and FT threats from outside the Union. The Authority will cooperate in this regard with the relevant European Commission services, the European External Action Service, as well as EU bodies, offices and agencies. A country designated by the FATF will also be listed by the EU. There will be two EU lists, a "black list" and a "grey list" reflecting the FATF list. Once listed, the EU will take measures proportionate to the risks posed by the country. The EU will also be able to list countries that are not listed by the FATF but pose a threat to the EU financial system on the basis of an independent assessment.

In this chapter, a selection of analytical and related perspectives with particular challenges for the emerging AML/CFT framework has been highlighted and briefly analysed. Two recurrent challenges identified in these analytical perspectives are, first, regulatory fragmentation. Regulation at different levels, such as global, regional and national levels, can lead to both application and efficiency problems. The new legislative package consists of four legislative proposals, three of which are directly applicable in the Member States. A new EU agency is proposed to be given specific competences, and power over the Member States' authorities active in the area, is established. On the one hand, predictability and effectiveness of the regulatory framework are likely to improve, while some enforcement problems may remain before national frameworks have had time to adapt to the new regulations and other relevant provisions.

Fragmentation of the regulatory framework that occurs due to the difficulty of drawing clear boundaries between what is private and what is public, or between what is administrative law and what is criminal law and associated challenges such as differences regarding the protection of rights in the relevant regulatory instruments, will probably continue to lead to some problems. If, for example, you are affected by a criminal sanction, you have access to higher protection and more rights than if you receive an administrative, although severe sanction. It is true that access to financial information will be subject to strong safeguards in the proposed Financial Information Exchange Directive, but how these will actually be implemented at the national level remains to be seen. Furthermore, the processing of individuals' personal data in EU-wide databases to which both national authorities focusing on prevention, and judicial and law enforcement authorities with a focus on control have access, poses a particular challenge. The data protection principle of purpose limitation must not be circumvented. However, as an EU body, the new AMLA authority will be subject to the relevant data protection regulation, Regulation (EU) 2018/1725, (European Parliament and the Council of the European Union, 2018b) in the sense that it can handle personal data.

This brings us to a second recurrent challenge, the protection of fundamental rights, and the balance between public interests such as financial market integrity, and individual rights and freedoms, as well as a number of related issues and challenges. Specific challenges linked to digitalisation, cooperation between authorities and exchange of information have been addressed in the legislative proposals that have now been developed. Here there is every reason to be critical of how individuals' fundamental rights are protected when the long-ongoing securitisation of ML and TF with increased competence to regulate and to take extraordinary measures risks weakening the system of fundamental rights guarantees in the Union. With the increased fragmentation and digitalisation of key parts of our modern world, newly updated regulatory frameworks are facing rapidly accelerating challenges. It is to be hoped that the variety of tools that the European Commission and AMLA will be able to use will allow the EU to keep pace with a rapidly changing and complex international environment with rapidly changing risks without restricting the protection of fundamental rights. The legislative package is currently being discussed by the European Parliament and the Council, and here there is every reason to pay attention to developments so that individuals' fundamental rights are not curtailed in response to the ever-changing threats to our society.

References

1AMLD. (1991). Council Directive 91/308/EEC of 10 June 1991 on prevention of the use of the financial system for the purpose of money laundering, OJ 1991, L 166/77.

2AMLD. (2001). Directive 2001/97/EC of the European Parliament and of the Council of 4 December 2001 amending Council Directive 91/308/EEC on prevention of the use of the financial system for the purpose of money laundering, OJ 2001, L 344/76.

3AMLD. (2005). Directive 2005/60/EC of the European Parliament and of the Council of 26 October 2005 on the prevention of the use of the financial system for the purpose of money laundering and terrorist financing [2005] OJ L 309/15.

4AMLD. (2015). Directive (EU) 2015/849 of the European Parliament and of the Council of 20 May 2015 on the prevention of the use of the financial system for the purposes of money laundering or terrorist financing, amending Regulation (EU) No 648/2012 of the European Parliament and of the Council, and repealing Directive 2005/60/EC of the European Parliament and of the Council and Commission Directive 2006/70/EC, OJ 2015, L 141/73.

5AMLD. (2018). Directive (EU) 2018/843 of the European Parliament and of the Council of 30 May 2018 amending Directive (EU) 2015/849 on the prevention of the use of the financial system for the purposes of money laundering or terrorist financing, and amending Directives 2009/138/EC and 2013/36/EU, OJ 2018, L 156/43.

BCBS. (1988). Basel Committee on Banking Supervision, Prevention of criminal use of the banking system for the purpose of money-laundering, December 1988.

Bergström, M. (2011). EU Anti-Money Laundering Regulation: Multilevel Cooperation of Public and Private Actors. In C. Eckes & T. Konstadinides (Eds.), *Crime within the Area of Freedom, Security and Justice: A European Public Order* (pp. 97–126). Cambridge University Press.

Bergström, M. (2013). The Place of Sanctions in the EU System for Combating the AML. In I. Cameron (Ed.), *EU Sanctions: Law and Policy Issues Concerning Restrictive Measures* (pp. 97–116). Intersentia.

Bergström, M. (2019). Legal Perspectives on Money Laundering. In V. Mitsilegas, S. Hufnagel, & A. Moiseienko (Eds.), *Research Handbook on Transnational Crime* (pp. 98–111). Edward Elgar.

Bergström, M., Svedberg Helgesson, K., & Mörth, U. (2011). A New Role for For-profit Actors? *The Case of Anti-Money Laundering and Risk Management, Journal of Common Market Studies, 2011*(5), 1043–1064.

Bergström, M. (2016). Money Laundering. In: Mitsilegas, V., Bergström, M. & T. Konstadinides (eds.) *Research Handbook on EU Criminal Law*, (pp. 335–354). Edward Elgar Publishing.

Bergström, M. (2018a). The Global AML Regime and the EU AML Directives – Prevention and Control, in King, C., Walker, C. & J. Gurule, (eds.) *The Palgrave Handbook of Criminal and Terrorism Financing Law*, (vol 1, pp. 33–56). Palgrave.

Bergström, M. (2018b). The Many Uses of Anti-Money Laundering Regulation – Over time and into the future, in Herlin-Karnell, E. & E. De Busser (eds.), Special Issue: EU Security Governance and Financial Crimes, *German Law Journal*, Vol. 19 No. 5.

Bergström, M. (2020). The Dynamic Evolution of EU Criminal Law and Justice – New Developments through the Lense of Past Experiences, in *20 Year Anniversary of the Tampere Programme – Progress and Future Priorities of the EU Area of Freedom, Security and Justice.* Collective Volume Incorporating the Contributions from the High Level Conference Part of Finland's Presidency Calendar and Co-organised by CEPS, the Migration Policy Centre (MPC) and the LW Department of the European University Institute (EUI), in cooperation with the Finnish Permanent Representation to the EU, CEPS, Brussels, 3 and 4 October 2019.

Bush, G.W. (2001). State of the Union Address to a Joint Session of Congress and the American People, 20 September 2001.

Cameron, I. (ed.) (2013). *EU Sanctions: Law and Policy Issues Concerning Restrictive Measures*, Intersentia.

CJEU. (2006). Case C-217/04 *UK v. European Parliament and Council*, EU:C:2006:279. European Court of Justice.

CJEU. (2007). Case C-305/05 *Ordre des Barreaux Francophones*, EU:C:2007:383. European Court of Justice.
CJEU. (2013). Case C-617/10 *Åkerberg Fransson*, EU:C:2013:105. European Court of Justice.
CJEU. (2014). Case C-270/12 *UK v. European Parliament and Council*, EU:C:2014:18. European Court of Justice.
European Parliament and Council of the European Union. (2018a). Criminal Law Directive: Directive (EU) 2018/1673 of the European Parliament and of the Council of 23 October 2018 on combating money laundering by criminal law, OJ 2018, L 284/22.
ECtHR. (2012). European Court of Human Rights. *Michaud v. France*, Application No 12323/11.
EDPS. (2017). European Data Protection Supervisor, Summary of the Opinion of the European Data Protection Supervisor on a Commission Proposal amending Directive (EU) 2015/849 and Directive 2009/101/EC Access to beneficial ownership information and data protection implications, OJ 2017, C 85/3.
Emmers, R. (2018). Securitization. In A. Collins (Ed.), *Contemporary Security Studies* (5th ed., pp. 173–188). Oxford University Press.
European Commission. (2015). Communication from the Commission to the European Parliament, the Council, the European Economic and Social Committee and the Committee of the Regions. The European Agenda on Security, COM (2015)185 final.
European Commission. (2016a). Commission's Action Plan to Strengthen the Fight Against Terrorist Financing of 2 February 2016, COM(2016) 50 final.
European Commission. (2016b). 'Fair Taxation: The Commission sets out next steps to increase tax transparency and tackle tax abuse' (Strasbourg, 5 July 2016) http://europa.eu/rapid/press-release_IP-16-2354_en.htm
European Commission. (2019a). Communication from the Commission to the European Parliament and the Council. Towards better implementation of the EU's anti-money laundering and countering the financing of terrorism framework, COM/2019/360 final.
European Commission. (2019b). Report from the Commission to the European Parliament and the Council on the assessment of the risk of money laundering and terrorist financing affecting the internal market and relating to cross-border activities, COM/2019/370 final.
European Commission. (2019c). Report from the Commission to the European Parliament and the Council assessing the framework for cooperation between Financial Intelligence Units, COM/2019/371 final.
European Commission. (2019d). Report from the Commission to the European Parliament and the Council on the interconnection of national centralised

automated mechanisms (central registries or central electronic data retrieval systems) of the Member States on bank accounts, COM/2019/372 final.

European Commission. (2019e). Report from the Commission to the European Parliament and the Council on the assessment of recent alleged money laundering cases involving EU credit institutions, COM/2019/373 final.

European Commission. (2020a). Communication from the Commission on an Action Plan for a comprehensive Union policy on preventing money laundering and terrorist financing, OJ 2020, C 164/21.

European Commission. (2020b). Communication from the Commission to the European Parliament, the European Council, the Council, the European Economic and Social Committee and the Committee of the Regions on the EU Security Union Strategy, COM/2020/605 final.

European Commission. (2021a). Anti-money laundering and countering the AML legislative package (europa.eu)

European Commission. (2021b). Remarks by Executive Vice-President Dombrovskis (europa.eu), 20 July 2021.

European Parliament and Council of the European Union. (2015). Transfer of Funds Regulation: Regulation (EU) 2015/847 of the European Parliament and of the Council of 20 May 2015 on information accompanying transfers of funds and repealing Regulation (EC) No 1781/2006, *OJ 2015, L 141/1.*

European Parliament and Council of the European Union. (2018b). Regulation (EU) 2018/1725 of the European Parliament and of the Council of 23 October 2018 on the protection of natural persons with regard to the processing of personal data by the Union institutions, bodies, offices and agencies and on the free movement of such data, and repealing Regulation (EC) No 45/2001 and Decision No 1247/2002/EC, *OJ 2018, L 295/39.*

FATF (2023a). FATF Statement on the Russian Federation (fatf-gafi.org), 24 February 2023.

FATF (2023b). The FATF Recommendations (fatf-gafi.org), last visited 27 March 2024.

FATF (2023c). FATF Methodology for assessing compliance with the FATF Recommendations and the effectiveness of AML/CFT systems (fatf-gafi.org), last visited 27 March 2024.

Franssen, V. (2018). The European Commission's E-evidence Proposal: Toward an EU-wide Obligation for Service Providers to Cooperate with Law Enforcement? *European Law Blog,* 12 October 2018, available at: https://europeanlawblog.eu/2018/10/12/the-european-commissions-e-evidence-proposal-toward-an-eu-wide-obligation-for-service-providers-to-cooperate-with-law-enforcement/

Herlin-Karnell, E. (2011). The EU's Anti-Money Laundering Agenda: Built on Risks? In C. Eckes & T. Konstadinides (Eds.), *Crime within the Area of Freedom, Security and Justice: A European Public Order* (pp. 76–96). Cambridge University Press.

Herlin-Karnell, E. (2016). Is Administrative Law Still Relevant? How the Battle of Sanctions Shaped EU Criminal Law, In: Mitsilegas, V., Bergström, M. & T. Konstadinides (eds.) *Research Handbook on EU Criminal Law*, (pp. 233–248). Edward Elgar Publishing.

International Monetary Fund. (2023). Anti-Money Laundering/Combating the Financing of Terrorism (AML/CFT) - Topics (imf.org), last visited 12 October 2023.

Joint Paper. (2020). Joint-Paper by the Ministers of Finance of Netherlands, France, Germany, Italy, Latvia and Spain on a European Mechanism to Enhance Anti-money Laundering Supervision Across the EU. Towards a European Supervisory Mechanism for Money-Laundering and Terrorist Financing | Publication | The Netherlands at International Organisations (permanentrepresentations.nl).

Kersten, A. (2002). Financing of Terrorism – A Predicate Offence to Money Laundering? In M. Pieth (Ed.), *Financing Terrorism* (pp. 49–56). Kluwer Academic Publishers.

Lenaerts, K., & J. Gutiérrez-Fons (2016). The European Court of Justice and Fundamental Rights in the Field of Criminal Law, In: Mitsilegas, V., Bergström, M. & T. Konstadinides (eds.) *Research Handbook on EU Criminal Law*, (pp. 7–26). Edward Elgar Publishing.

Mitsilegas, V. (2003a). Countering the Chameleon Threat of Dirty Money: "Hard" and "Soft " Law in the Emergence of a Global Regime against Money Laundering and Terrorist Finance, in Edwards, A., & P. Gill (eds), *Transnational Organised Crime: Perspectives on Global Security,* (pp. 195-211). Routledge.

Mitsilegas, V. (2003b). Money Laundering Counter-Measures in the European Union: A New Paradigm of Security Governance versus Fundamental Legal Principles, Kluwer Law International.

Mitsilegas, V. (2022). Criminal Justice and Security Cooperation after Brexit in Lazowski, A., & A. Cygan (eds.), Research Handbook on Legal Aspects of Brexit, (pp. 198–220). Edward Elgar.

MONEYVAL. (2023). Jurisdictions - Committee of Experts on the Evaluation of Anti-Money Laundering Measures and the Financing of Terrorism (coe.int), last visited 12 October 2023.

OECD (1998). *OECD Report on Harmful Tax Competition: An Emerging Global Issue* (1998).

Strasbourg Convention (1990). Council of Europe Convention on Laundering, Search, Seizure and Confiscation of the Proceeds from Crime, 1990.

Trade and Cooperation Agreement. (2021). Trade and Cooperation Agreement between the European Union and the European Atomic Energy Community, of the one part, and the United Kingdom of Great Britain and Northern Ireland, of the other part, OJ 2021, C 149/10.

UN Convention. (1999). International Convention for the Suppression of the Financing of Terrorism adopted on 9 December 1999.

UN Convention. (2000). The United Nations Convention against Transnational Organized Crime (UNTOC) adopted on 15 November 2000.

Vienna Convention. (1988). United Nations Convention against Illicit Traffic in Narcotic Drugs and Psychotropic Substances of 19 December 1988 (1582 UNTS 95).

Warsaw Convention. (2005). Council of Europe Convention on Laundering, Search, Seizure and Confiscation of the Proceeds from Crime and on the Financing of Terrorism of 2005, CETS No 198.

Winer, J. M. (2002). Globalization, Terrorist Finance, and Global Conflict – Time for a White List? In M. Pieth (Ed.), *Financing Terrorism* (pp. 5–40). Kluwer Academic Publishers.

CHAPTER 9

The European Security Order

Kjell Engelbrekt

Even before the Russian Federation launched its war of aggression against Ukraine on 24 February 2022, it was evident that the conflict also concerned the security order in Europe and the values and principles that underpin it since the middle of the last century. As 2021 came to a close, some 150,000 Russian troops were stationed along the border with Ukraine, and Sergei Lavrov, the Russian foreign minister, was demanding that the North Atlantic Treaty Organization (NATO) refrain from expanding to the east and from deploying offensive weapons in Russia's immediate vicinity (Kramer & Erlanger, 2021). Consequently, the sovereignty of individual European states within the realm of security and defence was called into question.

If Russia ultimately fails to subdue Ukraine by military means, then the conditions should be present for recreating a European security order, consolidating it, in part, by Finland and Sweden joining NATO. On a more general level, however, it is far less certain that most of the world's great powers, such as Russia, will relinquish their seemingly increasing demands that smaller states conform to their wishes. The effect of such a

K. Engelbrekt (✉)
Swedish Defence University, Stockholm, Sweden
e-mail: Kjell.Engelbrekt@fhs.se

A. Bakardjieva Engelbrekt et al. (eds.), *The Borders of the European Union in a Conflictual World*,
https://doi.org/10.1007/978-3-031-54200-8_9

trend, over the long run, will be to weaken the rules-based international order.

In this chapter, Russia's war in Ukraine will be treated as a concrete and specific threat to the continent's largest country (geographically speaking), but above all as a deliberate attempt to break up the current security order in Europe. The question of the inviolability of borders is thereby also raised at the level of global politics and of international law. Although Ukraine is not a member of either NATO or the European Union (EU), both of these institutions are now confronted with an antagonistic regional power that opposes, by military means, the vision of a 'European neighbourhood' with stable and increasingly prosperous societies in the east and south. While NATO had taken several steps and measures to deal with the situation that arose in 2014, with Russia's annexation of Crimea and its support for separatists in southeastern Ukraine, the large-scale war that broke out in February 2022 brought about an abrupt awakening for the EU as a political system.

This chapter begins with a description of what is usually termed the European security order from 1946 to 2021. It then proceeds to an examination of how this order was openly challenged by Russia's express demands in the late autumn of 2021, and above all by the decision of that country's leadership in February 2022 to order a large-scale war of aggression against a neighbour on the European continent. A third section discusses the various measures that the EU and NATO took during the spring and summer of the same year to defend the existing security order in Europe, and to preserve cohesion within both organisations on the subject. The focus of the fourth section is on the bilateral military support that Ukraine has received from a number of countries in order to resist the Russian invasion, and on what this concrete cooperation says about the prospects for more integrated policies among Europe's democracies in the area of security and defence. A fifth section looks at the demands made by great powers in a global perspective, as they may reinforce the trend towards European integration. Finally, in its last section the chapter returns to the overall question of Europe's security order, and whether the EU and the non-American part of NATO need to shoulder a greater responsibility for it, now that Russia has chosen direct confrontation and the involvement of the US in Asia, and the Pacific is steadily increasing.

European Security 1945–2021

According to two American political scientists, David Lake and Patrick Morgan, a regional security order consists of member states which are so intertwined in their security policies that actions by their individual governments, and significant events within each country, have a substantial impact on all of them (Lake & Morgan, 1997). It is this mutual dependence that distinguishes a regional security order, although many such arrangements are also strongly affected by external actors, in this case the United States and the Russian Federation (previously the Soviet Union). Global and regional institutions—such as the United Nations (UN), the EU, and NATO—may exert significant influence as well.

In part, it can be said that the European security order has existed since the late 1940s, as an extension of the rules-based world order that came about through the establishment of the UN. The victorious powers were prepared to guarantee this order through political, economic, and military means in countries and regions over which they exercised control. This reflected not least the commitment to reintegrating Germany and Japan—the two former 'Axis powers' that had tried to subjugate large parts of Europe and East Asia respectively during the Second World War—into the international community. The first and second articles of the UN Charter laid down that war is only legitimate for self-defence, or when conducted under a mandate from the UN Security Council. Furthermore, all UN members must undertake to observe certain principles for relations between states: above all, to settle disputes by peaceful means; to respect the sovereignty of states and their formal equality; and, in the words of Article 2(4) of the UN Charter, to 'refrain in their international relations from the threat or use of force against the territorial integrity or political independence of any State, or in any other manner inconsistent with the Purposes of the United Nations' (UN Charter, 1945).

However, precisely because the European continent had experienced two world wars within the space of less than a generation, such pledges were regarded as insufficient. With mainly American support, therefore, several joint organisations were established, for the primary purpose of reducing the risk for renewed serious conflict on the European continent. It may also be said here that Europe's security order gained credibility and grew deeper as a result of institutional innovations in several policy areas, in line with what is usually known as a 'collective security system'—with a common commitment to stability and the suppression of aggression, whether political or military (Kupchan, 1995; Inis, 2006).

The foundations for this security order were laid in 1949, with the establishment of NATO under American leadership. However, the Council of Europe and its European Court of Human Rights, created in 1949 and 1958 respectively, bear mentioning here as well. The European Coal and Steel Community was formed in 1952, and in 1967 the six founding countries of that body—Belgium, France, Italy, Luxembourg, the Netherlands, and West Germany—merged it with the European Economic Community (EEC) and the European Atomic Energy Community (Euratom), thereby forming the European Communities (EC). In 1993, finally, the latter were brought together in the European Union (EU), which then had twelve member states. NATO had sixteen members at the time (Wallace, 1994).

While the EU and NATO contributed the most to Europe's security order—alongside the Council of Europe, with its efforts to strengthen human rights and the rule of law—the importance of the Conference on Security and Co-operation in Europe (CSCE) should be recognised too. The CSCE provided diplomatic mechanisms for promoting security between the countries of Western Europe and their counterparts in the communist bloc, including the then-Soviet Union. The Helsinki Conference of 1975 was unique in this regard, as it resulted in a commitment by thirty-five European states, and by US and Canada as well, to recognise existing borders, to increase trade, and to respect human rights. Up until 1990, when a new charter was adopted that transformed it into the Organization for Security and Co-operation in Europe (OSCE), the CSCE was one of the few places where government representatives from both sides of the 'Iron Curtain' on the continent could meet (Flynn & Farrell, 1999).

At the beginning of the twenty-first century, the OSCE also functioned as a diplomatic buffer between the Russian political leadership under President Vladimir Putin, who took office at the New Year of 2000, and Western leaders. Cooperation with the US also proceeded well to begin with, following the terrorist attacks on New York and Washington on 11 September 2001. Then-President George W. Bush sought partners beyond the traditional ones, and he hoped to take advantage of Russia's geographical location and its knowledge about Islamist extremism in Afghanistan and the former Soviet Union. This collaboration then flourished within the framework of the G8, in the form of intelligence exchange. It was when 'colour revolutions' took place in Georgia and Ukraine, with demands for greater independence from Moscow, that Putin's suspicions seem to have been awakened (or sooner strengthened) that the US government was trying to curtail Russia's freedom of action. In 2007, at the Munich Security Conference, he decided to speak frankly, sharply criticising what he saw as intervention in Russia's sphere of influence (Fried & Volker, 2022).

After this, the OSCE too became the scene for constant Russian objections to the European security order (Engelbrekt, 2013). These objections have concerned attempts by Western leaders to encourage democratic reforms within Russia or in its immediate vicinity, and they have evinced strong irritation on the part of Russian leaders at criticisms aimed at the functioning of the Russian legal system, or at the corruption believed to be particularly widespread in countries that were formerly part of the Soviet Union. The Kremlin has felt an ever greater need to limit freedom of expression for political and social movements that have sought closer ties with Europe or the United States, or which have demanded political and economic reforms in line with how Western democracies function. Moreover, Russian officials have repeatedly claimed that the underlying motive for the concern displayed by governments in Europe and particularly the United States for the political freedoms of post-Soviet citizens has lain ultimately in a desire to expand Western geopolitical influence at Russia's expense.

The EU and NATO—Complementary Institutions

A great deal has been written about friction and organisational rivalry between the EU and NATO (see, for instance, Ewers-Peters, 2021). It has been difficult at times to sort out the distribution of roles and responsibilities in the security area. Viewed historically and on an overarching level, however, the two Brussels-based organisations have almost always taken complementary and mutually reinforcing approaches to the European security order. The EU has been 'liberated' from purely defence questions (such as how to achieve deterrence by military means), and NATO has not needed to take on complex foreign-policy issues like the Middle East.

NATO's expansion in the 1990s and 2000s paved the way for post-communist states to reach association agreements with the EU, and to become members of the Union after some years. To become a member of NATO, a country must have civilian control over its armed forces; it must respect democratic rights and freedoms; and its state administration must function according to the rule of law. There is also one thing it cannot have: namely, an unresolved border dispute with a neighbouring country. In reality, the post-communist states were asked to qualify for EU membership gradually—first by joining the Council of Europe, and then by joining NATO. In the case of the former organisation, the need for a well-functioning rule of law was the biggest stumbling block; in the case of the latter, it was the manner in which defence and security affairs were organised. As candidates in the 'Partnership for Peace' programme, finally, the countries in question received support from NATO members throughout their period of preparation.

Scholars of international relations often depict security policy as dictated by the interests and desires of great powers, such that the preferences of smaller states almost always have to take a back seat. John Mearsheimer, political scientist at the University of Chicago and renowned researcher in the theory-driven 'realist' school, has repeatedly argued that it was ultimately the US that pushed for NATO's expansion into Central and Eastern Europe (Mearsheimer, 2014). The empirical research, however, shows with all due clarity that it was sooner the other way round: i.e., that the expansion was demand-driven, reflecting the concern felt by voters and political decision-makers in these countries—dominated as they had been by the Soviet Union—about Russia's lingering imperialism and its military bullying of smaller neighbours.

It is true, however, that Russia rarely expressed opposition to the EU's eastward expansion until the 2010s (Engelbrekt & Nygren, 2010). Table 9.1 shows the progress of European integration following the formation, on 18 April 1951, of the European Coal and Steel Community by six countries: Belgium, France, Italy, Luxembourg, the Netherlands, and West Germany. In the years following the collapse of communism and the dissolution of the Soviet Union, Moscow too seemed to see increasing prosperity in Europe as offering economic opportunities for Russia itself. Between 2004 and 2007, a total of twelve states joined the EU, of which ten had been part of the Soviet sphere of influence and members of the Warsaw Pact during the Cold War.

The line went, however, at the borders of Belarus and Ukraine. This became clear already in 2004, in connection with the 'Orange Revolution' in the latter country. There is much to indicate that the Kremlin's involvement in Ukrainian politics from that time on has consisted both in open support for various leaders and parties and in covert attempts at exerting influence via economic policy, intelligence activities, and the like (Belton, 2020). In addition, the large pipeline systems that had been built in Ukraine during the Soviet era—for storing and exporting gas to a number of countries in Europe—have been the subject of recurrent conflict and tough negotiation (see the chapter on energy by Torbjörn Becker and Anders Åslund in this volume.) The same has been true of the Russian naval base in Sevastopol on the Crimean Peninsula—it too a legacy of the Soviet era.

Around the New Year of 2014, what the Kremlin described as a geopolitical tug-of-war between the West and Russia over the most important component in the latter's sphere of interest—namely Ukraine—grew more intense. Ukraine's then-President Viktor Yanukovych—who had promised in his election campaign to negotiate an association agreement with the EU, and who also received such an offer from Brussels—suddenly did a U-turn in favour of a proposal from Moscow for greater cooperation. The 'Maidan Revolution', born of the disappointment of many Ukrainian citizens with this reversal, became for Moscow a direct challenge to the idea of incorporating Ukraine into an economic union with its eastern neighbour. When Yanukovych fled to Russia in February 2014, Putin decided to take control over Crimea by military means, to annex it, and to support Russian-speaking separatists in the Donbass in southeastern Ukraine (Allison, 2014; Bukkvoll, 2016).

One way of describing the situation over the past fifteen years is to say that two rival conceptions of a security order have confronted one another. According to the one, coercive military power is the sole effective means for creating real stability, which must be based ultimately on the military might of a great power. According to the other, if regional actors prefer a multilateral order where diplomacy and economic relations play an important role, they can bring a more polycentric security order into being. The contrast between the two conceptions has been described by Derrick Frazier and Robert Stewart-Ingersoll, as they examined Russia's unilateral, paternalistic, and not seldom openly revisionist behaviour in the so-called post-Soviet sphere (Frazier & Stewart-Ingersoll, 2012). In the view of the two authors, Russia represents an almost stereotypical illustration of the first-mentioned approach.

The Kremlin's Repeated Demands for an Alternative Security Arrangement

There is thus a clear continuity between, on the one hand, Russian diplomacy in the OSCE for some fifteen years (Stronski & Sokolsky, 2020), and, on the other, the specific demands Moscow made in late 2021—i.e., prior to the war in Ukraine breaking out—that the European security order adapts to its desires (Kramer & Erlanger, 2021). Three demands were recurrent: Russia would have veto power over significant changes in the security regime; the deployment of weapons systems capable of hitting military installations deep within Russian territory would be banned; and NATO and EU countries would refrain from political intervention in the post-Soviet sphere.

Where the demand for a Russian veto over adjustments in the security order is concerned, the question of NATO membership for additional European states has been paramount. Ever since Putin assumed the presidency, the Kremlin has consistently demanded that no further NATO expansion take place without Russia's consent. This applies above all to countries with which Russia shares a border, as Moscow believes the effect thereof would be to shift geopolitical conditions to the West's favour. As a rule, any domestic debate about joining NATO in any country—whether Montenegro, North Macedonia, Sweden, or Ukraine—has resulted in criticism and threats of countermeasures from Russian officials (on threats against the non-NATO Nordic countries, see Roth, 2022).

The demand for a ban on the deployment of weapons systems has mostly been made in narrower contexts, in connection with negotiations over disarmament. Russian leaders have aimed their harshest criticism at the possible deployment of long-range missiles in NATO countries in Central Europe, and they have called attempts to differentiate between offensive and defensive systems into question. At the same time, the Russian defence industry has continually developed new robotic systems which, in the view of many experts, have violated agreements entered into—above all the 1987 agreement not to develop medium-range missiles (with a range from 500 to 5500 kilometres), due to the risk they pose of undermining the military balance on the European continent. In 2019, after the publication of documents detailing how certain types of Russian missiles had violated the terms of previous agreements, the US withdrew from the Intermediate-Range Nuclear Forces Treaty (Lopez, 2019).

However, it is the demand for political non-intervention in the post-Soviet sphere that has posed the greatest challenge for Western democracies, as it conflicts both with the European security order and with Russian commitments to respect sovereignty and territorial integrity. As noted above, the European security order is more 'finely meshed' than that of other regions, in the sense that the principles and rules of the UN Charter are reinforced in its case by additional agreements and institutions. These include the Council of Europe, with its Convention on Human Rights; the OSCE, with its Helsinki Accords and its 1990 Paris Charter; and the EU and NATO, with their respective frameworks for how their members are to act towards each other and in relation to third parties.

When countries like Georgia and Ukraine have chosen leaders who have tried to break away from economic and political dependence on Russia, formal and informal norms of behaviour have been broken, and the conflict between Europe and Russia has deepened. This was seen in 2003–2004, with the 'colour revolutions', and again with Russia's military intrusion into Georgian territory in 2008 and into Ukrainian territory from 2014 on. On the surface, the aim of official Russian statements may seem to have been to defend the rights of Russian-speaking populations—in connection, for example, with Ukraine's legislation on the standing of the Russian language in that country. Observers with knowledge, however, of how the opposition within Russia has not just been restricted but also eliminated—through politically controlled trials, repression by government agencies, forced exile, and even political assassination—realised early on that the Kremlin's actions evinced no true concern for the rights of Russian-speakers in the post-Soviet sphere (Snegovaya, 2023; Umland, 2021).

Despite a large number of clear signs of what was to come, relatively few outsiders read the situation correctly in the months leading up to the invasion in February 2022. Most observers expected a military operation limited to the Donbass—the area in southeastern Ukraine over which Russia already exercised considerable control. Others pointed to the enormous financial losses that members of Putin's inner circle would likely suffer in the event of open military conflict. It is well-known that Russia's political leaders are intertwined with the members of its economic elite, who control a wide range of industries—above all in oil and gas—and who have taken enormous assets out of Russia and placed them in a number of European countries instead. Observers expected both Putin and his closest confidants to take care first and foremost not to risk endangering such assets through actions that would elicit far-reaching economic sanctions or political isolation (Gardner, 2022).

European Security: Signs of Renewed Consolidation

The portrayal of the EU as a 'normative power' (Manners, 2002), has sometimes been criticised for expressing smugness or even a sense of moral superiority among EU citizens and leaders. In this understanding, the EU does not behave in the classical fashion of a great power: instead of practising power politics, it conducts a positive type of foreign policy—thereby exerting an 'attraction' over others in the world, rather than inspiring respect or fear for its military might or material strength (For a more extensive treatment of this concept, see Ann-Kristin Jonasson's chapter in this volume). It can be argued that the war in Ukraine has shown the potential strength of consistent action in accordance with strong moral conviction, which according to many is central to the concept of 'normative power'. Such moral conviction not only increases the power of resistance, the will to defend; it also boosts the fighting morale of the soldiers charged with defending a Ukraine oriented towards Europe and the EU. Similarly, many EU leaders and officials, and millions of EU citizens, strongly empathise with Ukraine's struggle in the face of tough military odds—a struggle to which citizens themselves are showing great commitment.

Russian political leaders clearly hoped that the 'special military operation', not unlike the takeover of Crimea in February 2014, would be accomplished quickly and with overwhelming force (Harris et al, 2022). There would be no time for any far-reaching mobilisation of Ukraine's armed forces or civil society; nor would outside assistance to the Ukrainian authorities be possible. This proved, however, not to be the case. Already in the first days of the combat, moreover, the lack of any justification for the invasion in terms of international law served to strengthen Ukraine's cause. At an emergency special session of the UN General Assembly on 2 March 2022, the Russian invasion was condemned by 141 votes to five; 35 countries abstained, while another twelve were absent (UN News, 2022). The resolution also demanded that civilians be protected and that access to humanitarian aid be ensured.

Unlike the case in the UN, the condemnation from NATO and the EU regarding the invasion was altogether unison, and emphatic besides. It was also quickly followed up by a series of concrete countermeasures. In the course of 2022 and 2023, as shown in Table 9.2, a series of joint decisions and sanctions 'packages'—coordinated with the US and a number of like-minded countries—expanded the breadth and depth of the Union's economic sanctions. The legal basis for EU action had already been laid in important respects in 2014, when sanctions were imposed in connection with Russia's takeover of Crimea (European Council Regulations 208/2014 & 269/2014). However, the Union's efforts in this regard were gradually expanded and specified through export bans on technology in the maritime, space, and aviation sectors; on technology and services in the area of energy; on electronics and machinery with a potential for strengthening Russia's industrial capacity; on trade in gold and gold products; on petroleum products via a so-called price cap; on Russian media companies broadcasting in Arabic; on the Wagner Group private military entity. Similarly, in several stages over the course of 2022, the access of Russian banks to the so-called SWIFT system was restricted.

Illustrating: implemented sanctions against Russia by the European Union and like-minded entities, autumn 2023.

Imports banned during the spring and summer of 2022 included wood, coal, cement, fossil fuels, petroleum products, and iron and steel products. Bans were then extended as well to other products that generate significant revenues for the Russian state—revenues that can be used in turn to finance Russia's warfare in Ukraine. Some of the most effective sanctions—the price cap on crude oil and a ban on maritime transport of Russian oil and petroleum products—took effect in late 2022 or early 2023. Already on 31 August 2022, the EU cancelled the relaxation of visa rules that had applied for Russian citizens since 2007.

One significant weakness in the sanctions regime in 2022 was the fact that several European countries—notably Germany, Italy, the Netherlands, and Poland—had grown dependent on imports of Russian fossil fuels through long-term agreements and shared infrastructure for the transport of natural gas (see Becker and Åslund this volume). The Kremlin was clearly aware of this weakness, and imagined it meant that European governments would not be able to put very great economic pressure on Russia. Greek shipping companies were allowed to continue transporting Russian oil, and Belgian diamond merchants could continue to import rough diamonds. However, these concessions were of minor importance for Russia's state revenues overall. Overall, the problem of sanctions-evasion had more to do with a lack of political support for EU objectives in parts of the Middle East, Asia, and Latin America.

Had the war ended quickly, the political calculation in European countries might not have changed. However, the protracted situation that followed Ukraine's successful resistance to the invasion meant there was enough time to mobilise structural countermeasures, and not least to take various steps to reduce dependence on Russian gas. The coordinating role played by the European Commission—and maybe also the fact that its current president, Ursula von der Leyen, was once Germany's defence minister—contributed to the ability of the Union's member states to come together and to mitigate the impact of reduced imports of natural gas. The problem here consists, however, not just in the dependence itself, but also in the enormous revenues that Russia generates through its combined energy exports—revenues that far exceeded the loans and aid offered to Ukraine until the fall of 2022.

While political solidarity with Ukraine has been unanimous, the readiness to supply Kyiv with military support has been more variable, both over time and as between different governments. Training assistance for Ukraine's armed forces has been ongoing since 2014. For the most part, however, the delivery of complete weapons systems was long conspicuous by its absence. This sluggishness was due in part to Ukraine's financial situation (the country struggled with deficits during the 2010s), and in part to political considerations (Goldberg, 2016). NATO countries have been aware all along that the Kremlin can cite the sale (or transfer) of advanced weapons systems to Ukraine in support of its claim that Western countries, especially the US, seek to advance their geopolitical position to Ukraine's eastern border and 'contain', and eventually threaten, Russia. Even the delivery of state-of-the-art defensive systems, such as the Javelin anti-tank missile, has come under constant scrutiny in arms-producing countries. It was first in early February 2022 that the UK started exporting the British-Swedish equivalent of the Javelin—the NLAW system—to the Ukrainian army.

The situation changed very soon after Russia's full-scale invasion in late February 2022. The governments first and foremost of NATO countries bordering on Russia, Belarus, or Ukraine itself started delivering various weapons systems. A 'triangular' pattern of export emerged, whereby Czechia, Slovakia, Romania, and Bulgaria supplied Ukraine with Warsaw Pact-era materiel; and Germany, the UK, and the US supplied more modern, NATO-compatible weaponry to the former countries. It could be a question of tanks, artillery pieces, or military vehicles. This way, the Ukrainian armed forces would not need to spend time practising with the equipment supplied; instead, they could start using it immediately. An accelerated modernisation of materiel within Central Europe's armed forces took place thereby—a modernisation which would otherwise, on the basis of regular methods of procurement, have taken a longer time.

A qualitative shift in terms of military support took place in the spring of 2022, when the US and France started transferring long-range missile and artillery systems—of the HIMARS, M777, and Caesar types respectively—to the Ukrainian army. These require time for training and for incorporation into logistics systems, which is why it was only in June and July that they could start being used. At that point, however, the military impact was considerable: Russian command centres and ammunition depots behind the front lines were attacked to great effect, and the Russian offensive in the Donetsk and Luhansk regions came to a halt. In addition, deliveries of American-made *Harpoon* anti-ship missiles—from among other sources the Danish military—helped persuade Russia's Black Sea fleet to stay further away from the Ukrainian mainland, as did an increasingly effective use of drones by Ukrainian armed forces.

It bears noting too that the EU and NATO, after decades of friction and mutual rivalry in the area of security, seem to have reached a new consensus as a result of the Ukraine war and their concerted action in 2022–23. This consensus applies not least to the need for an autonomous European conventional military capacity that can be deployed in the continent's immediate proximity. The two organisations have also taken a quite pragmatic stance where the shared utilisation of logistical resources is concerned.

Why a Security Order Is Ultimately Dependent on Military Capacity

The normative power of the Union is insufficient, however, when the adversary is a great power whose political leadership has already shown itself prepared to use military means to enforce its will, to conquer territories, and to destroy the infrastructure, economic life, and social institutions of its enemies—as well as to undermine the authority of the EU and NATO. There is no doubt that the European security order is at stake in the war between Russia and Ukraine. The demands that the Kremlin, with increasing intensity, has made on NATO, the EU, and all of their member states are extremely far-reaching. Moscow claims the right to veto the deployment of weapons systems in Russia's vicinity, as well as the membership of other countries in security organisations. It also aims, at least as much, to force former Soviet republics—especially those with Russian-speaking or other Slavic populations—to adhere to its preferred political and economic order. In other words, the Kremlin does not regard sovereignty or territorial integrity as valid principles for Russia's 'near abroad' (Deyermond, 2016).

As long, however, as these demands were made through diplomatic channels and within the framework of organisations like the OSCE—as they were until 2014—they could be dealt with by political means. Western powers have made various concessions over the years, without by virtue of that accepting any undermining of the European security order itself. Now, however—after Russia's invasion of Ukraine—there is a large consensus among observers that diplomacy is no longer an effective means. The tools of *Realpolitik* must be used in defence of Europe's security order. Since February 2022, moreover, it has been clear that they must be used before opposed military forces create realities 'on the ground' that are extremely hard to reverse (Bugayova, 2022).

As early as the fall of 2021, the administration of President Joe Biden seems to have had highly reliable information on the far-reaching plans of Russia's political and military leaders. US leaders understood early on that Europe's security order was under direct threat. They found themselves faced with several decision-making dilemmas, having among other things to do with the leaders of Ukraine, who wanted to keep their economy going as long as possible, and who therefore sought to avoid giving public expression to their unease. In addition, President Biden, Secretary of State Antony Blinken, Secretary of Defense Lloyd Austin, and National Security Advisor Jake Sullivan found it hard to convince their European partners that the intelligence was credible, and the attempt of US leaders to mislead the world before the invasion of Iraq in 2003 seems to have played a role here (Beaumont, 2022).

These dilemmas and past experiences were swept aside the moment Russian troops crossed the border on 24 February. Their place was taken by a consensus regarding the threat to Europe, and to the institutions that had more or less guaranteed peace on the continent—with exceptions such as the Cyprus conflict in 1974 and the violent disintegration of Yugoslavia in the 1990s—since the end of the Second World War. Achieving unity on the need to defend Ukraine's sovereignty was suddenly easy, and all were agreed on the need to provide humanitarian, political, and financial support to that country. As noted above, however, there has been less agreement on the provision of military support, or on what economic and other sacrifices the citizens of Europe should be called upon to make in order to help Ukraine resist Russia's territorial demands.

One manifest challenge for Europe's countries lies in the fact that political and economic commitments need to be aligned with the will to maintain the European security order (Engelbrekt & Hallenberg, 2007). This will is far from identical, for geographic and historical reasons, across the whole continent. Nevertheless, the experience of successful cooperation over several decades does furnish fairly firm ground on which to stand. Furthermore, Western countries are the time of writing (autumn 2023) providing resources—including military ones—needed to repel Russia's attack and thus to refuse its demands for an alternative security order. Anything that might be interpreted as a Russian 'victory' risk undermining the entire security order in the long run. In such a case, namely, rules and principles which are perceived as fundamental would be set at nought. Restoring the *status quo ante*—i.e., the situation that prevailed prior to 24 February 2022—was always viewed as a minimum requirement for being able to say that Russia's demands have been denied. By the autumn of 2023, President Volodomyr Zelenskyy told the UN Security Council that nothing short of full restoration of the 1991 borders including Crimea was acceptable to his fellow citizens (Lederer and Peltz 2023).

The stamina shown by European countries and their common institutions will likely be decisive for whether the security order on the continent lasts. Already after six months of warfare, it was clear that Ukraine had been the biggest loser, that the economy of the Union's member states had been negatively affected, and that the Russian Federation had mainly suffered losses in terms of reduced imports. Exports of gas, coal, crude oil, and petroleum products, which constitute Russia's main sources of income, fell only slowly, while their prices rose sharply. As a result, the country's revenues from its energy exports remained large until they began decreasing in early 2023, thus for many months helping to finance the war.

Due to a range of factors—military, geographic, economic, and politico-moral—Ukraine's ability to retake most of what Russian forces captured in 2022 is likely to be critical for the credibility of Europe's security order. To be sure, one can argue that the very failure of Moscow's most ambitious war goals—to take over the whole country save for a quarter portion in the west—demonstrates the viability of said security order. The fact that Ukraine and its European allies resisted the attack and were able to limit its success to less than half of Russia's original plans would thus be a sign that the security order largely endures, and that greater vigilance going forward may be sufficient to keep it alive. A more pessimistic view, in line with the predictions of Ukrainian leaders and of Russia experts, is that Putin and his sympathisers within and outside Europe will consider such an outcome to be a partial victory. The risk in that case is that Russia's leaders will try to conquer more Ukrainian territory at a later stage. Moreover, an outcome of this kind might inspire others who seek border changes in violation of Europe's current security order, e.g., rendering permanent the separate status of Transnistria from the Republic of Moldova.

European decision-makers were also increasingly worried about what they perceived as a greatly increased propensity on the part of Russian leaders to take risks. In the same way that European leaders viewed the continent's security as under challenge and as requiring defence by all available means, the Kremlin saw regime stability as dependent on a successful military campaign. That the stakes were seen as high was already evident in Putin's repeated warnings to Western leaders against intervening on Ukraine's side in the war. He announced, notably, that nuclear forces would be put on alert. When Russian troops occupied parts of Ukraine's Zaporizhzhya region and placed combat vehicles and artillery in the immediate vicinity of the nuclear power plant there, Europe's largest, the aforementioned propensity was confirmed again. In 2022 and 2023, representatives of the International Atomic Energy Agency (IAEA) repeatedly expressed great concern that the nuclear plant could be seriously damaged by the fighting, thereby causing a nuclear accident with consequences far beyond Ukraine.

Some of these fears nevertheless abated in the second year of the war, as Ukraine's armed forces were able to independently recapture large swaths of the Kharkiv and Kherson regions as part of the broader counteroffensive. Given that Russia's reputation as a major international power inevitably is at stake when allegations of war crimes, genocide and gross violations of the UN Charter have accumulated, restraining factors are assumed to be at work. As long as the United States and European allies and partners only gradually provided advanced military assistance to the Ukrainian armed forces in 2022–2023, this incrementalism was expected to reduce the risk of rash escalation on the part of the Kremlin. In the spring of 2023, however, voices urging Western governments to tip the scales in favour of Ukraine's armed forces grew stronger (see, e g, Schadlow, 2023).

The Demands of Great Powers in the Future, Both Within and Outside Europe

For more than two decades now, Putin's Russia has been calling for a multipolar world order where the US no longer plays the role of guarantor of regional stability, free trade, and freedom of navigation in Europe, the Middle East, East Asia, and Central and South America. It was with the aim of achieving such an order that, already in 2005, Russia entered into a 'special partnership' with the People's Republic of China (PRC). Subsequently, it spearheaded the establishment of the Shanghai Cooperation Organisation, as well as—together with Brazil, China, India, and South Africa—of the 'BRICS' group. Russia has also been very active in the informal body for cooperation between the world's twenty biggest economies, the *G*20, especially after it got expelled from the *G*8 in 2014 due to its annexation of Crimea. (The current *G*7 only includes countries—Canada, France, Germany, Italy, Japan, the UK, and the US—that recognise each other as functioning democracies, plus the EU.)

Although Russia in particular was the driving force behind the launch of bodies like BRICS and the Shanghai Cooperation Organisation, signs have been accumulating for some time that other regional powers wish to expand their own room for manoeuvre. Not least the BRICS countries have become more active in their neighbouring areas, even as they have worked together to support each other's interests vis-à-vis the US and its allies. For example, they have discussed the possibility of laying underwater cables between them, so as to offer an alternative communication infrastructure to the one in place (provided as the latter has been by the West and especially the United States) (Braw, 2023). Recent military investments by regional great powers, which have been significant in both quantitative and qualitative terms, suggest that diplomacy and trade policy may be marked in the future by an undertone of coercion—something of which neighbouring countries may need to take account in their security policy. The most important player here, not unexpectedly, is the PRC, with its ever larger defence budget.

The main arena within which the struggle between the US and the PRC may end up being fought out is currently Taiwan, to which Washington has made renewed security commitments in recent years. The PRC's line towards Taiwan, which it regards as a kind of apostate from the true fatherland, has hardened significantly under the current president, Xi Jinping. This in turn must be interpreted as aimed at the position of the US in East Asia generally. The fact that few members of the international community recognise Taiwan as an independent state facilitates attempts by the PRC to get other countries to discontinue their protests and expressions of solidarity with Taipei. The way in which Beijing managed to 'discipline' Hong Kong—by introducing several new laws (especially the Security Law that went into force in mid-2020) and revoking various rights and freedoms—looks like a dress rehearsal for what it hopes to achieve in Taiwan over the next few years.

It is logical and probably unavoidable for the EU and the European part of NATO to respond to such global and regional challenges in the future with a more robust security and defence policy, following the pro-Taiwanese example of Lithuania (Lau, 2023). Such a policy will need, moreover, to be accompanied by the development of a larger and more usable military capability. Relying on the Union's diplomatic voice seems naive here, particularly now that China's leaders and like-minded people have sided with Russia rather than Ukraine in connection with the most serious military conflict in Europe since 1945. In this regard, Germany's dramatic investment over the next few years in defence—to the tune of 100 billion euros, alongside its regular defence budget of 50 billion—stands out as the most important development (Fleischer, 2023). This special appropriation is intended for the German Air Force, which wants to acquire helicopters and more F-35 fighter jets. But it is not enough for European countries simply to increase their defence budgets. If they are to be capable of acting jointly vis-à-vis other parts of the world, they must also maintain their unity and internal stability.

The Americans, for their part, have long thought—since well before the outbreak of the war in Ukraine—that their European allies ought to increase their defence spending substantially. At least since Obama's first term as president (2009–2013), the US has sought to convince its European allies of the need to upgrade their defence capabilities significantly. Such a move would be particularly apposite, in the American view, given the steadily growing weight of Asia's economies in the world, and the consequent need to transfer American military resources to the region. It is only in recent years, however, that leading politicians and defence experts in NATO and the EU have started systematically collaborating to accomplish such a shift—now that they see an acute need and experience broader public support for European defence (Engelbrekt, 2022; Karampekios, 2015).

Building up a robust conventional military capacity in Europe capable of replacing the American one will take time. The same applies to getting the armed forces of the different countries to cooperate in the absence of any strong American component (which has always served as a common denominator in a NATO context). The funds which the EU is now prepared to invest in 'military mobility'—i.e., on being able to move troops and resources from one part of Europe to another—are a good start, as are the Permanent Structured Cooperation (PESCO) and the European Defence Fund (the last of which was added to the Union's budget in 2021) (Britz, 2023). The year 2022 saw the completion of the work of developing a 'strategic compass' within the EU, the aim of which was to get a better overview of various cooperative projects, to coordinate them more effectively, and thereby to strengthen the European Security and Defence Policy (ESDP). On this basis, it is hoped, cyber defence can be strengthened, cooperation on intelligence matters improved, defence expenditures utilised more effectively, and the fight against deception and disinformation expanded—thereby enhancing military capacity and operational readiness in the EU's immediate surroundings.

The European External Action Service (EEAS) headed by the High Representative—currently Josep Borrell of Spain—has been an important component of the Union's ambition to play a 'strategic role' in the world beyond Europe. The EEAS today has over 4,000 employees, of whom about half serve in more than 140 EU delegations in most independent states, with multilateral accreditation in the remaining countries represented in the UN, and in cities that host international organisations (Addis Ababa, Geneva, New York, Paris, Rome, and Vienna). Roughly half of the employees in these delegations are sent out by the various directorates-general of the European Commission or the EEAS; and their work is often in the areas of trade, migration, energy supply, counter-terrorism, or development assistance.

The British decision to leave the EU has the effect of temporarily undermining the latter's ambition to gain greater credibility as a strategic actor and to increase its independence vis-à-vis the US, the PRC, and a number of regional powers. Yet, in the shadow of the war in Ukraine, a more optimistic sense of the matter—that work can continue in the same spirit towards a Union that is 'sharper' and more capable of making and implementing decisions—may be showing itself to be warranted. It has really only been, after all, in the course of managing crises in connection with Brexit, the COVID-19 pandemic, and the war in Ukraine that the Union's main decision-makers and institutions have had to show clear and firm leadership. Not having given in to populist pressures from British negotiators; having agreed on the joint purchase and distribution of COVID-19 vaccines; and having instituted increasingly effective sanctions against Russia—these achievements seem to have resulted in greater self-confidence in Brussels.

The Road to a More Robust European Security Order

As long as Russia fails to renounce its political and military claims on Ukraine, as well as its efforts to dictate the terms of the foreign and domestic policies pursued by its Western neighbours, the acute threat to the European security order will persist. A change of regime in Moscow, combined with a Russian military collapse in southeastern Ukraine, could remove the short-term threat; but not even a new Russian government would necessarily take a different attitude. Nor would new leaders necessarily succeed in altering the views of those elements in society that support the country's aggression against Ukraine; or which are deeply suspicious of NATO, the US, and the Western world in general. In other words, the security problems that have resulted from the war in Ukraine, and from the demands Moscow has made in connection with it, are likely to last for quite some time.

As far as Europe and the EU are concerned, there is therefore no alternative at present to putting the house in order in terms of security and societal resilience. This means preserving political unity on the continent as best one can; further reducing the dependence on Russian oil, gas, fertiliser, rare metals and other income-generating exports; and preparing to defend Europe against the threat from the east with such societal and military means as may be necessary. It means working with several different types of question at the same time, so as to increase stamina and resilience in Europe as a whole. And it means taking defence issues more seriously than has been done over the last three decades—i.e., since the end of the Cold War.

Satisfaction is in order, to be sure, at Europe's relatively robust and unified response during the first eighteen months of this crisis: the sanctions imposed on Russia, the financial and diplomatic support extended to Ukraine, and so on. In this regard, as the situation looks now in the autumn of 2023, the Union's institutions, its member states, and Europe's civil society have passed the test with flying colours. Military defence, however, is clearly neglected in the majority of EU countries, and it will take a period approaching a decade to build up the capability to defend European territory with conventional forces without American help. In addition to joint investments in defence industries, in transport capacity, and in infrastructure, efforts are needed in the training of officers and the recruitment of soldiers and conscripts. Measures must be taken to ensure that, in the face of changing conditions on the labour market, members of the military are retained. Defence capabilities must be developed in close cooperation with industrial enterprises and academic institutions—ideally in European research networks and consortia—so as to achieve synergies and to ensure that scarce resources are well-spent.

Where the 'nuclear umbrella' over Europe is concerned, dependence on the US will continue for a longer time, largely irrespective of what measures are taken in Brussels in the coming years. Neither France, nor Germany, nor the UK is in a position to replace American nuclear weapons over the short or medium term. It is not least here that the transatlantic link needs to be nurtured (Engelbrekt, 2022). This will be necessary in order to ensure that the US, or indeed Europe, does not neglect over the long run to conduct successful cooperation on matters of security. To the extent that strategic and geopolitical rivalry at the global level continues to intensify over the next few decades, the value of a robust transatlantic link will likely increase rather than diminish.

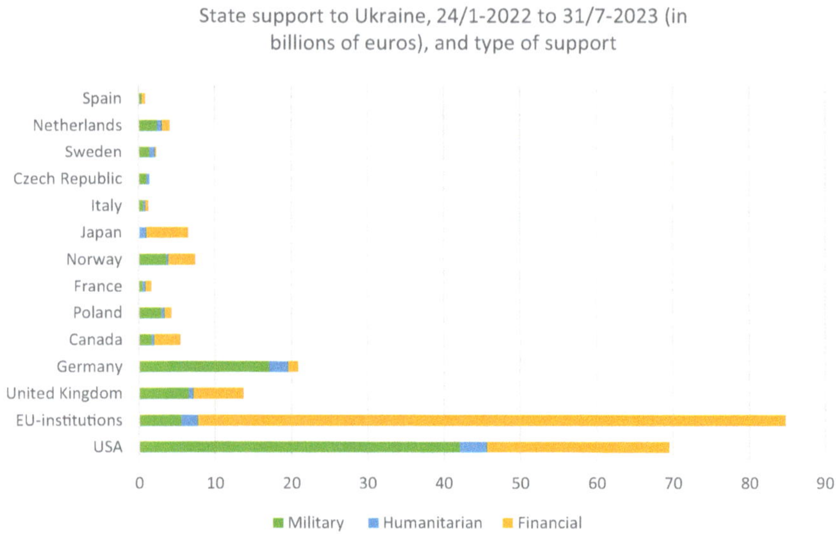

Fig. 9.1 Govermental support to Ukraine. *Source* 'Ukraine support tracker', website to a database on military, financial, and humanitarian aid to Ukraine, KIEL institute for the World Economy, 2023

Table 9.1 EU's enlargement following the signing of the European coal and steel community on april 18, 1951 (European Parliament 2023) EU's enlargement

January 1973	*Denmark, Ireland, and the UK*
January 1981	Greece
January 1987	Portugal and Spain
January 1995	Austria, Finland, and Sweden
May 2004	Cyprus, Czech Republic, Estonia, Hungary, Latvia, Lithuania, Malta, Poland. Slovakia, and Slovenia
January 2007	Bulgaria and Rumania
July 2013	Croatia

Source 'History of the EU', official EU homepage, European union

Table 9.2 Sanctions imposed on Russia by EU and like-minded countries, Fall 2023

Type of support for Ukraine	*Number of countries participating*	*Countries*
Imposed financial sanctions on Russia	45	EU's 27 member states, Albania, Australia, Bahamas, Canada, Iceland, Japan, Kosovo, Liechtenstein, Montenegro, New Zealand, North Macedonia, Norway, Singapore, South Korea, Switzerland, Taiwan, the UK, and the US
Restricted Russian banks' access to the SWIFT system for financial transactions	33	EU's 27 member states, Canada, Japan, South Korea, Taiwan, the UK, and the US
Closed airspace to Russian aircraft	36	EU's 27 member states, Albania, Canada, Iceland, Montenegro, North Macedonia, Norway, Switzerland, the UK, and the US
Adopted full suspension of visa facilitation with Russia.	34—full suspension 2—not full suspension, but in the process of implementation	EU - Announced full suspension of VFA as from 12 September 2022. Albania, North Macedonia, Norway, Switzerland, Taiwan and the US have aligned Montenegro—Aspires to align with EU. Have proposed cancellation of the visa-free regime for Russian citizens Kazakhstan—Ends unlimited stay for Russians
Agreed on level of price caps for Russian petroleum products	32	EU's 27 member states, G7 Countries (Canada, France, Germany, Italy, Japan, the United Kingdom, and the United States) and Australia

Source Official EU Homepage, European Commission 2023

References

Allison, R. (2014). Russian 'deniable' intervention in Ukraine: How and why Russia broke the rules. *International Affairs, 90*(6), 1255–1296.

Beaumont, P. (2022). The invasion of Iraq was a turning point on to a path that led towards Ukraine, *The Guardian*, 19 March, https://www.theguardian.com/commentisfree/2023/mar/19/2003-iraq-invasion-legacy-west-international-law-ukraine.

Belton, C. (2020). *Putin's People: How the KGB Took Back Russia and then Took on the West*. London: William Collins.

Braw, E. (2023). Decoupling Is Already Happening—Under the Sea, *Foreign Policy*, 24 May, https://foreignpolicy.com/2023/05/24/china-subsea-cables-internet-decoupling-biden/.

Britz, M. (2023). European Defence Policy: Between Flexible Integration and a Defence Union. In: Bakardjieva Engelbrekt, A., Ekman, P., Michalski, A. and L. Oxelheim (Ed.), *The EU between Federal Union and Flexible Integration: Interdisciplinary European Studies* (pp. 215–238). Basingstoke: Palgrave Macmillan.

Bugayova, N. (2022). The Window To Expel Russia From Ukraine Is Now. *Foreign Policy.* https://foreignpolicy.com/2022/05/19/russia-ukraine-war-west-military-aid/.

Bukkvoll, T. (2016). Why Putin went to war: Ideology, interests and decision-making in the Russian use of force in Crimea and Donbas. *Contemporary Politics, 22*(3), 267–282.

Deyermond, R. (2016). The Uses of Sovereignty in Twenty-first Century Russian Foreign Policy. *Europe-Asia Studies, 68*(6), 957–984. https://doi.org/10.1080/09668136.2016.1204985.

Engelbrekt, K., & Nygren, B. (Eds.). (2010). *Russia and Europe: Building Bridges, Digging Trenches*. London: Routledge.

Engelbrekt, K. (2013). Den «återställda» dialogen USA-Ryssland – Multilateral diplomati i OSSE och FN:s Säkerhetsråd 2009–2011. *Internasjonal politikk*, 71(4), 533–560.

Engelbrekt, K. (2022). Beyond Burdensharing and European Strategic Autonomy: Rebuilding Transatlantic Security after the Ukraine War. *European Foreign Affairs Review*, 27(3): 1–17.

Engelbrekt, K., & Hallenberg, J. (Eds.). (2007). *The European Union and Strategy: An Emerging Actor*. London: Routledge.

European Commission (2022). EU sanctions against Russia following the invasion of Ukraine. *EU Solidarity with Ukraine*. https://eu-solidarity-ukraine.ec.europa.eu/eu-sanctions-against-russia-following-invasion-ukraine_en.

European Council (2022). Seventh Progress Report on the Implementation of the Common Set of Proposals Endorsed by EU and NATO Councils on 6 December 2016 and 5 December 2017. *EU-NATO Progress Report*

(2022) 20 June 2022, https://www.consilium.europa.eu/media/57184/eu-nato-progress-report.pdf.

European Council Regulation 208 (2014). Regulation concerning restrictive measures directed against certain persons, entities and bodies in view of the situation in Ukraine, 5 March, https://eur-lex.europa.eu/legal-content/EN/TXT/?uri=celex%3A32014R0208.

European Council Regulation 269 (2014). Regulation concerning restrictive measures in respect of actions undermining or threatening the territorial integrity, sovereignty and independence of Ukraine, 17 March, https://eur-lex.europa.eu/legal-content/EN/TXT/?uri=CELEX%3A32014R0269.

European Parliament (2023). 40 Years of Enlargement. Who has joined the EU so far? European Parliament official homepage, https://www.europarl.europa.eu/external/html/euenlargement/default_en.htm.

Ewers-Peters, N. (2021). *Understanding EU-NATO cooperation: how member states matter*. Routledge, Taylor & Francis Group.

Fleischer, J. (2023). Bundeskanzler: „Wir machen Schluss mit der Vernachlässigung der Bundeswehr", German Ministry of Defence, 2 March, https://www.bmvg.de/de/aktuelles/ein-jahr-zeitenwende-bundeskanzler-gibt-regierungserklaerung-ab-5590270.

Flynn, G., & Farrell, H. (1999). Piecing Together the Democratic Peace: The CSCE, Norms, and the '"Construction"' of Security in Post-Cold War Europe. *International Organization, 53*(3), 505–535.

Frazier, D. & Stewart-Ingersoll, R. (2012). *Regional Powers and Security Orders: A Theoretical Framework.* London: Routledge.

Fried, D. & Volker, K. (2022). The Speech in Which Putin Told Us Who He Was, *Politico*, 18 February, https://www.politico.com/news/magazine/2022/02/18/putin-speech-wake-up-call-post-cold-war-order-liberal-2007-00009918.

Gardner, F. (2022). Ukraine crisis: Five reasons why Putin might not invade, *BBC News*, 21 February, https://www.bbc.com/news/world-europe-60468264.

Goldberg, J. 2016. The Obama Doctrine, *The Atlantic*, 10 March, https://www.theatlantic.com/magazine/archive/2016/04/the-obama-doctrine/471525/.

Harris, S., DeYoung, K., Khurshudyan, I., Parker, A., & Sly, L. (2022). Road to War: U.S. Struggled to Convince Allies, and Zelensky, of Risk of Invasion. *The Washington Post,* 16 August, https://www.washingtonpost.com/national-security/interactive/2022/ukraine-road-to-war/.

Inis, L.C. (2011). Collective Security as an Approach to Peace. In Goldstein, D. Williams P., & Shafritz M. (Eds). *Classic Readings and Contemporary Debates in International Relations*, (pp.289–302). Belmont Institute for the Study of War and AEI's Critical Threats Project (2022). Interactive Map: Russia's

Invasion of Ukraine, https://storymaps.arcgis.com/stories/36a7f6a6f5a9448496de641cf64bd375.

Karampekios, N. (2015). *The European Defence Agency: Arming Europe*. Routledge.

Kiel Institute for the World Economy. (2023). Ukraine Support Tracker, https://www.ifw-kiel.de/topics/war-against-ukraine/ukraine-support-tracker/?cookieLevel=not-set.

Kramer, A. & Erlanger, S. (2021). Russia Lays Out Demands for a Sweeping New Security Deal With NATO, *The New York Times*, 17 December, https://www.nytimes.com/2021/12/17/world/europe/russia-nato-security-deal.html.

Kupchan, C. & Kupchan, C. A. (1995). The Promise of Collective Security. *International Security* 20(1), 52–61.

Lake D., & Morgan M. P. (1997). *Regional Orders: Building Security in a New World*. University Park: Pennsylvania State University Press.

Lau, S. (2023). Lithuania defies China over Taiwan ties in new Asia strategy, *Politico*, 6 July, https://www.politico.eu/article/lithuania-defies-china-over-taiwan-ties-in-new-asia-strategy-xi-jinping/.

Lederer, E. & Peltz, J. (2023). Ukraine's president, at Security Council, lashes out at Russia but avoids face-to-face encounter, *AP News*, 21 September, https://apnews.com/article/ukraine-russia-war-un-general-assembly-9b8c2ab7b7cec53753b03fbbd8f0f973.

Lopez, T. (2019). U.S. Withdraws From Intermediate-Range Nuclear Forces Treaty, 2 August, U.S. Department of Defense, https://www.defense.gov/News/News-Stories/article/article/1924779/us-withdraws-from-intermediate-range-nuclear-forces-treaty/.

Manners, I. (2002). Normative Power Europe: A Contradiction in Terms? *Journal of Common Market Studies, 40*(2), 235–258.

Mearsheimer, J. (2014). Why the Ukraine Crisis Is the West's Fault: The Liberal Delusions That Provoked Putin. *Foreign Affairs, 93*(5), 77–89.

NATO. (2023). 'Milestones', NATO official homepage, https://www.nato.int/cps/en/natohq/topics_49212.htm#accession.

Roth, A. (2022). Putin issues fresh warning to Finland and Sweden on installing Nato infrastructure, *The Guardian*, 30 June, https://www.theguardian.com/world/2022/jun/29/russia-condemns-nato-invitation-finland-sweden.

Schadlow, N. (2023). Incrementalism Is Throttling U.S. Support for Ukraine, *Foreign Policy*, 9 March, https://foreignpolicy.com/2023/03/09/us-military-support-ukraine-war-russia-biden-incrementalism/.

Snegovaya, M. (2023). Why Russia's Democracy Never Began. *Journal of Democracy, 34*(3), 105–118.

Statista Research Department (2023). Russia-Ukraine War 2022 – statistics and facts. https://www.statista.com/topics/9087/russia-ukraine-war-2022/.

Stronski, P. & Sokolsky, R. (2020). Multipolarity in Practice: Russia's Engagement with Regional Institutions. *Carnegie Endowment for International Peace*, [online] 8 January, Available at: https://carnegieendowment.org/files/Stronski_Sokolsky_Multipolarity_final.pdf.

Umland, A. (2021) *Achievements and Limitations of the OSCE's Special Monitoring Mission to Ukraine*. The Swedish Institute of International Affairs, Stockholm.

UN Charter. (1945). Chapter I: Purposes and Principles. United Nations official homepage. The Charter was adopted in San Francisco 26 June 1945 and went in force since 24 October that year. https://www.un.org/en/about-us/un-charter/full-text.

UN News (2022). General Assembly resolution demands end to Russian offensive in Ukraine, 2 March, https://news.un.org/en/story/2022/03/1113152.

Wallace, W. (1994). *Regional Integration: The West European Experience*. Brookings.

CHAPTER 10

A European Marshall Plan for Ukraine on the Way to the EU

Anders Åslund and Torbjörn Becker

On February 24, 2022, Russia attacked Ukraine without any legitimate cause. Until the very end, Russia's President Vladimir Putin denied that he would attack Ukraine, but he did so anyway, starting the biggest war Europe has seen since World War II. At the end of 2023, the war is still in full swing, and its outcome remains unclear, but the start of the war united the EU like never before in its foreign policy in favor of Ukraine and against Russia.

Russia's war of aggression against Ukraine will affect Europe's borders for a long time to come. In June 2022, the EU declared that Ukraine had become a candidate to become a member of the EU (European Union, 2022). At the same time, the EU gave Moldova the same important status. Russia and Belarus, on the other hand, have ended up outside

A. Åslund
Georgetown University, Washington, USA

T. Becker (✉)
Stockholm School of Economics, Stockholm, Sweden
e-mail: Torbjorn.Becker@hhs.se

A. Bakardjieva Engelbrekt et al. (eds.), *The Borders of the European Union in a Conflictual World*,
https://doi.org/10.1007/978-3-031-54200-8_10

Europe for as long as their current authoritarian and lawless regimes remain.

Without predicting when the war will end, for our analysis we make three assumptions. First, we assume that the war will wind down or end in a reasonably near future that we believe is measured in months rather than years. It does not necessarily mean that a peace agreement is reached, but that regular fighting no longer continues. Second, we assume that a large part of Ukraine remains an independent state. Third, we assume that the EU's support for Ukraine will continue, and that Ukraine will eventually become a full member of the EU. Based on these three assumptions we propose a European Marshall Plan for Ukraine aimed at a combination of three important processes: reconstruction, reform, and EU accession.

In the second half of 2022, a Marshall Plan for Ukraine became a major topic, for which many argued. The first more comprehensive proposal was presented in Becker et al. (2022a) already in April of 2022. Based on that proposal we here outline our view on how a European Marshall Plan for Ukraine can be designed while planning for a future EU membership for Ukraine. The plan presented at the G7 and EU meeting in Berlin in October 2022 has many similarities to the proposals in the above-mentioned CEPR report, and these principles and ideas hold.

Several factors make Ukraine's case special. Russia's terror bombing of Ukraine has been crude and ruthless and it has caused enormous costs to Ukraine. How can these costs be financed? The reconstruction consists of many elements. How should it be implemented over time? For three decades, Ukraine has balanced between a post-Soviet system and a freer European system with actual rule of law. Can Ukraine get rid of the corrupt post-Soviet system and become a normal EU state when the war is over? Finally, is it realistic that Ukraine will become a member of the EU and how soon can it happen?

We tackle these questions by first describing the devastation of the war and expected costs of reconstruction. Then we set out the principles that we believe should guide the reconstruction process and the different phases of that process are addressed. Next, we go through how the reconstruction can be financed and what reforms are required. This leads to the central discussion of whether Ukraine can really become a member of the EU. This chapter ends with our conclusions about what should be done in the future to rebuild Ukraine and set out a clear path to the EU.

The Costs of War and Reconstruction

Russia's war on Ukraine has caused the country enormous costs. The Kyiv School of Economics has built up a database where all reported material damages are recorded, and the cost estimated. Of course, these are rough estimates based on what infrastructure has cost historically, but it is the most systematic analysis of the costs of devastation that we know of. It mainly concerns buildings and infrastructure. In June 2023, the Kyiv School of Economics (KSE, 2023) assessed the total direct damage to US$150 billion, which is dominated by destroyed buildings and infrastructure. It should be viewed as a lower mark of the physical damage since it will likely but much more expensive to rebuild than what the past values indicate and also the fact that some historical and cultural sites are hard to value more generally. In February 2023, the World Bank (2023) assessed the cost of Ukraine's recovery and rebuilding from Russia's invasion at $411 billion over the next decade. Given the great uncertainty associated with these calculations, this figure could be doubled. Added to this is the cost of tens of thousands of dead and perhaps three times as many injured and disabled. If the relatives of the dead are to be compensated, the amounts will be very large and the disabled need financial support anyway. In addition, the war has led to large migration flows, lost income, and missed investments that will affect the country's income for a long time.

Ukraine's gross domestic product (GDP) decreased by 29% in 2022, while it appears likely that the GDP will grow by a few percent in 2023 (see Constantinescu et al, 2022). Since Ukraine's GDP was $200 billion in 2021, this would mean a $58 billion shortfall in each of 2022 and 2023. Of course, waging war is also extremely costly and, apart from a large amount of support in the form of military equipment from Ukraine's partners in the West, about half of the state budget goes to the country's defense, according to Ukraine's Ministry of Finance (2023). The reduced production combined with the huge costs of defending the country against Russian aggression have also created immediate challenges for Ukraine's macro economy.

In Becker et al. (2022b), the authors go through these challenges and propose how best to deal with them under the grim constraint that the country must invest so many resources in its defense to survive the war. Hard priorities must be set on the government's expenditure side at the same time that new revenues need to be mobilized so that funding via the banknote press can be reduced. The alternative is a risky macroeconomic path that could lead to high inflation and a currency that falls sharply. The EU and other economic powers such as the US have much to gain by contributing foreign currency to Ukraine's public finances to avoid this scenario. This economic support both reduces the need to print money to manage the state finances internally and enables the import of many essential goods that cannot be produced domestically while the war is going on. Ukraine's government requested budget support from the West of $60 billion in 2022, but it received only $33 billion, which led to inflation of 27% year-over-year in the fourth quarter. Fortunately, the EU and the US have stepped up their financial support for the Ukrainian budget in 2023, so it appears that it will be fully financed with $40 billion in external support (Dragon Capital, 2023a). As a consequence, inflation more than halve in the first half of 2023.

Even before the 2022 war, Ukraine was Europe's poorest country after taking over the bottom spot from Moldova after Russia's first war in 2014, which cost Ukraine a 17% drop in GDP in 2014–15. Russia then occupied 7% of Ukraine's surface, but significantly more of its GDP in the densely populated and highly industrialized Donbass in eastern Ukraine. At the end of 2023, Russia occupied 17% of Ukraine's territory, but the territories occupied since February 2022 contain rather few people.

Ukraine's demographics are astonishingly fluid. The country had 52 million inhabitants in 1989 in the last Soviet census. The population has gradually decreased due to emigration and low birth rates as everywhere in Europe. Before the 2014 war, Ukraine had at most 44 million inhabitants. Furthermore, 5–6 million Ukrainians have occasionally worked abroad for many years but are usually included in the population of Ukraine. Crimea had a population of 2.3 million and the occupied Donbass probably 5 million, of which 1.7 million fled to Ukraine and 0.8 million to Russia. Summing up these figures, Ukraine's remaining population was at most 39 million. Our estimate, however, lands at about 34 million because an estimated 5 million Ukrainians worked in the EU, which was facilitated by visa freedom with the EU.

After the outbreak of war in February 2022, another 6 million Ukrainians fled to Europe, while approximately the same number have taken refuge elsewhere in Ukraine, mainly in western Ukraine. Almost half of the refugees, about 2.5 million, appear to have stayed in Poland. The large number of refugees means high costs in the short term for both

Ukraine and the host countries. As the refugees are primarily women, children, and the elderly and not entire families, many have already returned to Ukraine. For example, according to a presentation by Kyiv's Mayor Vitali Klitschko in April 2023, Kyiv had a population before the war of 3.8 million, which shrunk to 1 million soon after the start of the war, but it has at the beginning of 2024 recovered to 3.5 million, of whom 0.5 million are internally displaced people from the east and the south of Ukraine.

This discussion does not touch on the cost if Ukraine loses part of its land. Piketty (2014) estimates a country's capital relative to its GDP over long periods of time and finds that it averages four times GDP. In Ukraine, that corresponds to about $800 billion before the war started. In August 2022, the World Bank made its own calculations of the capital stock, which ended up at 1 trillion dollars (World Bank, 2022, p. 11). Currently, Russia occupies 17% of Ukraine's territory and if the capital were evenly distributed over the country, the loss of capital could be in the order of 160–200 billion dollars.

The war between Russia and Ukraine will also have major structural consequences. Before the 2014 war, Russia accounted for more than a third of Ukraine's foreign trade. Now this trade has fallen to a few percent, while Ukraine's trade with Europe has expanded. Therefore, Ukraine's entire infrastructure needs to be rebuilt for integration with Europe instead of with Russia.

Of course, the entire economy of Ukraine needs to be restructured and modernized. Its traditional strength was the armaments industry, but it was part of Russia's military-industrial complex, which was broken up in 2014. Instead, the new Ukrainian economy consists of modern large-scale agriculture, high technology, and integration into Europe's supply chain, notably the production of auto parts in the West Ukraine. All this modernization and integration with Europe is of course an important part of Ukraine's accession process to the EU.

Principles of Ukraine's Reconstruction

The principles of Ukraine's reconstruction have been discussed in many different contexts. The principles advanced in Becker et al. (2022a) have gained wide support and can be summarized in the following points:

1. The aid should be rapid but conditional. Ukraine is suffering from a humanitarian disaster. Therefore, speed is important. At the same time, the aid must be associated with reasonable conditions so that the international aid really helps the country, not least in fighting corruption.
2. Since Ukraine's debt burden is already high, the bulk of aid must consist of grants rather than loans. If Ukraine takes out large new loans, it will be forced to renegotiate its sovereign debt, which would likely delay aid.
3. Coordination. Given the multitude of aid sources, close coordination across funding sources and with the recipient will minimize waste and delays.
4. The aid should be administered by a self-standing EU-affiliated agency. Ideally, it should be a new Marshall Plan-style institution.
5. Ukraine must feel that it owns the reconstruction. The aid must be designed in line with Ukraine's democratic processes and not implemented without Ukrainian participation.
6. Ukraine's EU accession should guide institutional reforms. It creates the conditions for the legal framework to be adapted to EU standards, which, among other things, promote free trade and attract foreign direct investment, which are important complements to international aid.
7. The reconstruction offers Ukraine a unique opportunity to modernize its infrastructure and production apparatus. It should raise Ukraine's technological level and integrate Ukraine into the world economy.
8. Finally, reconstruction must be organized so that corruption is controlled and reduced. While the Marshall Aid was a positive experience, the recent aid to Afghanistan and Iraq has been discouraging. High demands must be made with regard to transparency and accountability, while such procedures must not become too bureaucratic and time-consuming. The sums that will be involved are likely to be very large. Ukraine has had many corruption scandals, which is a good indicator of openness, but corruption scandals can easily lead to international opposition to support for Ukraine. Since the funds come from foreign donors, they will demand full transparency on how the funds are used.

The Ukraine aid differs from a normal macroeconomic stabilization program. The IMF has led Ukraine's reform processes and the Ukrainian institutions that work the best, after the military and the church, are probably the central bank, the finance ministry, and the fiscal service. The big issues in 2024, are instead reconstruction (widely defined but with a heavy focus on critical infrastructure and green transition), reform of the legal institutions, and EU accession. Therefore, the IMF is not suitable to be the leading institution in this phase of Ukraine's development. Moreover, international financial institutions, such as the IMF, provide loans, but Ukraine mainly needs grant aid. As EU accession is the central issue, it is natural that the EU takes a central position, but considering that the contributors are many, they should all be given a role in Ukraine's reconstruction.

The best model seems to be the Marshall Plan, which was administered by an American-led team from the Hotel de Talleyrand on the Rue de Rivoli in Paris (see Hogan, 1987). A new governing body needs to be set up. The two largest donors, the EU and the US, should take the lead, but all other major donors should also be invited, i.e. the United Kingdom, Canada, Japan, Norway, Switzerland, and other interested countries as well as the international financial institutions IMF, World Bank, European Development Bank (EBRD) and European Investment Bank (EIB). Russia's role in the IMF and the World Bank should not be problematic because Russia is regularly voted down on matters concerning Ukraine. All of these institutions have important specialist skills that must be engaged.

Since 2017, various Western countries have held annual Ukrainian reform conferences. On July 4–5, 2022, the Swiss state organized a Ukrainian reconstruction conference in Lugano. This meeting should have had three main tasks. First, the Ukrainian government should have presented its plans for reconstruction, which it did. A second point should have been a donor conference, but such did not take place. No new promises of aid were presented. Thirdly, the parties should have presented their ideas on the organization of a coordinating body for the aid to Ukraine, but this did not happen either. As the main speaker was European Commission President Ursula von der Leyen, it appeared that the EU alone would be the coordinator, but the EU did not propose a clear structure.

Several proposals have been put forward in different forms about how the long-term aid to Ukraine should be administered. Initially, the Ukrainian government argued that it should receive all the funds and administer them itself. Since Ukraine has had major problems with corruption, this Ukrainian approach was met with firm Western opposition and, if implemented, it would have led to the delay of foreign aid due to Western mistrust. Suggestions for how the risks of corruption can be reduced through, among other things, how aid is organized and monitored to how procurement is managed and how state enterprises are handled in the reconstruction process are discussed by Becker et al. (2022c). As EU accession has become a central issue for Ukraine's reforms and development, the European Commission has come to play the most prominent role among the Western parties. But the US has contributed with both more financial and military support, so the US and other Western parties should also be involved in deciding how aid to Ukraine be administered. Since January 2023, the G7 has become the effective coordinating group for Ukraine's economic reconstruction. They hold monthly meetings ad hoc.

While it is good that such a body has been formed, it is unfortunate that not all the donors can be at the table as is the case with the monthly Ramstein roundtables for military support, where the United States has taken a firm stance with some fifty countries that provide military aid to Ukraine. The main reason for the G7 taking the lead is that the United States so desires, and it is important that the US is fully engaged.

On June 21–22, 2023, a new Ukraine Reconstruction Conference was held in London. It was a huge event co-chaired by the British and Ukrainian prime ministers with 61 government represented at high levels, mostly by their foreign ministers. All the G7 foreign ministers attended. President of the European Commission Ursula von der Leyen committed €50 billion in EU support for Ukraine for the four years 2024–27. She and many others have called for Russian war reparations to Ukraine. Antezza et al. (2022) provide regular updates on the military and financial aid Ukraine receives from different countries. The European Commission has set up a special Ukrainian Service, which appears as if it will become the actual Ukraine reconstruction agency, while the US has done little. In 2024, a Ukraine Reconstruction Conference is to be held in Germany.

Three Phases of Reconstruction

At the previously mentioned Ukraine conference in Lugano, the Ukrainian government presented a detailed and ambitious reconstruction plan for 2022–2032 (see Ukraine's National Recovery Council, 2022). It contained a lot of details about how much should be spent on various projects and which government agencies should be responsible for them.

The Ukrainian government divided its reconstruction plan into three phases—2022, 2023–25, and 2026–2032. The government specified how much funding it wanted for each of these phases. It called for $60–65 billion for 2022, which did not include security and defense, $300 billion for the three years 2023–25, and $400 billion for 2026–32. The amounts that donors have envisaged and actually paid out in 2022 are about half of what the Ukrainian government has pleaded for. However, two central elements were missing from the government's plan, namely where the funds are to come from and how these funds are to be administered.

The end of 2023 is approaching, but no end of the war is in sight. This means that the Ukrainian needs have increased. The draft Ukrainian budget for 2024 requires current budget financing of $39 billion for 2024 (Dragon Capital, 2023b). It remains impossible to predict for how long the war will last—or how it will end, but it is clear that Ukraine's reconstruction consists of two completely different phases: the current crisis phase, and hopefully a more predictable reconstruction phase. The latter, in turn, can be divided into a medium-term reconstruction phase and a long-term development phase. The international organization of these phases needs to be completely different.

In large parts of Ukraine, the war appeared to be over by early autumn 2022 and reconstruction had already begun. This changed in October 2022 when Russia began a period of widespread terror bombing of civilian targets far from the front lines, trying to kill civilians in the whole country. The Russians bombed electrical infrastructure, hospitals, and grain port infrastructure. Nevertheless, reconstruction needs to begin as soon as possible so that people can return and businesses can resume work and critical infrastructure be restored. Thanks to Ukraine's strong local self-government, the local mayors can initiate this work and many countries have decided to cooperate with specially selected cities.

For long-term support, a different structure with a central strategy is required, where the Ukrainian government sets its development goals, and Western donors cooperate with the Ukrainian government. The planning of how best to distribute aid cannot be fully decentralized, although most of the construction work should be decentralized.

Financing Needs in the Short and the Long Term

The Ukrainian government's funding target of $750 billion over a decade, nearly four times Ukraine's GDP in 2021, is extraordinarily ambitious. Well managed, however, it is possible. This funding could come from many sources: confiscation of Russian Central Bank foreign reserves in the West, possible confiscation of frozen assets of sanctioned Russian oligarchs in the West, bilateral aid, multilateral aid, and private investment.

The financing should be discussed in two phases, the first crisis phase while the war is going on and the more long-term reconstruction over the following ten years. During the crisis phase, funding must necessarily be decentralized. Ukraine needs to obtain the necessary resources quickly. Each donor country decides how to support Ukraine with humanitarian and military aid without much coordination.

The IMF (2022) estimated that Ukraine needed $5 billion a month or $60 billion in 2022 to cover its budget financing, as tax revenues had fallen sharply since the start of the war. In the end, Ukraine received only $33 billion, which led to higher inflation as discussed above (Dragon Capital 2023a, p.2). The US did its part, regularly paying $1.5 billion a month, and all US aid consists of grants. The US Congress legislated a total of 66 billion dollars for Ukraine in 2022. The main part goes to military aid and the rest goes to budget support and humanitarian aid. Unfortunately, the EU delivered less and not even what it had promised in May 2022 (EU Neighbours East, 2022). As a result of the meager and late European payments in 2022, Ukraine was forced into monetary financing, which led to inflation rising to 27% from October to December 2022.

For 2023, the Ukrainian government estimated that it will need a total of $40 billion in budget support. Fortunately, the EU managed to mobilize macro-financial support of €18 billion for the whole of 2023, and the US Congress legislated $ 9.9 billion for the first nine months. With some additional bilateral and IFI financing, it looks at the end of 2023 as if the Ukrainian budget deficit will be fully financed by international donors. As a consequence, inflation had fallen to 8.7% in August 2023.

In the longer term, even greater funding is required. The most important thing for Ukraine's financing is whether the foreign currency reserves of the Russian Central Bank in the West that have been immobilized can be confiscated and used for the reconstruction of Ukraine. The moral argument is obvious. Russia has started an unprovoked war of aggression against Ukraine and committed all kinds of war crimes. The relevant bodies of international law are the UN International Court of Justice in The Hague and the United Nations. On March 16, 2022, the court issued a first preliminary ruling that Russia must stop military operations in Ukraine (United Nations, 2022a). This ruling was supported by thirteen of the fifteen judges. Only the Russian and Chinese judges went against the majority. A later, definitive ruling could establish that Russia has committed an unacceptable act of aggression and that the country should pay war reparations.

The UN General Assembly has adopted numerous resolutions condemning Russia for its war of aggression against Ukraine. On November 14, 2022, it went further and called for Russia to pay war reparations to Ukraine and its members to set up the appropriate institutions for facilitating the reparations (United Nations, 2022b).

These two rulings give all Western countries a good basis for domestic legislation to confiscate the Russian central bank reserves, but the countries that have reserves can act without this UN sanction. Canada has already passed a law for the confiscation of sanctioned Russian reserves in Canada. European Commission President Ursula von der Leyen has advocated for the EU to adopt such a law, which would cover Russian central bank reserves in the EU. Belgium alone holds some $200 billion in the Euroclear system. In the United States Congress, multiple members of both parties have filed an act confiscating Russian sovereign assets in the US. Britain and Japan also need to act. In the fall of 2023, some legal developments in this area are likely, primarily US legislation.

The Russian Central Bank's foreign exchange reserves, which Western countries have immobilized, are held in a very liquid form, mainly in government bonds from various Western countries, with the central banks of various countries. According to the statistics of the Russian Central Bank for January 1, 2022, these assets amounted to 316 billion dollars, which were held by seven countries: 96 billion dollars in Germany, 61 billion in France, 57 billion in Japan, 39 billion in the United States, 31 billion in the United Kingdom, 15 billion in Austria, and 17 billion in Canada (Hufbauer and Schott, 2022). In Europe, most of this money has been moved to Euroclear in Belgium. The official Russian reactions, for example by Foreign Minister Sergey Lavrov, indicate that the Russian central bank was caught off guard by the *G7*'s hasty decision to freeze these reserves at the end of February 2022.

Several arguments have been advanced against the confiscation of Russian Central Bank reserves. One is that other countries, such as China, Saudi Arabia, and Nigeria, would be discouraged from holding their foreign exchange reserves in Western countries or in dollars or euros if those countries confiscated Russia's reserves. A counterargument is that the US has already confiscated central bank reserves from Iraq and Afghanistan without deterring anyone. President Joe Biden confiscated some of Afghanistan's central bank reserves as late as 2021 and he did so by decree based on previous laws.

Another argument against confiscation is that it would undermine private property rights, but central bank reserves are clearly government and not private property. Furthermore, Russia has been guilty of obvious war crimes, although they have not yet been determined in an international court. In practice, confiscation of central bank reserves faces strong silent resistance, making it difficult to push through the necessary legislation.

An argument that has more weight is where the confiscated reserves should be sent. So far, no Marshall Plan administration exists and Western countries are reluctant to transfer large resources to the Ukrainian government without full control over the intended use of the money. Both donor countries and Ukraine have a great interest in a strong administration for Western aid to Ukraine being set up soon and in full transparency.

The EU, UK, US, and Canada have imposed sanctions against a large number of Russian government officials and oligarchs. Many voices have been raised that these assets should be confiscated and used for Ukraine's warfare and reconstruction. In total, Russian private financial assets abroad are estimated at around $1 trillion. However, while these ideas enjoy great popularity, they are not very practical.

To begin with, it is difficult to establish in court whether the rich oligarchs are to blame for the war in Ukraine, which they will surely dispute. Controversial Russian businessmen have usually hidden their assets in layers of 20–30 shell companies registered in a dozen obscure tax havens. It is extremely difficult to determine who owns what without the owner's assistance. The various tax havens, especially the two most important, Dubai and the Cayman Islands, are likely to do everything they can to prevent assets there from being confiscated.

Our estimate is that the oligarch assets that should be frozen amount to some $500 billion, but by the end of 2022 only $30 billion worth of assets had been frozen. To a large extent, these are illiquid assets such as luxury yachts, palaces, and jets, which would fetch significantly less than their estimated value at an executive auction.

The frozen oligarch assets give rise to a number of other problems, as few countries have dealt with such large frozen assets before. Who will cover the often large administrative costs? How can these assets be insured? Who is responsible if frozen properties are burned down? All of these issues are likely to lead to new legislation and a large number of expensive court cases, where states with inferior lawyers will find it difficult to defend themselves against wealthy oligarchs with the best lawyers money can buy. Our conclusion is therefore that, due to these factors, one should not count on any major gains from any sale of oligarch assets in the foreseeable future.

Canada has passed a law allowing the confiscation of all sorts of frozen Russian assets but it has not confiscated anything yet. Other countries are discussing the issue but not very actively, although the Russian Central Bank reserves should be confiscated. We have both participated in the Yermak-McFaul International Working Group on Russian Sanctions which, among other things, has published a White Paper which was largely written by Anders Åslund and which advocates the confiscation of the Russian Central Bank reserves in the West (International Working Group on Russian Sanctions, 2023).

Normally, the international financial institutions—the IMF, the World Bank, and the EBRD—provide the bulk of the financial assistance. The IMF usually takes the lead because macroeconomic stabilization is the central concern. The World Bank focuses on general development issues, while the EBRD deals primarily with privatization, private investment, and corporate governance. In Ukraine, however, the situation should be different because vast sums will be required for reconstruction and they need to consist mainly of grant aid and not loans, which means that bilateral aid should become more important than multilateral aid, and the focus should be on reconstruction rather than macroeconomic stabilization. However, it is important that the impressive expertise of the international financial institutions is fully engaged.

The five major bilateral donors should be the EU, USA, UK, Japan and Canada. The EU has pledged to assist with 100 billion euros, but it is still unclear how much will consist of loans and gifts respectively. In 2022, the US allocated $66 billion in grants to Ukraine. A large number of Western countries have up to the end of 2023 given bilateral aid, mainly in the form of grants, and many intend to give more.

Of course, all the relevant international financial institutions should also play their traditional roles to the maximum. The IMF with its expertise and funding is needed to maintain Ukraine's financial balance. The World Bank can potentially play a major role as a coordinator of Ukraine's reforms and reconstruction together with the European Commission. The EBRD and the EIB should contribute with large investments. The EBRD is also important for assisting with privatization and improving the governance of the large state-owned enterprises. All these international institutions should expand and maximize their frameworks for financing Ukraine during reconstruction.

The Ukrainian government holds high hopes for significant foreign direct investment. However, in the last two years before the war, Ukraine had almost no foreign investment due to that the state complicated all business activities. In the initial talks on reconstruction, the Ukrainian state promises far better business conditions, simplified state administration, and a better legal system (see for example Ukraine's National Recovery Council, 2022). If that really happens, Ukraine could attract 5 percent of GDP a year in foreign investment, which would mean $10 billion a year to begin with. But that would require far-reaching reforms.

Unless special support measures are undertaken, it will be some time before foreign private companies dare to invest in Ukraine. Therefore, a series of such measures should be introduced, above all insurance against political risks, which bilateral export agencies as well as some international financial institutions stand for.

How Can Ukraine Be Reformed?

The most important factor for a country's future development is institutional transformation, the development of a free democratic society with free information and a strong rule of law that can guarantee private property rights. For three decades, Ukraine has strived to build a rule of law with democracy, freedom, and a market economy, but progress has at the beginning of 2024 been mixed.

The central national interest was to build a Ukrainian state after centuries of rule from Moscow. By and large, it has succeeded, as evidenced by Ukraine's successful resistance to the strong Russian military power. Ukraine has a functioning state administration at all levels. One of the most important reforms after Euromaidan 2014 has been a decentralization of power and funding to the local level, while the too many and too small municipalities have been merged to become viable.

Another major advance has been that Ukraine has built strong macroeconomic institutions—a strong central bank, a well-functioning finance ministry, a computerized tax system, and a solid banking system—in good cooperation with the IMF and the World Bank. Ukraine has had a large number of IMF agreements since 1994. Although they generally did not last for long, they gradually built up Ukraine's financial institutions. Yet, at the beginning of 2024 Ukraine still does not have a functioning stock market.

The two central problems for Ukraine remain to fight corruption and to secure private property rights. The independent non-governmental organization Transparency International produces an annual index of perceptions of corruption. According to the latest survey (Transparency International, 2022) Ukraine was ranked as a not-so-honorable 116th out of 180 countries, while thoroughly corrupt Russia was ranked 137th. All international institutions involved in Ukraine focus on these problems, but with slightly different angles. Although the corruption indicators for Ukraine before the war were poor, significant improvements in these indicators have been achieved after Euromaidan 2014, when Ukraine ranked below Russia.

In June 2022, the European Commission recommended that Ukraine should not only receive a membership perspective but also receive candidate status, which is a prerequisite for starting negotiations for full EU membership (see European Union, 2022). The EU demanded that Ukraine took seven important steps by the end of 2022 to meet the Copenhagen criteria, which have now been postponed until the end of 2023. The EU's demands were unusually concrete.

1. To legislate on the selection of judges to the Constitutional Court of Ukraine;
2. To complete the examination of the integrity of the candidates for the members of the Supreme Council of Justice that appoints the Supreme Judge of Ukraine;

3. To strengthen the fight against corruption, especially at high levels, through effective investigations, prosecutions and convictions, and to appoint a new head of the specialized anticorruption prosecutor's office and appoint a new director of the National Anti-Corruption Bureau of Ukraine;
4. Ensuring that anti-money laundering legislation complies with the Financial Action Task Force (FATF) standard;
5. To implement the law against oligarchs to limit the influence of oligarchs in economic, political, and public life, but this should be done in a legally correct way;
6. Addressing the influence of special interests by adopting a media law that aligns Ukrainian legislation with the EU's audiovisual media services directive and strengthens the powers of the independent media regulator;
7. To secure the rights of national minorities.

The EU assumes that Ukraine will meet all seven of these conditions by December 2023. Tellingly, the first four EU conditions are of a legal nature, while the other three are democratic principles. Either the EU is satisfied with Ukraine's macroeconomic achievements or it leaves such issues to the IMF. The preliminary EU judgment in June 2023 was that Ukraine had fulfilled two of the conditions (anticorruption appointments and law on media freedom) and had initiated work on all the remaining five conditions.

An important political issue missing from the EU's list is the reform of the Ukrainian state apparatus. The problem is not only corruption but also old-fashioned Soviet bureaucracy that needs to be reformed and simplified, but this is a big complex, which Ukraine's EU adaptation should be able to solve.

Ukraine needs several major economic reforms to make its economy competitive. First and foremost, the bulk of Ukraine's 3500 still state-owned enterprises must be privatized. Privatization is always controversial no matter how it is being done, but it is necessary for a normal market economy to be built. Half of Ukraine's state-owned enterprises are not active but really just ruins that should be auctioned off as real estate. About one hundred state-owned companies are of real value and several of them need to remain state-owned for the sake of national security. In these companies, Ukraine needs to develop transparency and good corporate governance. Attempts have been made but their success appears to have been limited.

Finally, the Ukrainian market needs to be opened up to more domestic and foreign competition. Too many markets in Ukraine are monopolized or exposed to little competition. The explanations vary. Some complain about the oligarchs, others about state bureaucracy. In any case, Ukraine needs a strong competition policy, which is traditionally one of the EU's strengths.

Ukraine's political leadership does not pronounce any economic ideology, as demonstrated by the fact that President Volodymyr Zelenskyi's first government in 2019–20 had a clear liberal stance, while the current government is fairly traditional and state-oriented. It is unclear which line Ukraine will choose and it depends to a large extent on Western influence and demands for reform.

Ukraine's First Deputy Prime Minister and Minister of Economy Yuliya Svyrydenko published a sensational liberal programmatic article in July 2022 (Svyrydenko, 2022). She declared that Ukraine's main task was to achieve an average growth rate of 7 percent per year over the next decade. The country would do this through three measures. First, the government tax burden on the economy would be reduced from 45 percent of GDP to 30 percent of GDP in one year. Second, Ukraine would minimize economic regulation and let the economy run free, which she calls the "philosophy of the free steppe". Third, she advocated a radical reform of Ukraine's judiciary so that it can guarantee all entrepreneurs their property rights. This is an extraordinarily liberal program and very much reflects what bureaucratic Ukraine needs, but it remains to be seen whether this program will have President Zelensky's support.

Can Ukraine Really Become a Member of the EU?

Before Russia attacked Ukraine on February 24, 2022, only a few enthusiasts advocated Ukraine's membership of the EU. The EU had not even promised Ukraine a "membership perspective", let alone a candidate status. As friends of Ukraine have always pointed out, a declaration of membership perspective is not very important because Article 49 of the EU Charter states that any "European" country can apply for membership in the EU and however Europe is defined, Ukraine is clearly a European country.

Article 6 of the EU Charter also clarifies that a country that wants to become a member of the EU must fulfill certain principles. They were established by the European Council in Copenhagen in June 1993 and are therefore called the Copenhagen criteria. They are fairly simple and consist of three criteria, one political, one economic, and one administrative:

1. The political criterion requires that the applicant country has stable institutions, which guarantee democracy, the rule of law, human rights, and the protection of minority rights.
2. The economic criterion requires that the applicant country has a functioning market economy that can cope with competitive pressure and market forces within the Union.
3. The administrative criterion requires that the applicant country has the capacity to undertake the obligations arising from membership.

Ukraine's main supporters have always been Poland and the three Baltic states. Russia's attack changed everything. On the same day that Russia attacked Ukraine, the EU agreed to support Ukraine and impose far-reaching sanctions against Russia. Above all, the President of the European Commission, Ursula von der Leyen, and the President of the European Council, Charles Michel, strongly committed themselves to Ukraine. On 23 June 2022, the EU offered Ukraine (and Moldova) not only a European membership perspective but also candidate status. Former Prime Minister of Lithuania and now member of the European Parliament Andrius Kubilius, who is deeply involved in Ukraine, has suggested that Ukraine can become a full member of the EU in 2029. He bases his assessment on the best past experiences of EU accession (Kubilius, 2022).

The next critical step is for the EU to open negotiations with Ukraine on membership. For this to be possible, the government of Ukraine must first fulfill the seven aforementioned conditions that the EU has identified as the basis for Ukraine to become a candidate. The European Commission then needs to confirm that all these seven conditions have been met in a report by the end of 2023. In that case, the EU can at best formulate its negotiating mandate and start negotiations in the first half of 2024. However, the EU can delay the start of negotiations indefinitely, and it is likely to happen if Ukraine does not meet the EU's seven basic conditions. The most important of these is the reform of the Constitutional Court.

Then, negotiations should begin. Kubilius sees the big EU enlargement in 2004 as the model to be followed. The actual EU negotiations with Lithuania lasted for three years and with Poland for four years. For Ukraine, it would mean that the negotiations could be completed in 2027–28 at best. After the negotiations are completed, it normally takes two years to prepare and ratify the accession agreement, which means that 2029 would be the earliest possible time for Ukraine's EU accession.

However, for this to become possible, the EU must change its enlargement philosophy. After 2007, when Bulgaria and Romania became EU members, the EU has become stuck in the Western Balkans. Since then, only Croatia has managed to join the EU, which happened in 2013. EU member states must realize that it is in the EU's political, security policy, and economic interest that Ukraine becomes a member.

The EU's previous enlargements have all strengthened the Union in so many ways. The fundamental purpose of the EU was to ensure that war was not possible for long in Europe, which has succeeded so well that Europeans tend to forget it. We argue that after Russia's unjustified war of aggression in Ukraine, no security policy act in Europe is more important than Ukraine becoming a member of the EU. Of course, a new expansion of the EU will increase the Union's security policy strength and weight. Ukraine has one of Europe's strongest military forces (if we do not include Russia and Turkey). As the EU increases its defense and security policy ambitions, it becomes increasingly important to include a country with such military competence.

Central Europe's integration into the EU contributed to Europe's great economic growth during the record years 2004–2007 (European Commission, 2014). Ukraine's entry into the EU will, according to our assessment, lead to a similar expansion of the European market and stimulation of growth as European companies establish themselves in Ukraine and thus can expand both sales and production. The reconstruction of Ukraine will also be a strong economic driving force in which many companies from the EU will be involved.

The EU needs to analyze its mistakes in the Western Balkans and correct its organization and policies so that it can assist applicant countries more effectively in making the necessary reforms to become a member of the EU. These EU reforms are of all kinds. To begin with, the European

Commission must start working faster on enlargement. At the beginning of 2024, the EU has a Commissioner for Enlargement who is so negative about enlargement as such that he has rightly been sidelined by the Commission's leadership. Secondly, EU countries should be deprived of the right to oppose enlargement negotiations with countries with which they had old neighborly disputes.

For many reasons, Ukraine's EU accession will be different from previous EU accessions. First, the process will begin with a major reconstruction. While this entails a large cost, it also offers new opportunities. The infrastructure—roads, railways, power lines, and pipelines—needs to be rerouted so that they lead to Europe and not to Russia. Ukraine's power grid has already made the transition to continental Europe's power grid. A major strategic investment issue is whether Ukraine should switch from Russia's railway width of 1520 cm to Europe's 1435 cm. Many of Ukraine's old industries are hardly possible to modernize. While Ukraine has all the prerequisites for steel production in the future as well, new technology with electric steel furnaces is probably required instead of the old-fashioned blast furnaces. Ukraine has many skilled engineers, but as in Central Europe, they should move to new industries. Ukraine already has an excellent software industry, which should expand.

Another reason why Ukraine's EU accession should be special is that the reconstruction will hopefully involve large sums of money, which should lead to strict financial rules and great dynamism.

Like any other EU accession, Ukraine's will require major reforms. Many of these reforms have been discussed for thirty years, but for many years Ukraine has not had the relevant human capital to carry out these reforms. In the last decade, this has changed and the country has access to all the relevant experts and can carry out the necessary reforms if only the political will is there. The EU and other foreign donors need to ensure that the Ukrainian authorities stay on track and make the necessary reforms.

Ukraine has three important advantages in joining the EU. First, the Ukrainian nation is more positive about the EU than any other nation. Remember that 125 Ukrainians died in their fight for an EU Association Agreement during Euromaidan in January and February 2014. Has anyone died for the EU anywhere else? More than 80 percent of Ukrainians are consistently in favor of EU membership in credible opinion polls (see for example Kyiv International Institute of Sociology, 2022).

Another advantage is that Ukraine already has a very far-reaching association agreement with the EU of more than 2,135 pages. Negotiations began in 2007, after which the agreement was adopted in 2014 and entered into force in 2016 (European Union, 2014). The main part of this agreement is a "Deep and Comprehensive Free Trade Agreement", but the association agreement also contains several hundred pages detailing hundreds of reforms that Ukraine has committed to implementing. This part includes a large part of the EU's *acquis communautaire*, and the Ukrainian government claims that it has already adopted the bulk of the reforms required by the EU. This applies to a large extent to technical legislation, while the main politically sensitive issues, such as control over the courts and the police, have not been implemented.

An EU accession consists of several important elements, perhaps above all institutional development, free trade, free travel, and large inflows of EU grants. They are all interrelated, and the first three factors occur before a country becomes a member of the EU. Adopting the *acquis communautaire* means adopting all the laws a country needs to build a stable legal society.

The EU's greatest attraction is perhaps its large internal market. The EU has traditionally been generous in opening its vast market to candidate countries at an early stage. Already in 1994, the Baltic and Central European countries had more than two-thirds of their foreign trade with EU countries, while they joined the EU only in 2004. Until 2000, Ukraine had minimal trade with the EU, only one tenth of its exports because Ukraine's exports were dominated by two commodity groups, steel and agricultural products, which have traditionally been subject to far-reaching protectionism.

The most important short-term EU action is to fully open the single market to Ukraine. To a large extent, this has already happened. As mentioned, the EU's free trade agreement entered into force in 2016, but it contained 36 import quotas for all of Ukraine's most important export goods, i.e. agricultural commodities and steel. Gradually, these quotas were eased, but only on a limited scale. In 2021, the EU still accounted for only 45% of Ukraine's foreign trade, while Moldova already had 70 % of its trade with the EU. In 2022, the EU's share of Ukraine's trade in goods had risen to 55%, a doubling since 2016, and it is set to rise further.

The war with Russia has accelerated the liberalization of EU trade with Ukraine. Temporarily, the EU has released all these import quotas and introduced true free trade. Hopefully, the EU will preserve this full free trade with Ukraine and incorporate Ukraine into the single market. As Russia blockaded all of Ukraine's Black Sea ports from February 2022, shipments from Ukraine could only go by truck or rail to Eastern Europe, mainly to Poland and Romania. Due to a number of reasons, this led to queues that took several days to cross these borders. Twenty kilometers long lines of trucks on both sides of the Polish-Ukrainian border are unfortunately common. The EU has too many bureaucratic controls and too few customs officials. The EU has tried to improve that situation, but the lack of infrastructure and the different gages of the railways remain a problem.

In early 2023, a new problem arose. Five neighboring countries - Poland, Slovakia, Hungary, Romania, and Bulgaria—protested against large cheap grain imports from Ukraine and blocked them, receiving EU acceptance to this violation of EU trade rules. To Ukraine, this was costly. The EU ended these grain export restrictions on September 15, 2023, but then Poland, Slovakia, and Hungary introduced unilateral illegal import restrictions, which led to severe acrimony between especially Poland and Ukraine.

The cooperation with the EU that Ukrainians generally attach the most importance to is the EU's visa freedom, which was introduced in 2017. This means that Ukrainians can spend 90 days in an EU country without applying for a special permit. Even before the war, some EU countries attracted large numbers of Ukrainians, especially Poland, which had an itinerant Ukrainian population of perhaps 1.5 million, the Czech Republic, which had at least half a million Ukrainians, Germany, and the southern European countries. Several EU countries gave the Ukrainians work and residence permits, which is a national prerogative, while the EU takes responsibility for Schengen visas. In practice, Ukrainians replaced the Central European workforce that had moved to Western Europe to earn more. Germany suffers from a substantial labor shortage and therefore wants half a million Ukrainian workers. The Ukrainians mainly worked temporarily in the construction industry, agriculture, the restaurant industry, and in households. Because they worked well and did not cause any problems, they were appreciated and attracted surprisingly little public attention. According to a report by Perspektywy Education Foundation, a non-profit national organization supporting education, 48,100 students from Ukraine are studying in Poland in 2022–23 (Erudera News, 2023).

The many Ukrainians who work, study, and temporarily live in Europe are a great asset for Ukraine's future development that receives too little attention. In a similar fashion, millions of Poles spent long periods in Europe during the 1980s but only for a limited time and they mainly returned home with European values and insights. These millions were an important reason why the Polish transformation was so successful.

However, many argue that Ukraine neither can nor should become a member of the EU as quickly as after seven years. They refer to the situation in the Western Balkans, problems with the justice system in Bulgaria and Romania, and the decline in Hungary and Poland. But none of these protests should stop Ukraine's membership negotiations.

The weakest argument concerns the Western Balkans because the main problem is that the EU has not driven the process due to internal EU opposition. First, Greece opposed enlargement to North Macedonia out of purely nationalist concerns about the name of that country. Next France slowed the candidate status of North Macedonia and Albania out of rather vague wishes for a reform of the EU, which had nothing to do with the potential candidates. Then the Bulgarian government protested against North Macedonia, claiming that the Macedonians were in fact Bulgarians. The EU's lack of interest in the Western Balkans has naturally reduced this region's interest in the EU. Ukraine's commitment to the EU should not be questioned but be welcomed by the EU. Tellingly, the EU's commitment to Ukraine has also led to the EU finally starting its accession negotiations with North Macedonia and Albania twenty years after they were declared candidates for EU membership.

Another argument against quick EU accession for Ukraine is that Bulgaria and Romania still have major difficulties with their legal systems. Bulgaria has severe organized crime and Romania has had great difficulties with high-level corruption. However, this is not an argument against reforming the legal system in Ukraine, but rather a reason to do so more firmly and decisively.

A third argument is the democratic and legal regression of Hungary, but the EU seems to be solving that problem of members who stop behaving in line with the EU's treaties by limiting transfers to such members. The EU cannot end all requirements after a country has become a member of the EU. It must have an effective auditing operation and it must have the ability to impose meaningful penalties on governments that abandon normal legal norms.

Ukraine's Path into the EU

On February 24, 2022, Russia started the biggest post-World War II war in Europe when it attacked Ukraine without any legitimate reason. This war has drawn Europe's new outer border for a long time to come. Ukraine belongs to Europe, while Russia has placed itself outside.

The principles we have outlined here are in line with Becker et al. (2022a) and they have been largely repeated in the Lugano and London meetings. At the beginning of 2024, a broad Western consensus reigns that the support needs to be delivered quickly but be conditional. It should mainly consist of grants and not loans. Good coordination is central and requires a joint organization of donors and the Ukrainian government. It is important that Ukraine feels ownership of the reconstruction, and the process must be transparent and control corruption. A central element of the reconstruction process should be Ukraine's entry into the EU, and this should not only be a reconstruction but a modernization of the entire Ukrainian state and economy. The principle that is sometimes questioned is whether the institution that will coordinate the reconstruction should be linked to the EU or some other organization, such as the *G7* or the World Bank. Given that the long-term goal for Ukraine is EU membership, we argue that it must be an EU-affiliated institution to provide the right planning horizon and steering mechanism.

The Ukrainian government foresees that the reconstruction will be divided into three phases. The first phase is the crisis phase while the war is going on. A second phase is predicted to be three years, probably 2023–25 but the start may be delayed by the war, and that is the actual reconstruction. The third phase is modernization 2026–32. The government has tentatively estimated the cost of this program at $750 billion, which sounds reasonable.

If such financing is to become possible, a Russian war reparation must account for a large part of it. Thanks to Western countries freezing $316 billion of the Russian central bank's foreign exchange reserves, these funds can be confiscated and used for war reparations (Hufbauer and Schott, 2022; Zelikow and Johnson, 2022; Summers, Zelikow & Zoellick, 2023).

Ukraine has so far not adopted a clear reform plan, but it will likely be largely driven by the EU's demands after the EU gave Ukraine a membership perspective and declared the country a candidate for membership. In the next step, the EU should open negotiations on membership. At best, Ukraine could become a member of the EU in 2029.

In Åslund (2022) the author suggested that in 2023 the EU should focus on five points that well summarize our view on how Ukraine can be rebuilt and become a member of the EU:

1. Ensure that the EU contributes EUR 1.5 billion a month to Ukraine's state budget. This has been fulfilled for 2013 and that will probably be the case also in 2024.
2. Insist that the West confiscate the Russian Central Bank's foreign exchange reserves in the West of $316 billion and that these funds be used as Russian war reparations to Ukraine. This is increasingly discussed but has not been done as yet. Canada and the US have moved faster, but two-thirds of this money sits in Belgium
3. Push through that the EU starts membership negotiations with Ukraine. Hopefully this will happen in December 2023, but that might be too optimistic.
4. Help the West set up a joint Marshall Plan and authority to coordinate the reconstruction of Ukraine. The European Commission is laudably setting up a large Ukraine Service, and in October the US finally appointed a special representative of the President for Ukraine's reconstruction, former Secretary of Commerce Penny Pritzker.
5. Secure long-term Western funding for Ukraine's reconstruction. In June 2023, the European Commission pledged €50 billion for 2024–27. Hopefully, this will be approved by the European Parliament and the EU Council in the fall of 2023.

References

Antezza, A. et al. (2022). "Ukrainian Support Tracker," Kiel Institute for the World Economy, August. https://www.ifw-kiel.de/topics/war-against-ukraine/ukraine-support-tracker/

Åslund, A. (2022). "Ett EU-ordförandeskap för Ukrainas sak", (An EU-presidency for Ukraine's cause) Fri Värld, October 18.

Becker, T., B. Eichengreen, Y. Gorodnichenko, S. Guriev, S. Johnson, T. Mylovanov, K. Rogoff and B. Weder di Mauro (2022a). "A Blueprint for the Reconstruction of Ukraine", Centre for European Policy Research

(CEPR), April 6. https://cepr.org/sites/default/files/news/BlueprintReconstructionUkraine.pdf

Becker, T., B. Eichengreen, Y. Gorodnichenko, S. Guriev, S. Johnson, T. Mylovanov, K. Rogoff and B. Weder di Mauro (2022b). "Macroeconomic policies for wartime Ukraine", Centre for European Policy Research (CEPR), August 12. https://cepr.org/about/news/new-ebook-macroeconomic-policies-wartime-ukraine

Constantinescu, M., K. Kappner, and N. Szumilo (2022). "Estimating the short-term impact of war on economic activity in Ukraine", VoxEU.org, 21 June.

Dragon Capital (2023a). The Dragon Daily, January 3.

Dragon Capital (2023b). The Dragon Daily, September 18.

Erudera News (2023). Report: Poland Attracts Over 105,000 International Students in 2022/23, Ukrainians Largest Group. July 21, 2023. https://erudera.com/news/report-poland-attracts-over-105000-international-students-in-202223-ukrainians-largest-group/#:~:text=According%20to%20the%20report%20by,students%20in%20Polish%20higher%20education

EU Neighbors East (2022). "EU Releases its First Tranche of $1 billion Macro-Financial Assistance for Ukraine," August 1, https://euneighbourseast.eu/news/latest-news/eu-releases-first-tranche-of-new-e1-billion-macro-financial-assistance-for-ukraine/

European Commission (2014). "10th Anniversary of the 2004 Enlargement – Strategic Benefits, Impact and the Current Enlargement Agenda", Memo, 30 April, Brussels. Available at https://ec.europa.eu/commission/presscorner/detail/en/MEMO_14_325

European Union (2014). "ASSOCIATION AGREEMENT between the European Union and its Member States, of the one part, and Ukraine," *Official Journal of the European Union*, 29 May.

European Union (2022). "EU Commission's Recommendations for Ukraine's EU candidate status," 17 June. https://www.eeas.europa.eu/delegations/ukraine/eu-commissions-recommendations-ukraines-eu-candidate-status_en?s=232

from the destruction caused by Russia's military aggression against Ukraine as of June 2023", available at https://kse.ua/wp-content/uploads/2023/09/June_Damages_ENG_-Report.pdf

Hogan, M. J. (1987). *The Marshall Plan*. Cambridge University Press.

Hufbauer, G. C. and J. J. Schott (2022). "The United States Should Seize Russian Assets for Ukraine's Reconstruction," Peterson Institute for International Economics, Washington D.C., April 21.

IMF (2022). Opening Remarks by the Managing Director – Ukraine Roundtable April 21, 2022, available at https://www.imf.org/en/News/Articles/2022/04/21/opening-remarks-by-the-managing-director-ukraine-roundtable-april-21-2022

KSE (2023). "Report on damages and losses to infrastructure

Kubilius, A. (2022). "Ukraine: Our Next Steps," Vilnius, July 6. https://elpnariai.lt/en/a-kubilius-ukraine-our-next-steps/

Kyiv International Institute of Sociology (2022). "Geopolitical Orientations of Residents of Ukraine, Poll July 6–20", Press release. Available at https://www.kiis.com.ua/?lang=eng&cat=reports&id=1125&page=5

Piketty, T. (2014). *Capital in the Twenty-First Century*. Belknap Press.

Summers, L. H., P. Zelikow, and R. B. Zoellick (2023). "The Other Counteroffensive to Save Ukraine," *Foreign Affairs*, June 15.

Svyrydenko, J. (2022). "Kakuyu ekonomiku my stroim? (What kind of economy are we building)?" *Ukrainskaya pravda*, July 8.

The International Working Group on Russian Sanctions (2023). "Why and How the West Should Seize Russia's Sovereign Assets to Help Rebuild Ukraine," Stanford, Working Group Paper #15, September 4.

Transparency International. (2022). Corruption Perceptions Index. http://transparency.org.

Ukraine's Ministry of Finance (2023). "Budget 2024 is a solidarity document for financing national needs in the context of martial law", Available at https://mof.gov.ua/en/news/v_umovakh_dii_rezhimu_voiennogo_stanu_biudzhet-2024__solidarnii_dokument_finansuvannia_zagalnoderzhavnikh_potreb_-_denis_uliutin-4209

Ukraine's National Recovery Council (2022). "Ukraine's National Recovery Plan", Lugano July, https://www.urc2022.com/urc2022-recovery-plan

United Nations. (2022a). "International Court Orders Russia to 'Immediately Suspend' Military Operations in Ukraine," *UN News*, March 16. https://news.un.org/en/story/2022/03/1114052

United Nations. (2022b). "General Assembly Adopts Resolution on Russian Reparations for Ukraine." *UN News*, November 14. https://news.un.org/en/story/2022/11/1130587

World Bank. (2022). *Ukraine: Rapid Damage and Needs Assessment*. World Bank, August.

World Bank (2023). "Ukraine: Rapid Damage and Needs Assessment," Washington, DC: World Bank, August. Available at https://documents1.worldbank.org/curated/en/099184503212328877/pdf/P1801740d1177f03c0ab180057556615497.pdf

Zelikow, P. and S. Johnson (2022). "How Ukraine Can Build Back Better," *Foreign Affairs*, April 19.

CHAPTER 11

The EU's Internal and External Borders in a World Torn by Conflict

Antonina Bakardjieva Engelbrekt, Per Ekman, Anna Michalski, and Lars Oxelheim

The Increasing Precariousness of Open Borders

Physical borders are salient in a world marked by threats to security, the movement of migrants, and economic and technological competition between states (Andreas, 2003). Many contemporary threats are cross-border in character, among them pandemics, climate change, and organized crime in all its forms (Bakardjieva Engelbrekt et al., 2022). The precariousness of maintaining open borders within the EU has become

A. Bakardjieva Engelbrekt
Faculty of Law, Stockholm University, Stockholm, Sweden

P. Ekman
Department of Government, Uppsala University, Uppsala, Sweden

A. Michalski (✉)
Department of Government, Uppsala University, Uppsala, Sweden
e-mail: anna.michalski@statsvet.uu.se

L. Oxelheim
Research Institute of Industrial Economics, Stockholm, Sweden

A. Bakardjieva Engelbrekt et al. (eds.), *The Borders of the European Union in a Conflictual World*,
https://doi.org/10.1007/978-3-031-54200-8_11

apparent in recent years, as some internal borders have reappeared as a response to various threats. First, for reasons of domestic security to hinder the movement of terrorists and migrants. Later, as an ultimately futile attempt to keep the COVID-19 virus from spreading across borders (Bengtsson, 2022). Some of these measures remain in force, albeit as exceptions to the principles of open borders, but because of their longevity have become a challenge to the freedom of movement of people. The EU continues to exert an attraction across its external border for goods, capital, and people seeking a way into Europe and as long as that is the case, the pressure on its external border will persist. Within the EU, meanwhile, a reinforcement of the external border is seen as necessary for preserving the freedoms that membership brings to people and businesses inside Europe, and for defending liberty within from threats to security from the outside. For these reasons, the derogations from the policy of open border within the EU in the wake of the COVID-19 pandemic are problematic although the states upholding them are not questioning the principle of open border per se (see, Pettersson Fürst in this volume).

As seen in Chapter 1, the borders of the EU have fluctuated greatly during its 70 years of existence. The EU has seen its membership widened to include new members seven times since 1973 when the United Kingdom (UK), Ireland, and Denmark first joined. Thereafter, the EU's membership further increased from nine to 28 member states, then reduced to 27 as the UK withdrew from the Union in 2020. With enlargement has the geopolitical importance of the EU as a global actor grown. From previously being concerned mainly with international trade and development aid to the countries in Africa, the Caribbean, and the Pacific, along with the stability and economic development of the countries in its neighbourhood (see also Jonasson in this volume), it is in the 2020s involved in most major issues of international politics.

Since the creation of the Common Foreign and Security Policy (CFSP), the EU has carved out a role as a post-sovereign actor with diplomatic capabilities deployed in areas of particular concern, many of which have links, direct or indirect, to the pressures on the EU's external borders. In this regard, the EU is taking concerted action on the global agendas on climate change and sustainability under the auspices of the UN with the aim of promoting and assisting climate change mitigation, sustainable social and economic development, and stability in developing countries. With time, the migration-security nexus has become increasingly prominent and the EU's ambition to tackle the drivers of migration in a long-term perspective is clearly linked to these global agendas (Bremberg et al., 2019; Michalski, 2020). In this vein, the EU has developed a more advanced partnership with the African continent going beyond the traditional development agenda by establishing the EU-Africa strategic partnership and the joint EU-Africa Strategy in 2007, and engaging African leaders in recurrent summit diplomacy, involving also the African Union (AU) (Council of the EU, 2007). The EU's renewed focus on Africa is partly in response to China's increasingly influential position on the African continent, partly to find solutions to problems related to the EU's southern border caused by a lack of development, political repression, and security concerns in African countries. In this concluding chapter, we widen the perspective of the role of the EU's internal and external borders to review a number of challenges and opportunities which have impact on the future of the EU's border policy. We put particular emphasis on external developments in the EU's neighbourhood and the ongoing shift in international politics because of their significance for the EU's ability to extend its borders further through enlargement.

Implications of the Geopolitical Shift

Since the mid-2000s, an ever more palpable geopolitical shift is taking place. The rules-based international system is being broken down gradually by states that do not respect its principles. These states wield power in the pursuit of their national interests, to the detriment of cooperation on the basis of common rules and practices (Finnemore et al., 2021; Han & Paul, 2020; Johnston, 2019; Mearsheimer, 2019; Sørensen, 2011). The concept of the rules-based international system has been used more and more often in the new millennium to describe the multilateral order from the 1990s up until the mid-2000s when the international norms and rules underpinned interstate cooperation and global governance. The rules-based international system as a concept bears comparison with the earlier concepts of Pax Americana, used in reference to the security community created after World War II for Western countries under the protection of the United States (US), and the Bretton Woods system which refers to the American economic hegemony which underpinned the economic and financial institutions set up to manage the international (until the fall of the Berlin wall in 1989, in practice, western) economic system, chiefly the

International Monetary Foundation (IMF), the World Bank (WB) and the forerunners to the World Trade Organization (WTO).

A closely related concept is that of the 'liberal world order', which has its origins in the political dominance and consequent hegemony of the US during the Cold War. Liberal values, such as political rights and freedoms linked to liberal democracy, make up the backbone of the order, along with the rule of law and the market-based economy which were used as reference points to distinguish between the political models of liberal democracy of the US and its allies, and the command economy of the authoritarian Communist regime of the Soviet Union and its satellite states (Ikenberry, 2011, 2018). In the golden days after 1991 and the fall of the Soviet Union, the rules-based system was credited to instil stability and predictability into the international system, and nourished a belief in the strength of liberal democracy which other states sought to emulate (Kagan, 2018). It was also associated with the imagery of the 'free world' inspired by the Kantian perpetual peace theory based on the belief that democratic nations are less likely to start a war between them. The liberal world order has not been purely 'good', to be sure. Geopolitical tensions in the Cold War led to so-called proxy wars in Asia and Africa, or even outright wars, as in Vietnam and Korea, as well as the bullying of weaker states in Latin America and elsewhere. These originated in the tug of war between the US and the Soviet Union, each of which attempted to shape the world in such a way as to strengthen its own security and economic and military dominance.

The rules-based international system as a concept rests, however, more on the theory of liberal institutionalism set forth in the 1980s by American political scientists, such as Robert Keohane, John Ruggie, Stephen Krasner, and Robert Axelrod (see for example Keohane & Martin, 1995). How is it, these researchers asked, that cooperation between states arises and then persists over time? The solution to the puzzle that they proffered is that the inherent risks of international cooperation—that other states will not fulfil their commitments—can be obviated through the establishment of regulatory frameworks enforced by international organizations. These scholars and others have found that, over time, international organizations have established durable regimes that have made it possible to hold member states accountable for their commitments, and to persuade them to comply with common rules. This is perhaps most evident in the case of the WTO, which has given rise to a strong international trade regime based on common rules and lasting commitments. Trade has grown as a result, forming the foundation for economic globalization and making the advantages of multilateral cooperation clear, even for countries, such as China whose spectacular rise to an economic superpower bears witness to. When EU leaders speak of defending the rules-based international order, they are referring to principles, such as multilateralism and the rule of law, as well as to norms like human rights and democracy (Dworkin & Leonard, 2018). Moreover, they insist international organizations need to be strengthened, and bodies like the WTO must be reformed in view of a changing international order.

Why does the rules-based international system need to be defended, and against whom? If we are to answer this question, we must first note that the multilateral system is founded on mutual trust—trust that all states taking part will follow the rules and carry out the commitments made (Kydd, 2005; Natorski & Pomorska, 2017). If there are repeated violations of the rules, or recurrent patterns of behaviour are at odds with them, such trust will be eroded, and the belief that cooperation always pays off in the long run will be undermined. It is therefore something of an anathema that possibly the gravest threat to the liberal world order came from within in the guise of Donald Trump, who as President of the US between 2016 and 2020, undermined the rules-based international system, for example by refusing to appoint judges to the WTO's appellate court or threatening to withdraw support to military alliances with Japan, South Korea, and Europe (Hicken et al., 2021). Since Joe Biden came to power in 2021, the economic dimension of American foreign policy has remained orientated towards domestic interests in line with his predecessor. Concerning security and defence, the US has followed a double-edged strategy of withdrawal (Afghanistan) and engagement (Ukraine).

Yet, it is the rise of autocratic great powers which has captured the attention of policy-makers, not least due to their ambition to change many of the premises of the rules-based order (Cooley & Nexon, 2020). From the mid-2000s onwards, China's economic success has upset the equilibrium of the global system. For a number of years now, China has accounted for the largest single share of world trade, with large trade and investment surpluses vis-à-vis other countries and the EU, which registered a record trade imbalance with China of almost 400 billion euros in 2022 (Moritsugu, 2023). The vast country also has a high-tech advantage in certain sectors, and it dominates the production of rare earth metals.

The hope that China would accommodate itself to the rules-based international system as a consequence of its entry into the WTO in 2001 has failed to bear fruit. Growing problems with steel dumping, forced technology transfer, trade-distorting subsidies, infringements of international intellectual property laws, and more recently the arbitrary enforcement of new security laws, are among the recurring complaints heard from companies operating on the Chinese market. Dumping and unfair price competition are recurring grievances of industries whose home-market position has been weakened by imports of Chinese goods. China dominates the European market for solar panels, and perhaps in the future, also for electric vehicles. To make things worse, despite being the world's second-biggest economy behind the US, China protects its WTO status as a developing country in order to enjoy the advantages that follow from that. This stands in stark contrast to China's claim in the WTO that it should have been automatically recognized as a market economy at the end of the transition period in 2016. Western WTO member states, including the EU and the US, opposed granting China a market economy status and the issue was not yet solved in 2023, further undermining necessary reforms.

From De-Coupling to De-Risking: The EU and the Challenges from a Weakening Rules-Bound System

The problems surrounding the weakening of the rules-bound system could have been mitigated, perhaps resolved, within the framework of the WTO, if only the two great powers, China and the US, would agree on using the available instruments. Since Xi Jinping came to power in 2012, China has increasingly exploited its dominant position in certain sectors, such as in the extraction of rare earth metals and in the production of solar cells and batteries, in order to influence the shape of the rules-based international order. This became evident not least during the early stages of the COVID-19 pandemic, when China used its dominance in certain production lines to break value chains and to influence the view expressed by various countries of its responsibility regarding the origins of the pandemic. China's efforts in this regard included benign measures, such as the donation and sale of face masks, as well as punitive measures, such as trade bans (which it imposed on some Australian products, for example).

Even before the pandemic, China imposed sanctions on countries that took a stance it viewed as insulting or disrespectful, or that raised questions about human rights violations in Tibet and Xinjiang or the status of Taiwan. One such punitive measure—a ban on salmon imports from Norway—was introduced after political dissident Liu Xiaobo was awarded the Nobel Peace Prize in 2010. Another example concerns China's decision to temporarily suspend diplomatic relations with Denmark in 2009 in the run-up to the COP15 climate summit in Copenhagen to express its displeasure that Danish Prime Minister Løkke Rasmussen had met with the Dalai Lama in May the same year (Sverdrup-Thygeson, 2015). In December 2021, moreover, China removed Lithuania from its customs registry, rendering that country unable to export goods to China. It did so in response to Lithuania's decision to allow Taiwan to open a representative office in Vilnius in its name (Reuters, 2022). This type of punishment is part of economic coercion, a strategy of weaponizing economic interdependence that flies in the face of global free trade.

Since the war in Ukraine broke out in February 2022, weaponized interdependence and various types of economic coercion are becoming more ubiquitous (see Sjöholm in this volume). Its origin is an unforeseen deviation of the global economic system and the integration of markets and the extension of the just-in-time method of production (Drezner et al., 2021). As global economic interdependence grew certain states could dominate value chains by controlling access to critical natural resources, production facilities etc. This control could also be used as a weapon against strategic rivals. Strategic use of economic dependence is of course not a new phenomenon, but the scope and depth of economic tics between countries in the global economy of the early 2020s has greatly worsened states' potential vulnerability. The EU felt the impact of the dependency of several of its member states on Russian gas, fertilizers, oil, and other products at the onset of the war in Ukraine (see also Becker and Åslund in this volume). Russia has been known to use to control the dependency on its gas against neighbouring countries, such as Ukraine, starting in the early 2000s but up until the war in Ukraine, EU member states had not been directly concerned, except for a short gas dispute between Russia and Ukraine in 2009 (Pirani et al., 2009). However, after Germany's decision in early 2022 not to complete the certification of Nord Stream 2 in reaction to Russia's actions in Ukraine, gas deliveries via Nord Stream 1 were greatly reduced. Then, in September 2022, both gas pipelines were badly damaged in an explosion, and deliveries were stopped altogether. For EU members dependent on Russian gas for a large portion of their energy needs, the sudden lack of access to Russian gas had significant consequences. Germany in particular, which despite international warnings had increased its dependence on Russian gas by co-financing Nord Stream 1 and 2, had left itself vulnerable to Russian pressure (Sturm, 2022). In May 2022, the European Commission presented a strategy for energy security—REPowerEU—the aim of which is to diversify gas imports, eliminate dependence on Russian oil and gas, and invest in energy efficiency and renewable energy sources. Since then, the import of Liquefied Petroleum Gas (LPG) has increased significantly to make up for the shortfall of Russian gas, and disused coal power plants have been reactivated.

Russia and China are the countries most often in focus when the shift from a rules-based world order to one based on power is discussed. They have a so-called geopolitical worldview, which affects how they see relations with other countries. In their way to see the world, borders and territory play a prominent role, because the control over transport routes and the possession of natural resources yield power. Countries fall hierarchically into spheres of political dominance, and instruments of power are both economic and military. China's strategy for international economic development—the Belt and Road Initiative (BRI)—has drawn considerable attention in this regard, because countries in receipt of this aid have become dependent in many cases on China, both economically and politically (Rolland, 2017). China expects loyalty in return (not least on the issue of Taiwan) in various international and regional forums, such as the United Nations General Assembly or the 16 + 1 group. China has also secured access to natural resources through the BRI, as well as markets for the products supplied by state-owned companies. Russia, for its part, has sought to draw former Soviet republics into the Commonwealth of Independent States and the Eurasian Economic Union, in order to establish a sphere within which it can exercise power and dominance. A consequence of the geopolitical turn in the international system is the great power rivalry between the US and China for hegemonic dominance, with the issue of Taiwan and the dominance of maritime transportation routes in the East and South China Seas as potential flashpoints. The rivalry has also spilt over to the economic realm as the US under Donald Trump introduced tariffs on Chinese goods, chiefly steel. Under Joe Biden, the US's aggressive stance towards China has continued and taken the form of various investment bans, for instance the prohibition to sell strategic goods, mainly for the production of microchips and armament, to China. For China, the American stance is seen as a blatant attempt to halt its rise to power by adopting a strategy of containment while for the Americans its policy towards China is a necessary pushback on its territorial claims and de-coupling of their bilateral economic ties.

From the standpoint of the EU, these international developments are worrying. The Russian regime has been taking a more and more extreme approach towards neighbouring countries that were once part of the Soviet Union, and the significance of this shift has sunk in only slowly (Götz, 2017). It was not until the war in Ukraine in 2022 that its full import was revealed. Likewise, it has taken several years for EU leaders to realize the implications of China's international norm dissemination and its territorial ambitions in the South China Sea to control access to international sea transport routes. Nevertheless, for the Europeans, the greatest factor generating uncertainty, finally, was the less-than-friendly attitude towards NATO and the EU expressed by Donald Trump, then president of the US. This attitude on Trump's part, together with his tendency to break agreements entered into, seemed to call the durability of American commitment to Europe's security and international free trade into question (Cooley & Nexon, 2020). Taken together, these developments have prompted Europe's leaders to take a greater interest in the idea of European strategic autonomy. Since the beginning of the 2020s onwards, the EU has gradually equipped itself with various instruments to meet the threat of weaponizing economic interdependence, punitive statecraft directed at individual EU member states and companies, and balancing the competitive disadvantages for domestic firms which need to comply with the EU's stricter environmental and climate mitigation rules. Among these instruments are the anti-coercion instrument of 2023 with the aim of protecting member states that fall victim to coercive measures, the Foreign Direct Investment (FDI) regulation, operational since October 2020, with the aim to equip the EU to identify, assess and mitigate potential risks for security or public order, and the carbon border adjustment mechanism, approved by the EU Council in 2022 which puts a levy on imports that originate in countries with lax environmental and climate mitigation regimes (European Commission, 2021a, 2021b, 2021c; European Commission, 2022; Council of the EU, 2019; Council of the EU, 2020; Allenbach-Ammann, 2023). In December 2020, the EU adopted a new global human rights sanctions regime which makes it possible to pursue individuals who are in breach of human rights (Council of the EU, 2020). This regime is distinct from the sanctions that the EU has adopted in accordance with the UN Security Council (international sanctions) or against specific countries, such as those adopted against Russia since its invasion of Crimea and later in the war in Ukraine, which have been taken on the basis of article 29 of the Treaty on the European Union and article 215 of the Treaty on the Functioning of the EU (Ecks, 2018).

For the EU, the American strategy of de-coupling economically from China carries too big a risk to its economy given that many European firms, especially in Germany, are dependent on the Chinese market for their turnover and profit. The EU has therefore been reluctant to follow the US down the road of de-coupling from the Chinese economy. However, China's refusal to condemn Russia for its invasion of Ukraine, its continued restriction of access to sought-after raw materials and its stepped-up discriminating treatment of European firms in China, prompted a response from the EU. To this end, the European Commission President von der Leyen held a speech in April 2023 where she called for a de-risking of the EU's relations with China starting with 'recognizing how China's economic and security ambitions have shifted' (von der Leyen, 2023b). Economic de-risking for von der Leyen implied making the European economy more competitive and resilient, using the existing instruments in the EU's toolbox, including defensive trade measures in certain sectors, and teaming up with partners around the world which grapple with similar concerns regarding China. In September 2023, the European Commission opened an investigation into the threat of dumping of Chinese electric vehicles in the EU (Blenkinsop, 2023). This action was followed by the visit to China in September 2023 of the European Commissioner Valdis Dombrovskis to convey the concerns of the EU regarding issues with access to the Chinese market and the conditions for European companies operating there. He also addressed the growing imbalance in bilateral trade and the necessity to rebalance the EU–China economic and trade relationship on the basis of transparency, predictability, and reciprocity (European Commission, 2023a).

The changed geopolitical map and the new adjacent political mindset are also reflected in the investment policies of global multinational firms (MNEs). As pointed out by Ghauri et al. (2024), the increased tensions after the financial crisis of 2008–2009 and the development in geopolitics in the wake of Russia's invasion of Ukraine have contributed to reducing the assumptions for a well-functioning global value chain. The reappearance of border frictions calls for careful adaptation of corporate strategies and government policies. As a result, the 2020s onwards will witness a dramatic reorganization of investments. Ghauri et al. (2024) point to five corporate strategies. These strategies reside on various means at the disposal of companies to divest and bring back their investment to the home market to escape the uncertainty surrounding border passages. Another means available to companies is to opt for a regionalized strategy of which one region may be the EU. The corporate abandonment of the efficient use of global resources inherent in the principle of the global value chain or global factory will come at a huge welfare cost. However, on the positive side, the reorganization of global value chains provides an opportunity to meet the United Nations Sustainable Development Goals (SDGs) and to make sustainable investment decisions by internalization of environmental, social, and governance (ESG) considerations.

Russia's War Against Ukraine. The Implications for Europe

Russia's invasion of Ukraine on 24 February 2022 will go down in history as the fateful day when Europe's contemporary security order was shattered (see also Engelbrekt in this volume). This order emerged during the final phase of the Cold War, when the Soviet Union lost its grip on the countries of Central and Eastern Europe, and thereupon collapsed as a result of internal frictions caused by the Soviet regime's mismanagement of the economy and its inability to achieve social, cultural, and political development. For the EU, the geopolitical shift in Europe at the beginning of the 1990s led to a new era, marked by deeper political integration, a far-reaching enlargement of the EU's membership, and an expansion of the powers and policy areas in the hands of Union institutions.

Russia's war against Ukraine has prompted the EU's institutions and its member states to mobilize—morally, economically, and militarily—in support of the Ukrainian people and their government (European Commission, 2023b). Russia's actions pose a great challenge to the member states, worsening the security threat they face and unleashing an energy crisis. The latter fuelled the rate of inflation, and created economic uncertainty for both companies and the population at large in the winter of 2022–23. In the first 18 months into the war, EU, with the European Commission at the forefront, responded in an unexpectedly resolute fashion to these challenges. In her State of the Union address in 2022, the president of the European Commission, Ursula von der Leyen, expressed her satisfaction with the EU's efforts at crisis management as follows: 'Fifteen years ago, during the financial crisis, it took us years to find lasting solutions. A decade later, when the global pandemic hit, it took us only weeks. But this year, as soon as Russian troops crossed the border into Ukraine, our response was united, determined, and immediate. *And we should be proud of that*' (von der Leyen, 2022. Emphasis in original.)

At the beginning of 2024, the war against Ukraine has soon raged for two years, and the contours of a new world order can be discerned. As discussed earlier in the chapter, the emerging order is based less on cooperation and more on competition and rivalry, not least between China and the US. What does this geopolitical shift mean for the EU's ability to act in the international arena? We can expect attempts to strengthen multilateralism to face great difficulty, and norm competition to remain a permanent aspect of interchange between states. As we have seen, on many fronts the EU has adjusted its approach to foreign policy accordingly to stand a better chance to achieve its goals. In accordance with the global trend, its main foreign-policy instrument—external trade policy—is now focused mainly on regional and bilateral trade ties. In a number of areas, moreover, it seeks to achieve certain political objectives, both internal and external, and to help promote greater strategic autonomy for Europe. In its trade agreements, therefore, the EU includes clauses on human rights (although there are exceptions), the rule of law, sustainable development, and adaptation to climate change (see also Öberg in this volume). Less directly, by the sheer size of its market and its considerable regulatory capacity, the Union exerts a powerful unilateral effect on other countries and private companies extending its regulatory standards in areas such as sustainable fisheries, forestry, product safety, data protection and competition policy (Damro, 2012).

On the diplomatic level, the Union aims to create alliances with like-minded states and partners in Asia, Africa, the Pacific, and Latin America. Moreover, faced with the war in Ukraine, and Russia's ever closer alignment with China, the Union has embraced the discourse according to which the world is witnessing a struggle between autocracy and democracy. It has also supported the French initiative for a European Political Community. Ursula von der Leyen's (2019) vision of a geopolitical Commission, which she set out at the start of her term of office, has thereby been fulfilled. She has set the European Commission's sights on breaking vulnerability and dependence in energy, technology, and raw materials; on taking a harder line on strategic investments, economic coercion, and harassment of states and companies; on pursuing joint diplomatic initiatives on human rights, climate issues, and sustainable development; and on strengthening the strategic autonomy of the Union. Finally, with Finland and Sweden having joined NATO, conditions are improving further for close cooperation between the EU and NATO, as the two organizations seek to build a new European security order in the wake of the war in Ukraine.

Despite the stronger consensus that has prevailed within the West since the outbreak of the war in Ukraine, the place of the EU in a new world order is far from secured. Regulatory competition at the global level in advanced technology and digitization is fierce. The Union can invest, for example, in the manufacture of microchips and batteries in Europe, but it cannot thereby guarantee that Europe will become a world leader in these areas, or that its industries will be able to withstand the global competition. China is far ahead in certain sectors, and many organs of international standardization are now dominated by that country, which seeks, and sometimes succeeds, to have its norms and standards adopted globally (Rüling, 2021). Where the climate transition is concerned, major powers such as the US and China have faltered, and the commitments they have made to help achieve the UN's climate goals have failed so far in the early 2020s to bear fruit. The question is how far the Union's climate diplomacy of forming partnerships with countries in Asia and Africa can persuade said countries to adopt European objectives on climate, sustainable development, and the environment. The EU's goals in these areas, after all, are ambitious, and the economic and political incentives it offers are not necessarily more lucrative than those extended by China.

A European Security Order and the Future Enlargement of the Union

As discussed in Chapter 1, when Russia invaded Ukraine in February 2022, it broke definitively with the security order that had prevailed since the dissolution of the Soviet Union in December 1991 (see also Engelbrekt in this volume). With the fall of communist regimes in Central and Eastern Europe at the end of the 1980s, the task fell to the EU and NATO to integrate the new democracies into the political, economic, and security order of Western Europe. Since Russia's annexation of Crimea in 2014, the European security order has been under challenge, not least with regard to the principle of the inviolability of borders which was laid down by the Conference on Security and Cooperation in Europe (CSCE) in 1975. The invasion of Ukraine is a direct violation of international law breaking, not least, with the principles of the UN Charter of 1945. It has made close relations between Russia and Ukraine impossible for a long time to come, and it has decisively accelerated the latter country's orientation towards the West.

NATO's eastern enlargement took place in several rounds, beginning in 1990 with the reunification of Germany, followed by the Czech Republic, Hungary, and Poland, which became members in 1999. The Baltic States followed in 2004, together with four countries in Eastern Europe, namely Bulgaria, Romania, Slovakia, and Slovenia. In the years since, four Balkan nations have joined the alliance as well. NATO has applied an open-door policy in principle towards the admission of new members, and Europe's security community has gradually expanded thereby, although in practice both European states and the US were quite circumspect towards the inclusion of Ukraine throughout the 2010s which made known its membership aspirations already in 2002 (D'Anieri, 2023). Countries that wish to join must meet the requirements set forth in the North Atlantic Treaty regarding 'democracy, individual liberty, and the rule of law'; and they must be able to contribute to NATO's mission and mutual defence. To be sure, the successive enlargements have given rise to debate among NATO's member states, and Russia has protested throughout (Marten, 2023). Otherwise, the process has been relatively uncomplicated. In the case of Ukraine, however, the prospect of enlarging NATO to a country still at war is impossible. At the summit in Vilnius in July 2023, the NATO member states reconfirmed NATO's open-door policy and its unwavering support for Ukraine, but did not open up for a fast-track enlargement, simply noting that it 'will be in a position to extend an invitation to Ukraine to join the Alliance when Allies agree and conditions are met' (NATO, 2023).

The incorporation of new member states in the EU is a long and complex process that puts far-reaching demands on candidate countries to adjust their legislation and policies to EU standards. In connection with the Eastern enlargement that began in the late 1990s, the EU developed a policy with four phases: (1) an evaluation of the applicant country's eligibility—economically, socially, and politically—to become a member of the Union, followed in the favourable case by a decision to grant the country candidate status; (2) preparations in the candidate country, with financial and administrative support from the EU, to adjust its national legislation to EU law, to strengthen its administrative capacity, and to consolidate its democratic system; (3) negotiations on membership, which in practice means granting the candidate country exemptions for a limited period in certain sectors—since adjusting to EU laws and policies is not negotiable; and (4) entry into the Union, together with a follow-up of the adjustment process in specific areas where the Union has not granted full membership to the candidate country—e.g., in connection with the Schengen Area or the third stage of monetary union (i.e., transition to the euro) (Michalski, 2014; Pridham, 2008). It is telling that the candidate countries in the western Balkans have made very slow progress towards the goal of EU accession, and their adoption of the EU rules and legislation is characterized by fits and starts. Since the eastern enlargement in 2004 and 2007, the EU has become much more circumspect with the candidate countries' genuine economic, political, and social adaptation to membership. Problems with corruption and political instability in Romania and Bulgaria, as well as the democratic backsliding of Poland and Hungary, the latter of which maintains good strategic relations with Putin's regime in Russia, are real causes of concern for the EU.

The EU has long-standing principles for enlargement (European Union, 2023; Michalski, 2014). In order to join the Union, a country must satisfy the so-called Copenhagen and Madrid criteria. These criteria, adopted in 1993 and 1995, specify that a country that seeks to join the EU must have a democratic political system, with guarantees for human rights, the rule of law, and protection for minorities (Cremona, 2003; Hillion, 2004). It must also have a functioning market economy that can cope with competitive pressures on the internal market as well as possess sufficient administrative capacity to assume the obligations of membership and to adhere to the aims of political, economic, and monetary union. It must incorporate EU laws and policies, the so-called *acquis*, into its own legislation before it can become a member. Finally, it must have no unresolved border disputes at the time of its entry into the Union. The last-mentioned criterion has been applied with greater flexibility than the one pertaining to the adoption of EU legislation, as can be seen in the case of the admission of the Republic of Cyprus (which did not extend to the Turkish Republic of Northern Cyprus). This criterion was tightened, however, in the case of Serbia, which must normalize its relations with Kosovo before it can become a member.

On 28 February 2022, the government of Ukraine submitted an application for EU membership. In June of the same year, after a decision-making process of record speed, the European Council conferred official candidate status on Ukraine. Moldova and Georgia followed soon thereafter, submitting their respective applications for membership in March 2022 (Petrequin & Corder, 2022). Moldova was granted candidate status at the same time as Ukraine, while Georgia would first need to meet certain requirements set by the EU before achieving this status. The European Commission has signalled that membership negotiations with Ukraine may take a long time, and that adjustment to EU legislation and fulfilling the Copenhagen criteria for membership is a huge task for a country still at war. Given the criteria regarding border disputes, there is no realistic prospects that Ukraine could accede to the EU as long as there is no permanent border settlement with Russia. Therefore, it is to be expected that the Union and its member states take the initiative for Ukraine's reconstruction once a peace agreement with Russia has been reached and that this will be integrated with the requirements for membership. However, this does not preclude that the EU and Ukraine begin with the long preparation for fulfilling the European *acquis* well before that moment. It is, for instance, of utmost importance that Ukrainian authorities convince Western benefactors and sponsors that it is getting on top of the endemic corruption, which for a long time has been a problem in Ukrainian politics and within its public administration. In this vein, the European Commission published in June 2022 its opinion on the capacity for Ukraine to fulfil the criteria for EU membership (European Commission, 2022). The Commission recommended that Ukraine is granted candidate status and that a path towards membership is staked out on the understanding that Ukraine make progress on continued judicial reform, strengthening the fight against corruption and money laundering, implementation of the Anti-Oligarch Law, tackling the influence of vested interest by adopting a Media Law, and finalizing the reform of the legal framework for the protection of national minorities. Some commentators expected the European Council in December 2023 to take a decision to open formal negotiations with Ukraine on membership which it subsequently agreed to (Bastasin, 2023).

In Agenda 2000—a report produced in 1997—the European Commission (1997) not only assessed the then candidate countries' readiness to become members of the EU, but also laid out the consequences for the EU of a near-doubling of the number of members. This was the first time in the history of European integration that the EU evaluated its own readiness to enlarge, or as it was called at the time: its absorption capacity. Three issues were highlighted where the EU needed reform: the EU institutions, the EU decision-making, and a settlement of the costs of enlargement, including the financial position of the member states after accession. The last issue was particularly tricky as some of the then existing member states who benefited from EU funding, chiefly Spain and Portugal, stood to lose their status as net recipients as the prospective new member states were poorer, and many of them had important agricultural sectors which at the time absorbed large sums of the EU's budget. The issue was settled by setting a cap on financial transfers from the structural funds and the cohesion fund of 4 per cent of GDP. The EU's overall absorption capacity is highly relevant in the context of future enlargement of the EU to Ukraine, Moldova, and the other candidate states on the Balkan Peninsula. Without comparison, the integration of Ukraine, given its size, in terms of geography, population, and agricultural sector, as well as its needs as a war-torn country will be very demanding (see also Åslund and Becker in this volume). The implications of enlargement are huge for the functioning of the EU institutions and decision-making procedures, which will need recalibration. However, the most difficult sticking point will probably be over the allocation of EU funds as the prospective newcomers will, unless the current rules are changed, become net beneficiaries while the present beneficiaries will become net payers to the EU budget. Given the uproar in Poland over the cheap grain imports from Ukraine in the autumn of 2023, which saw a long-standing supporter of Ukraine turn into an adversary by blocking Ukraine imports against EU rules, it is evident that the political sensitivity of the access to EU funding, the rules of the Common Agricultural Policy, and other market access issues are very significant in certain EU member states. To solve these issues while at the same time anchor Ukraine, Moldova and the Western Balkan states within the sphere of the EU, the Union might feel obliged to come up with alternatives to full EU membership, at least temporarily.

Closer in time looms the issue of the reconstruction of Ukraine (see Åslund and Becker in this volume). The European Commission (2022), together with the World Bank, and the Ukrainian government estimated, in a first report on 9 September 2022, the cost for the country's reconstruction at 349 billion euros—a cost that increases with each day the war continues. The economic resources needed for Ukraine's reconstruction are thus colossal, and the complexity of implementing such a project will naturally be enormous as well. Ursula von der Leyen has promised that the EU 'will support Ukraine every step of the way towards our Union' (von der Leyen, 2023a). There is a clear ambition to coordinate Ukraine's reconstruction with its adjustment to EU laws and regulations. It remains unclear, however, how the Union's promises of help with reconstruction and EU entry are to be balanced against the need for Ukraine to meet the criteria for membership. The EU's commitment to Ukraine is long-term, but the challenges are great. Security and stability in the region are crucial, but a deep democratization of political processes is needed too, as is a more secure rooting of the rule of law within the country. There must be modernization of the state apparatus, greater transparency in economic life, and a greater willingness among economic actors to follow the rules. During this long process, it is of great importance that the EU's external border with Ukraine does not become a dividing line, but rather serves as an area for contact—for trade, for the dissemination of norms, for interchange between people, and for joint projects in green energy, sustainable development, and adaptation to climate change.

Closing in on the mid-2020s, the EU has a great many challenges on its hand which are in the main caused by external events and crises but with significant implications for the political cohesion among its member states and in extension its ability to face up to, and deal with, their consequences. The EU's external borders are likely to remain the physical flashpoint of the insecurity and war in the neighbourhood as well as the instability and lack of economic and social development further afield. Moreover, the calamities caused by global warming and increasingly unstable weather patterns will further drive people away from their own countries towards Europe and the illusion of a better life. In this perspective, the EU's external borders are likely to become even harder than today and therefore the difference to be inside or outside the EU even greater. The EU needs to find a way to enlarge its membership to countries which fulfil the criteria to become a membership without erecting hard borders towards those which do not. Internally, the dismantlement of national frontiers in the late 1980s was an act of faith in other European states and a conviction that together the EU member states could trust each other to guard each other from unwanted border crossings. This trust is now being eroded and internal borders are again being erected. Yet, to withstand the external challenges, the EU is dependent on the willingness of its member states to uphold their joint commitment to the common management of open borders.

References

Allenbach-Ammann, J. (2023). EU Agrees on Anti-Coercion Instrument to Fight Foreign Interference. *Euroactive*, 28 March, Accessed on 2 October 2023 at: https://www.euractiv.com/section/economy-jobs/news/eu-agrees-on-anti-coercion-instrument-to-fight-foreign-interference/.

Bastasin, C. (2023). Want Ukraine in the EU? You'll Have to Reform the EU too. The Brookings Institution. Accessed on 2 October 2023 at https://www.brookings.edu/articles/want-ukraine-in-the-eu-youll-have-to-reform-the-eu-too/

Bengtsson, L. (2022). COVID-19 and the EU's Ability to Manage and Prevent Health Crises. In Bakardjieva Engelbrekt, A., Ekman P., Michalski, A. and L. Oxelheim (eds.) *Routes to a Resilient European Union* (Basingstoke: Palgrave Macmillan), pp. 89–113.

Blenkinsop, P. (2023). EU to Investigate 'Flood' of Chinese Electric Cars, Weigh Tariffs. Reuters. 13 September. Accessed on 2 October 2023 at https://www.reuters.com/world/europe/eu-launches-anti-subsidy-investigation-into-chinese-electric-vehicles-2023-09-13/

Bremberg, N., Sonnsjö, H., & Mobjörk, M. (2019). The EU and climate-related security risks: A community of practice in the making? *Journal of European Integration*, Vol.v41. *No.*, *5*, 623–639.

European Commission. (2021a). EU Strengthens Protection Against Economic Coercion. Brussels. Accessed on 6 March 2023 at https://ec.europa.eu/commission/presscorner/detail/en/ip_21_6642

European Commission. (2022). European Green Deal: Agreement reached on the Carbon Border Adjustment Mechanism (CBAM), Press release, 13 December 2022, accessed on 2 October 2023 at https://ec.europa.eu/commission/presscorner/detail/en/ip_22_7719

European Commission. (2023a). EU Calls for Greater Market Access and Fair Competition at EU-China High-Level Dialogue. Accessed on 2 October 2023 at /https://ec.europa.eu/commission/presscorner/detail/en/ip_23_4609

European Commission. (2023b). EU Solidarity with Ukraine. Brussels. Accessed on 6 March 2023 at https://eu-solidarity-ukraine.ec.europa.eu/index_en

Cooley, A., & Nexon, D. (2020). *Exit from Hegemony*. New York, NY; Oxford University Press.

Council of the EU. (2007). *The Africa- EU Strategic Partnership. A Joint Africa-EU Strategy*. 2007/16344, 9 Dec. Brussels.

Council of the EU. (2019). Regulation Establishing a Framework for the Screening of Foreign Direct Investment (FDI) into the EU, 2019/452, 19 March, Brussels, accessed on October 2 2023 at https://eur-lex.europa.eu/legal-content/EN/TXT/PDF/?uri=CELEX:32019R0452&qid=1695822905475

Council of the EU. (2020). Regulation concerning restrictive measures against serious human rights violations and abuses, 2020/1998L 410 I/1, 7 December 2020. *Brussels: Official Journal*, 2020.

Cremona, M. (2003). *The Enlargement of the European Union.* Oxford University Press.

D'Anieri, P. (2023). *Ukraine and Russia. From Civilized Divorce to Uncivil War* (2nd ed.). Cambridge University Press.

Damro, C. (2012). Market Power Europe. *Journal of European Public Policy, 19*(5), 682–699.

Drezner, D., Farrell, H., & Newman, A. (2021). *The Uses and Abuses of Weaponized Interdependence. Washington.* Brookings Institution Press.

Dworkin, A. & Leonard, M. (2018). Can Europe Save the World Order? *European Council on Foreign Relations.*

Eckes, C. (2018). The Law and Practice of EU Sanctions. In S. Blockmans and P. Koutrakos (eds.) *Research Handbook on the EU's Common Foreign and Security Policy* (Edward Elgar, 2018), pp. 206–229.

European Commission. (2022). Joint Press Release: Ukraine Recovery and Reconstruction Needs Estimated $349 Billion. Brussels, 9 September. Accessed on 6 March 2023 at https://ec.europa.eu/commission/presscorner/detail/en/ip_22_5428

European Commission. (1997). Agenda 2000 - Volume I - Communication: For a Stronger and Wider Union. DOC/97/6. 15 July.

European Union. (2023). Joining the EU. Brussels. Accessed on 6 March 2023 at https://european-union.europa.eu/principles-countries-history/joining-eu_en

Finnemore, M., Kenneth Scheve, Kennth A. Schultz and Erik Voeten, 'Preface', *International Organization,* 75:2 (2021), pp. iii-iv.

Ghauri, P. N., Oxelheim. L., and, Randøy. T. (2024). "The Changed Geopolitical Map: Implications for Business Policy in a Sustainable Finance Perspective". In Gugler. P. and Tavares. A. (Eds.), *Handbook on International Business Policy.* Cheltenham: Edward Elgar Publishing.

Götz, E. (2017). Putin, the state, and war: The causes of Russia's near abroad assertion revisited. *International Studies Review., 19*, 228–253.

Han, Z., & Paul, T. V. (2020). China's Rise and Balance of Power Politics. *Chinese Journal of International Politics, 13*(1), 1–26.

Hicken, A., Jones, P., & Menon, A. (2021). The International System After Trump and the Pandemic. *Current History, 120*(822), 3–8.

Hillion, C. (2004). *EU Enlargement. A Legal Approach.* Hart Publishing.

Ikenberry, J. G. (2011). *Liberal Leviathan: The Origins, Crisis, and Transformation of the American World Order.* Princeton University Press.

Ikenberry, J.G. (2018). The End of Liberal International Order? *International Affairs*, Volume 94, Issue 1, January, pp. 7–23.

Johnston, A. I. (2019). China in a World of Orders: Re-Thinking Compliance and Change in Beijing's International Relations. *International Security, 44*(2), 9–60.

Kagan, R. (2018). *The Jungle Grows Back: America and Our Imperiled World*. Knopf.

Keohane, R. & Martin, L. (1995). The Promise of Institutionalist Theory. *International Security* (1995) 20 (1): pp. 39–51.

Kydd, A. H. (2005). *Trust and mistrust in International Relations*. Princeton University Press.

von der Leyen, U. (2019). 2022 Speech by President-Elect von der Leyen in the European Parliament Plenary on the Occasion of the Presentation of Her College of Commissioners and Their Programme. Brussels. Accessed on 6 March 2023 at https://ec.europa.eu/commission/presscorner/detail/es/speech_19_6408

von der Leyen, U. (2022). 2022 State of the Union Address by President von der Leyen. Brussels. Accessed on 6 March 2023 at https://ec.europa.eu/commission/presscorner/detail/en/speech_22_5493

von der Leyen, U. (2023a). Statement on Twitter about Ukraine. 9 February. Accessed on 6 March 2023 at www.twitter.com/vonderleyen/status/1623609001580560384

von der Leyen, U. (2023b). Speech on EU-China Relations, Brussels, 30 March 2023, accessed on 2 October 2023 at: https://ec.europa.eu/commission/presscorner/detail/en/speech_23_2063.

Marten, K. (2023). NATO Enlargement: Evaluating Its Consequences in Russia. In: Goldgeier, J., Shifrinson, J.R.I. (eds) *Evaluating NATO Enlargement*. Cham: Palgrave Macmillan.

Mearsheimer, J. (2019). Bound to Fail: The Rise and Fall of the Liberal International Order. *International Security, 43*(4), 7 50.

Michalski, A. (2014). The Enlarging European Union. In D. Dinan (Ed.), *Origins and Evolution of the European Union* (2nd ed., pp. 274–301). Oxford University Press.

Michalski, A. (2020). The EU and Global Development Policy in Challenging Times, *UI Report* 4/2020. https://www.ui.se/globalassets/butiken/ui-report/2020/ui-report-no.-4-2020.pdf

Moritsugu, K. (2023). EU Commissioner Calls for More Balanced Trade With China and Warns That Ukraine Could Divide Them. AP News. 23 September. Accessed on October 2, 2023, at https://apnews.com/article/eu-china-trade-dombrovskis-31d10030134f46429e10cf40273a20ea

NATO. (2023). Vilnius Summit Communiqué. Press Release. 11 July. Accessed on October 2, 2023 at https://www.nato.int/cps/en/natohq/official_texts_217320.htm

Natorski, M., & Pomorska, K. (2017). Trust and Decision-Making in Times of Crisis: The EU's Response to the Events in Ukraine. *Journal of Common Market Studies, 55*(1), 54–70.

Petrequin, S. & Corder, M. (2022). European Union Makes Ukraine a Candidate for EU Membership. *AP News*. June 23. Accessed on 6 March 2023 at https://apnews.com/article/russia-ukraine-brussels-european-union-ff560e01c6b3e4f9c70777fad97be397

Pirani. S., Stern., & Yafimava. K. (2009). *The Russo-Ukrainian Gas Dispute of January 2009: A Comprehensive Assessment*. Oxford: Oxford Institute for Energy Studies.

Pridham, G. (2008). The EU's Political Conditionality and Post-Accession Tendencies. *Journal of Common Market Studies, 46*(2), 365–388.

European Commission. (2021c). Proposal for a Regulation Establishing a Carbon Border Adjustment Mechanism, COM(2021) 564 final 2021/0214 (COD). 4 July 2021. Brussels.

European Commission. (2021b). Proposal for a Regulation on the Protection of the Union and its Member States From Economic Coercion by Third Countries, COM(2021) 775 final 2021/0406 (COD), Brussels, 8 December 2021.

Reuters. (2022). Lithuania Demands China Revoke Sanctions Against Official Over Taiwan Visit. August 18. Accessed on 6 March 2023 at https://www.reuters.com/world/lithuania-demands-china-revoke-sanctions-against-official-over-taiwan-visit-2022-08-18/

Rolland, N. (2017). China's "Belt and Road Initiative": Underwhelming or Game-Changer? *The Washington Quarterly* Volume 40, 2017 - Issue 1, pp. 127–142.

Rüling, T. (2021). China, Europe and the New Competition over Technical Standards, *UI Brief* 1/2021, Stockholm: The Swedish Institute of International Affairs.

Sørensen, G. (2011). *A Liberal World Order in Crisis: Choosing Between Imposition and Restraint*. Cornell University Press.

Sturm, C. (2022). Between a Rock and a Hard Place: European Energy Policy and Complexity in the Wake of the Ukraine War. *Journal of Industrial and Business Economics., 49*, 835–878.

Sverdrup-Thygeson, B. (2015). The Flexible Cost of Insulting China: Trade Politics and the "Dalai Lama Effect". *Asian Perspective*, Vol. 39, No. 1 (Jan-Mar), pp. 101–123.

Index

A

African Union, 132
AMLA, 195–198
Anti-globalization movements, 50
Anti-money laundering, 178, 192

B

Balkans, 8, 9
Belt and Road Initiative, 268
Bordering, 25, 26
Borders, 1–6, 8–14, 16, 18, 19
Bretton Woods system, 263
Brexit, 9, 74, 81, 85–88

C

China, 263, 265–270, 273
Climate action, 94, 107, 109–111
Coal, 150, 151, 153, 154, 160, 163, 166
Cold War, 4, 6
Common Foreign and Security Policy, 262
Conditionality, 97–99, 102, 104, 105, 238, 256
Coordination, 238, 242, 256
Counter-terrorist financing, 185, 186
COVID-19, 24, 27, 29–31, 41, 42, 262, 266
Cultures of civilisations, 126

D

Damages, 235
Democracy, 4, 10, 13, 14, 93–96, 99, 101–107, 111–113
Democracy promotion, 102, 104–107, 110
Digitalisation, 178, 186, 188, 197, 198
Digitisation, 38
Donors, 238–242, 246, 252, 256

E

Economic interdependence, 267, 269
Economy, 218, 219
Energy balance, 150–152

A. Bakardjieva Engelbrekt et al. (eds.), *The Borders of the European Union in a Conflictual World*,
https://doi.org/10.1007/978-3-031-54200-8

Energy, 147–172
Energy security, 166
Enlargement, 94–96, 99, 103–105
Entry-Exit System (EES), 39
EU accession, 234, 238–240, 250–253, 255
EU-Africa Strategy, 263
EU Asia relations, 120, 139
EU association, 6, 9
EU Association Agreement, 73
EU DCFTA, 74
EU enlargement, 5, 7
EU external relations, 74, 78, 82, 142
EU industrial policy, 50, 63
Europe, 205–214, 217–225
European Border and Coast Guard Agency, 33. *See also* Frontex
European Coal and Steel Community, 5
European Commission, 7, 96, 103, 105, 109
European Community, 5, 13
European Economic Area, 78, 83
European Economic Community, 5, 6
European Free Trade Association, 83, 84, 88
European history, 1, 2
European integration, 24–27, 29, 30, 32, 42, 44
European Union (EU), 5, 49–51, 53, 56, 57, 59, 62, 63, 65, 66, 68, 69, 147–164, 166, 167, 169–172, 206–211, 214–218, 221–225, 261–263, 265–267, 269–278
EU security policy, 179, 190
External border, 24–28, 31–39, 41–43, 262, 263, 278
Externalisation, 37, 38, 42, 43

F

Flexible integration, 90
Freedom of movement/free movement, 24, 27, 29, 30, 36, 41–44
Frontex, 24, 32–36, 38–40, 42
Frozen assets, 242, 245
Fukuyama, Francis, 125

G

Gas, 147–154, 156, 163–168, 171
Gazprom, 148, 149, 154, 163–165
Geopolitical shift, 263, 271, 272
Globalization, 49–51, 53–57, 62, 64, 69
Global trade liberalization, 62, 69
Grants, 238, 242, 246, 253, 256
Great power politics, 205, 206, 211, 217
Green transition, 166, 239

H

Huntington, Samuel, 125, 126

I

Instrumental adaptation, 98
Integration, 73–90
Internal border control, 24, 26–32, 35, 41–43
Internal borders, 261, 278
Internal market, 5, 6, 9, 12, 13, 19
Internal market *acquis*, 74, 75, 78, 79, 81–87, 89
Internal market functioning, 50, 69
Invasion of Ukraine, 10, 14

K

Kyiv School of Economics, 235

L

Loans, 238, 239, 245, 246, 256

Logic of appropriateness, 98, 99, 101, 106, 109
Logic of consequentiality, 98–101, 104, 106, 108

M
Marshall Plan, 234, 238, 239, 244, 257
Migration, 24, 27, 29, 30, 33, 36–39, 41, 44
Military means, 205–207, 209, 211, 217, 225
Modernization, 237, 256

N
National borders, 49, 66
NATO, 6, 17, 18, 205–210, 212, 213, 215–218, 222–224
Neighbourhood policy, 78, 79, 85
Neutrality, 6
Normative power, 94–98
Norm diffusion, 98–101, 112
Norm promoter, 101
Norms, 93–95, 97–101, 105, 108, 110–113
Nuclear, 220, 225
Nuclear power, 150, 151
Nye, Joseph, 122, 123

O
Oil, 147, 148, 150–154, 159–162, 164–169, 171
OPEC+, 153, 164
OSCE, 208, 209, 212, 213, 218

P
Paris Agreement, 107–110
Pax Americana, 263
Pipelines, 147, 149, 152, 154, 160, 164
Political attitudes towards globalization, 69
Political leadership, 208, 217
Protectionism, 50, 53, 60, 62, 63
Public-private cooperation, 178

R
Realpolitik, 121
Reconstruction, 234, 235, 237–246, 251, 252, 256, 257
Reforms, 234, 238, 240, 246–248, 251–253
Refugees, 236, 237
Re-nationalisation, 24, 32
Renewable energy, 151, 167
Reparations, 240, 243, 256, 257
REPowerEU, 167
Rule of law, 7, 10, 14
Rules-based international system, 263–265
Russia, 9, 10, 12, 14, 15, 17, 147–172, 205, 206, 208–213, 215–222, 224, 225, 233–237, 239, 241, 243, 244, 247, 249–254, 256

S
Sanctions, 147, 149–152, 156–163, 168–171
Schengen Agreement, 27, 31, 32, 39, 41
Schengen area, 24, 27, 28, 30, 33, 39
Schengen Information System (SIS), 39, 40
Securitisation, 37–39, 179, 190, 191, 198
Security order, 205–209, 211–213, 217–220, 224
Security policy, 7–9, 17, 18

Social market economy, 120, 127, 128, 130, 132, 142
Soft power, 122, 123, 127, 129–131
Southern Neighbourhood, 94, 101, 102, 105–107, 110–112
Soviet Union, 264, 269, 271, 273
Supervision, 180, 184, 192, 193, 195
Switzerland, 83, 84, 86

T
Technological competition, 261
Technological developments (digitalization, AI), 54, 69
Territory, 3
The European Neighbourhood Policy, 96, 102, 103
The Global Strategy, 94, 96
Trade barriers, 50, 53, 60, 62, 68, 69
2008–09 financial crisis, 50, 51, 54

U
Ukraine, 205, 206, 209–226, 233–257
United Kingdom, 74, 85
United Nations (UN), 207, 221
United States, 263, 264
US-China trade dynamics, 50, 69

V
Values, 93–97, 102, 103, 105, 106, 113

W
World Trade Organization (WTO), 50, 53, 55, 59–62, 65–69, 121, 125, 137–142
World War II, 4, 6